Jamaica Travel Guide, Caribbean

Tourism

Author
Caleb Gray.

SONITTEC PUBLISHING. All rights reserved. No part of this publication may be reproduced, distributed, or transmitted in any form or by any means, including photocopying, recording, or other electronic or mechanical methods, without the prior written permission of the publisher, except in the case of brief quotations embodied in critical reviews and certain other noncommercial uses permitted by copyright law. For permission requests, write to the publisher, addressed "Attention: Permissions Coordinator," at the address below.

Copyright © 2019 Sonittec Publishing
All Rights Reserved

First Printed: 2019.

ISBN:

Publisher:
SONITTEC LTD
College House, 2nd Floor
17 King Edwards Road,
Ruislip
London
HA4 7AE.

Table of Content

- **SUMMARY** 1
- **INTRODUCTION** 4
- **PAST AND IN THE PRESENT** 6
  - CULTURE 8
  - ECONOMY 12
  - EVENTS & FESTIVALS 19
  - HISTORY 27
    - British Colonialism 28
    - Freeing the Slaves 29
    - Entering the 20th Century 30
    - Moving to Independence 31
  - RELIGION 32
    - Creole Religions in Jamaica 34
    - Protestantism in Jamaica 36
    - Rastafarianism in Jamaica 37
    - Jamaican Roman Catholicism 41
  - CRIME 42
- **TRANSPORTATION** 47
  - AIR TRAVEL 51
  - BUSES 56
  - FERRIES 59
  - RENTAL CARS 60
  - SAILING & BOATING 70
  - TAXIS 77
- **JAMAICA VACATION PLANNING** 83
  - BOOKING 84
  - BUDGETING 86
  - GETTING INFO 89
  - MAKING DECISIONS 91
  - PACKING 93
  - BEST TIME TO VISIT 98
- **WEATHER** 101
- **JAMAICA ACTIVITIES** 104
  - BIKES & MOPEDS 114
  - DIVING 116
  - FISHING 122
  - GOLF 125
  - NIGHTLIFE 128

- Shopping...136
- Snorkeling..145
- Spas..150
- Sports...153
- Tennis..156
- Other Activities...157

JAMAICA ATTRACTIONS......................................160
- Beaches...163
- Casinos..170
- Landmarks..174
- Natural Attractions..178

JAMAICA ACCOMMODATIONS............................186
- All Inclusive..190
- Eco Tourism...197
- Hotels...200
- Villa Complexes..217
- Villa Rentals...222

CRUISING TO JAMAICA...241

WEDDINGS IN JAMAICA..247
- Budgeting for a Wedding in Jamaica..................251
- Wedding Locations and Venues in Jamaica......256
- Weddings Traditions and Requirements in Jamaica......262

WHY NOT GO TO JAMAICA?....................................266

TRAVEL BASICS...271
- Clothing...273
- Currency...276
- Customs..277
- Driving...280
- Electricity..281
- Embassies...281
- Health..283
- Hours of Operation..285
- Languages..286
- Passports..287
- Telephones...293
- Tipping..294

Summary

The importance of travelling in our life?

Everyone has their very own reasons to travel. Some people travel for work, some travel for pleasure while for others it is just a way of life. They travel to live and to escape at the same time.

Whatever might be the reason to travel, here are few ways in which travelling would definitely change you and I think that is why travelling becomes so important in life:

<u>Enjoy being alone</u>: There is something therapeutic about being alone and being at peace with it. While you soak in a new culture, you also connect with your own inner self.

<u>Learn to adapt</u>: It is a different world out there, literally. Be it the pace of life, the language or simply the change in weather, it is always a change and you have to adapt to it. This is what makes travelling truly beautiful as you break away from the routine and adapt to something totally new.

<u>Experience a new culture</u>: Every place comes with its distinct cultural habits, you cannot think about New York without talking about its fast paced life and about Italy without enjoying its relaxed lifestyle. Similarly, while visiting the UK you might have to be a bit formal in your interactions with the locals, on the other hand, while greeting the people in Thailand, one can be really warm and casual.

Broaden your taste buds: Travelling without experiencing the local food is just not complete. It is not only a culinary experience but a cultural one as well.

Get out of comfort zone: From simple experiences like the weather, way of life or food to the more adventurous ones like trying a new sport, travelling really pushes ones boundaries to the core. You might end up participating in a street carnival in Brazil just like the locals or trying the local delicacies (read insects) in Thailand.

Indulge in Photography: It does not matter whether you are a professional or not. It is also irrelevant whether you have a DSLR or a very basic camera, while travelling what matters is the love and quest for seeing beautiful places and the sheer joy of capturing them in your lense. Travelling would in return give you your very own collection of amazing postcards of beautiful sunsets, snow laced mountains or sunny beaches.

Learn to escape: Travelling is the best way to break the routine. If you are in a bustling city, go ahead and experience the country life. If you are in a rural place, travel to a bustling city and experience its madness. Stressed with the city life or work pressure? A spa break in Himalayas or Kerala is a must try.

Appreciate Nature: The quest to explore more when one is travelling always leads to a sense of amazement about nature. While most of us keep a track of technological advancements, Nature has its own ways of outshining all of these. The Antelope Canyon in Arizona or Turquoise Ice in Russia are the finest examples of this. For more, check out the most unbelievable places around the world.

Get closer to your own roots: While one travels and experiences a lot of different cultures and practices, it definitely brings one closer to his or her own roots. Travel helps one appreciate one's identity and culture.

Travelling is all about experiences. They can happen in terms of culture, people, places but most importantly with one's own self and this was all about

Caleb Gray

Introduction

Jamaica is the largest English speaking island in the Caribbean. It is 150 miles long and approximately 50 miles at the widest point, covering an area of 4,411 square miles. The interior is mountainous and gives rise to many rivers. The Blue Mountain, running east to west, reach a peak of 7,402 ft.

The island has a maritime tropical climate and temperature range from approximately 80 degrees 90 degrees at sea level and from 50 to 60 degrees in the mountains. June through September are the warmest months and the traditionally rainy months are May and October.

Jamaica's original inhabitants are the Arawaks who came from South America some 2500 years ago. They names the island "xayamaca", which means 'land of wood and water'. Christopher Columbus came upon the island in 1492 and claimed it for Spain. They substituted X for J and the island became Jamaica. The Arawaks were gentle, peaceful; people who loved dancing, hunting and playing ball games. The Arawak population was totally wiped out by the brutality of the Spanish settlers. They were replaced with African slaves.

The island was invaded in 1655 by the British expedition who failed to conquer Santo Domingo. Instead of going away empty handed, they took Jamaica as a consolation prize. The African slaves of the Spanish colonists escaped to the hills and lived a free life, they were called the Maroons. They harassed the British conquerors to such an extent they were granted independence and their own lands by treaty in 1734, and are in part autonomous even today.

English is the official and commercial language, although a local patois is widely spoken. The vast majority of Jamaicans are of African descent or mixed race Negroes, Indians, Caucasians, and Chinese. Jamaica has more churches per square mile than anywhere in the world. The largest religious body is the Anglican church and the others include Baptists, Roman Catholics, Methodists, Presbyterians, Seventh Day Adventists and Moravians. There are also other religious groups such as Hindus, Bahia's and Rastafarians.

Jamaica has two political parties, the Peoples National Party formed in 1938 and the Jamaica Labour Party formed in 1943. The Road to self government was paved in 1944 when adult suffrage was granted to all people of the age of 21 and over, giving them the right to vote. The first election under Universal Adult Suffrage was held in 1944 and the Jamaica Labour Party was victorious in the polls.

In January 1962, a draft if the Independence Constitution was unanimously approved. At midnight, August 5, 1962, the British flag was lowered and the Jamaican flag was hoisted for the first time. On August 6, 1962 Jamaica became an independent nation.

Past and in the Present

A link to the past in the present, Jamaica is known for its proud culture, shaped by history and economy

An intriguing cultural heritage defines the spirited people of Jamaica, a place Columbus is said to have called, "the fairest isle mine eyes ever beheld." But peace would be rare after Columbus feasted his eyes on this fair isle.

Jamaica is located 90 miles south of Cuba, and has a total area of 4,213 square miles. This makes it the largest island in the Commonwealth Caribbean. Jamaica arose from the sea millions of years ago as a result of volcanic activity, and has a terrain comprised of high mountains, low valleys, and coastal plains.

History

From the relative calm of its early Arawak inhabitants to the slavery and revolt brought on by the Spanish and British, no group who touched Jamaica's shores left without leaving an indelible print on the country's fabric. You can still see the influence of the past today, all over the island and in its people.

Some may argue that Jamaica's struggles began after the Great Depression, when Marcus Garvey spoke out about Black Nationalism, but political strife can be traced back to many years before when slavery was introduced to the island. After years of poor treatment, island slaves began to fight back, taking strength from the knowledge that the French and American revolutions had been successful.

Jamaica saw more slave uprisings than any other island in the Caribbean, and emancipation was finally granted in 1834. You can learn more about the history of Jamaica by clicking here.

Culture

People from around the globe have settled in Jamaica over the years, making it a true melting pot. From English colonist to Africans who were originally forced to the island as slaves, and even the most resent influx of West Indian immigrants, the blend of so many different cultures has made the island of Jamaica a truly dynamic locale. The island's language is a great way to see how much each different culture has effected the island's own. While the official language is English, dialects with African, Spanish, and European lilts showcase the melding of languages from around the world.

Music is a hugely important part of Jamaican culture. It is hard to think of Jamaica without immediately equating the island to reggae music, though many other forms such as traditional African dance and dancehall are popular means of expression as well. Another association that most foreigners make with Jamaica is the island's huge Rastafarian following. Rastafari focuses on the cultivation of the inner spirit, and is well-known for its use of marijuana for spiritual an medicinal purposes. What many people don't know is that a large number of other religions have their home in Jamaica, including Judaism, Hindi, Muslims, Bahai, and various Christian sects.

Economy

The political and social history of the island is closely tied to the economy, which has had a very shaky past. Once the world's largest producer of sugar, Jamaica had endured slave revolts and racial inequality while plantation owners prospered off the fruits of the land and the backs of the workers. Economic depression followed emancipation, and political splits and gang warfare peppered the 20th century, but Jamaica has kept itself afloat with banana and bauxite exports and tourism.

Jamaica has been marketing itself to the outside world as a pleasure and health retreat since the 1890s, and tourism has been a major industry since even before that time. Today, over 26 thousand guest rooms at numerous hotels accommodate well over one million vacationers each year during the tourist season alone, and new rooms are popping up every year. Tourism is such a major industry in Jamaica that one in four residents works directly in the industry.

Despite intense political strife and racial divide, the people of Jamaica have maintained the relaxed attitude for which the Caribbean is famous. Jamaicans are proud of who they are and pride themselves on their native culture. When you visit Jamaica, you will understand the complexity and the joy of the local spirit, which embraces its past through expressions such as music, dance, and joyful celebrations.

Culture

The Culture of Jamaica

The unique Jamaican culture is kept alive by its extraordinary people
Nowhere else on earth will you find a culture as dynamic as the one visitors encounter in Jamaica. Its people are a mixture of the many ethnicities that have landed on the island's shores over the past several centuries. Weathering enslavement and oppression, the Jamaicans are survivors, and their past is full of fascinating stories just waiting to be told.

Cultural Heritage
Whether they are the descendants of the colonists or recent immigrants from the Middle East, people of all nationalities live and work together in Jamaica. Cultures have been mingling on Jamaica's shores for hundreds of years. And while this mixture inspires pride, it is also the source of Jamaica's characteristically brassy banter that, to an outsider, might seem inappropriate at times. The Taíno, who inhabited the island long before European discovery, also left behind a cultural history.

Most Jamaicans are always willing to talk about subjects most find uncomfortable, peppering their speech with terms such as 'browning,' 'redman,' 'coolie,' 'whitey,' 'blacka' or 'Miss Chin.' It is not uncommon to find people of all ethnic backgrounds on Jamaica, and the islanders are comfortable with their outward racial differences because they know this is part of what makes their culture unique.

Dig into the island's past and learn more about its present by reading our guide to Jamaica's History.

Language
Language is another way in which Jamaica demonstrates its melded culture. Although Jamaica's official language is English, many of its residents speak with their own linguistic style. There are even differences from village to village. The main ingredients of Jamaica's language stew are Spanish, African, English (including Irish, British and American idioms), and even Rastafarian. On Jamaica you might hear your shoes referred to with the Spanish word, "*zapatos*," and you might talk about where to "*nyam*," an African word meaning "eat." However, you may also hear terms you're more familiar with, like "cool." The language also has roots in slavery, as the slaves found ways to combine the language of their owners with their own African tongues.

Traditional Clothing
Traditional wear includes colorful and usually handmade dresses from calico cloth. Calico is generally striped, similar to a plaid. These dresses include tiered skirts, but another important aspect is the head scarf. This scarf is carefully wrapped around the head to keep hair in place. Rastafarian-influenced clothes are of particular interest to tourists and generally include red, green, and gold, which are the colors of the Ethiopian flag. One of the most important aspects of Rastafarian clothing is that it is made from natural fibers. Also important in this attire is the "tam," a hat that covers the dreadlocks.

You can learn more not only about the island's traditional clothing style, but also how locals dress today and tips on what you should wear as a visitor by reading the page on Jamaican Clothing.

Traditional Food

Jamaican culture is also richly flavored by its cuisine. The aromatic spices of the Caribbean have allowed the island's kitchens to create one of the most unusual fusions of flavors in the world. Most popular on the menu is jerk, a marinade that can be added to almost anything, but usually meat. The spicy sauce includes many of the island's native ingredients. Seafood is also prevalent on the island, but most truly Jamaican dishes, which intimidate most visitors, include cow foot stew and goat's head soups.

Religion

Spirituality takes many forms in Jamaica, but all are reflected in the local culture. The Guinness Book of World Records determined Jamaica to have the most churches per square mile of any place on the planet. The island hosts many different Christian denominations, including Anglicans, Baptists, Catholics, Methodists, Seventh Day Adventists, and Presbyterians. But the religious are not only Christians: Jews, Hindus, Muslims, Bahai's, and Rastafarians all call Jamaica home.

Visual Arts

Jamaicans take pride in their artistic style. Influenced by the island's unique culture as well as European, American, and African art forms, islanders have mastered a style all their own. The nation has produced many famous artists including sculptor and painter Edna Manley, painter Albert Huie and the self-taught artist Kapo.

Crafts

Although equally artistic, local crafts fall out of the visual arts category and into one of their own. On the island, there are many artisans who create goods of local, natural materials and they do so by hand. You can get your own hands on any number of these goods by visiting a local crafts fair where you will find such items as glazed pottery animals, straw hats made of palm leaves, embroidered linens and batik clothing, and shell jewelry. If the Rastafarian culture is of particular interest to you, you'll also be able to find wood carvings that are typically made of red hard woods.

Dance

Of course, Jamaicans are also known for their willingness to dance. Dances found on Jamaica fuse the styles of Europeans and Africans into a unique form. Some of the local dances are the "jonkonnu," a dance practiced by slaves at Christmas time, "bruckins," from the period after emancipation, and the newer "ska." European dances like the maypole and quadrille are performed with "mento" music, while African dances like the "gerreh," "dinki-mini," and "ettu" were turned into commentaries on plantation living. New dances crop up constantly, but these older styles are the basis for new moves. Dance halls are the best places to find new styles, but the traditional dances of Jamaican culture are kept alive by organizations such as the National Dance Theater Company.

Music

Where would dancers be if it weren't for music, the most popular form of Jamaican music is reggae, which has a sound is so easy to enjoy that it has gained popularity throughout the world. Many reggae musicians have grown to international fame, most notably Bob Marley, who worked with and influenced many other local musicians before his death in 1981. The popularity of this genre has continued to this day. Dancehall, a variation of reggae, is also growing in popularity.

Reggae may be the most well-known style of music, but there are many more. Jamaican folk music has come from many sources over the years. The most notable influence on many of the sounds found here is Africa, in celebrations of birth, death, and harvesting. However, the different types of music performed now fall into three groups: dance, religious, and work and entertainment.

Film

Thanks to the picturesque landscape and the unique culture, Jamaica has always been a popular location to shoot scenes for Hollywood films. There have also been films made by locals in recent years that discuss social issues and every-day-life on the island. If this is a subject of interest to you, you can read more and get a full list of movies that have been shot even partially in Jamaica by reading on Jamaican Film page in this book.

Theater
It may come as a shock to some visitors, but Jamaica has a very rich theater history. The island's first theater opened back in the 17th century, hosting theater troops from Europe and America. Locally put on performances were not popular at first, but soon writers that lived on the island found their niche in discussing the tumultuous social issues and popularity boomed. Today, there are more than a half a dozen live theaters on the island, and visitors are always invited to stop in and see a play or musical.

Literature
The literary world of Jamaica got its start with folk tales told as a form of oral history that was passed down from generation to generation, often as cautionary tales for youths to hear and heed. What we find in the literary world of Jamaica today, however, is that the local dialect is interwoven with elevated prose to create pieces of written work that is unlike anything you'll find elsewhere in the world. Like many things that become important to the arts and culture scene of the island, it is discussion of social issues that catapults local literature to the top.
A more in depth discussion of the past and present of local literature can be read on Literature page in this book.

From painting to music, language to food, the Jamaican people have so much to offer the world. Once you leave, you'll never lose the lasting influence of Jamaica's multifaceted culture.

Economy

The Economy of Jamaica
Jamaica's cultural strength is a great support for its economy

Jamaica's rich economic history has shaped the population's unique strength of character. From leading the world's economy in sugar production to bankrupt socioeconomic turmoil, the Jamaica you see today is a country shaped by a tumultuous economic past.

Economic History

Sugar has always been the most abundant crop on the island, and for most of Jamaica's history, sugar production was the top industry. Spanish settlers started sugar cultivation in 1520 until the British invaded in 1655 and took over the island. In 1670, the "Peace of Madrid" gave Britain official rule of the island, but the English weren't the most merciful of leaders.

Slavery led to the first significant uprising in 1690, a year that marked the beginning of a long history of social unrest and racial divisiveness. During the times of slavery, Jamaica experienced more revolts and uprisings than any other Caribbean colony. In 1760, a now famous slave by the name of Tackey led one of the largest slave revolts in history when more than 600 slaves rioted, killing whites and burning farms.

Still, profits and production soared. As the world's largest single producer of sugar, Jamaica became known as the "jewel of the British crown" in the 18th century. The island exported 22 percent of the world's sugar supply, and plantation owners prospered.

In 1830, mulattoes, or people of mixed race, were enfranchised. Many used their new rights to fight for the still-oppressed blacks. One such defender, a Baptist deacon named Sam Sharpe, led a slave revolt in 1831. The revolt was put down harshly by the government; hundreds were killed, and Sharpe and other key players were captured and hanged. Others caught in the fray were beaten or flogged.

The brutality of the retaliation stirred sympathetic sentiments in England, and in 1834 slavery was abolished with a six-year program of apprenticeship to smooth the transition. The program didn't work as well as planned, however, because most blacks would rather have been released to fend for themselves than stay on the plantation and be reminded of their slavery.

In 1838, unconditional emancipation was declared, two years earlier than intended. This mass exodus from plantation life left the plantation owners without cheap labor and put a tremendous strain on the economy. From 1830 to the early 1900s, indentured servants from India and Japan immigrated to Jamaica.

In 1846 the British government passed the Sugar Duties Act, putting a tax on Jamaica's sugar export and forcing the island's sugar prices to compete worldwide. That, along with the development of the sugar beet in Europe, reduced demand and further depressed the Jamaican economy. Unemployment rose and wages fell.

As conditions continued to worsen into the 1860s, mulattoes like George William Gordon fought for improvements for the predominantly black lower class. The American Civil War from 1861-1865 brought further depression as the Union's blockades of the Confederacy prevented Jamaica from trading with its chief trading partner.

By 1865, the economic and social conditions came to a head when Gordon and Paul Bogle led the Morant Bay Rebellion. The governor of Jamaica at the time, Edward Eyre, retaliated with such ferocity, by burning houses and killing 437 people including Bogle and Gordon, that he was removed from his position in 1866 and Jamaica adopted a Crown Colony system of government. The new government promised many social reforms, which never happened, and the disappointment led to further social unrest.

By the early 1900s, the economy started a recovery fueled by a developing banana crop. Some prosperity returned to the island, but most of it stayed in the hands of the landowners, and poverty still remained high. The Great Depression halted recovery in the 1930s, and unemployment rose again, resulting in strikes and riots. One such strike was led by Alexander Bustamante at the West Indies Sugar Company and resulted in the founding of Jamaica's first labor union, the Bustamante Trade Union (BTU). This spawned a political party called the Jamaican Labor Party (JLP), and about the same time, Bustamante's cousin, Norman Manley, founded the People's National Party (PNP).

The 1940s saw an economic upturn once again started by World War II when the Caribbean islands were supplying Britain with food and raw materials. Bauxite, the primary component of aluminum, was discovered on the island. Jamaica was also starting to be seen as a vacation spot. This was the launch of Jamaica's two current largest industries: tourism and mining.

In 1944, the first election was held with universal adult suffrage and was won by the JLP, which adopted an increasingly capitalist philosophy. Prosperity was seen on the island with greater diversity than ever before. With developing industries and increased exports, the port cities became bustling centers of commerce and rural dwellers flocked into the cities in pursuit of 'the good life.' Into the 1960s, tourism continued to take an increasingly significant role in the economy, and both bauxite and agricultural exports grew.

In 1962, Jamaica became an independent nation and, led by the JLP, continued to prosper and develop. By the early 1970s, Jamaica was the world's leader in bauxite, exporting to Canada, the United States, Norway and the USSR.

In 1972, however, power changed hands. The PNP, led by Norman Manley's son, Michael, won the election, and Michael Manley led the nation toward democratic socialism. The industrialization of Jamaica halted in mid-stride, and while the nation was on the fence, trying to decide whether to industrialize or return to its agricultural roots, the economy faltered.

The cities didn't have the housing or jobs to support the massive influx from the countryside. Inflation soared more than 50 percent, unemployment skyrocketed, the older neighborhoods that these people settled in became today's inner city slums, and society became increasingly polarized.

A full-fledged war broke out leading up to the election of 1976. Gangs terrorized towns to show their support for the JLP or the PNP, pressuring innocents to sway their votes and breaking into gunfights in the streets. Manley and the PNP won the election, and continued the progress of their socialist agenda, developing ties with Cuba, a move that elicited ire from the United States. America sanctioned Jamaica and prepared to topple the government.

The sanctions proved effective, however, in-and-of themselves. Businesses pulled out of the Jamaican economy, tourism dropped, and the economy plummeted. The increasingly poor conditions led to further civil unrest, and in the most violently warred election yet, there was a regime change in 1980. Leading up to the 1980 elections, nearly seven hundred people were terrorized or killed in gang wars, but Edward Seaga of the JLP emerged victorious.

In the 1980s Seaga began the process of trying to boost the economy once more, but faced several obstacles. The recovery was slow and difficult due to uncontrollable factors. Reduced world demand for aluminum depressed the bauxite industry, and in 1988 Hurricane Gilbert dealt a blow to the island that damaged nearly every industry in the nation, especially tourism.

In 1989 Michael Manley reinvented himself as a "mainstream realist" and won yet another election, but due to health problems he relinquished power in 1992, passing the helm to Percival James Patterson, Jamaica's longest running prime minister. Patterson won both the 1993 and the 1997 elections by a landslide and remained in power until 2006 when Portia Simpson Miller became the first female Prime Minister in Jamaica. She lasted for only one year, when Bruce Golding of the Jamaica Labour Party was elected into office. He remains Prime Minister today.

Present Day Economics

In 1992, Patterson's government inherited one of the largest per capita national debts in the world and started a comprehensive economic program to reduce inflation and unemployment. Jamaica now has a very strict fiscal policy and is open to trade and free markets. A floating exchange rate, which at times can be quite unstable, is maintained with the United States, and there are reduced restrictions on foreign investments.

In 1996, Jamaica went through an economic crisis that left the economy stagnant for four years. The GDP didn't increase again until 2000 and only then by 0.8 percent, accelerating slightly to 1.7 percent of growth in 2001. But the global recession that followed the Sept. 11 attacks on the World Trade Center slowed the growth again to 0.8 percent in 2002.

The GDP of Jamaica is made up of three primary industries: Services make up 65 percent of GDP, manufacturing and mining make up 28 percent, and agriculture accounts for 7 percent. Interestingly enough, agriculture, which is very labor intensive, accounts for 21 percent of the workforce in spite of being the smallest major industry on the island.

Tourism and Services

One of every four employed workers in Jamaica works in tourism and services. In 2000, Jamaica hosted 1.3 million visitors, and tourism and services contributed $1.33 billion to the economy, which was up 4.2 percent from 1999. The September, 11 attacks and political rioting that followed, which accounted for 32 deaths, reduced tourism in 2001 and the following years. The majority of vacationers, 71.3 percent, are from the United States. The United Kingdom sends 10.2 percent, and 8.1 percent come from Canada.

Mining and Manufacturing

Mining accounts for 9 percent of the GDP and employs 6,000 people. Two thirds of the island is made of limestone, and Jamaica is the world's third largest producer of bauxite, following Australia and Guinea. There are also mineable deposits of gypsum, marble, silica, sand, and clays. Bauxite production fell in 1999 by 7.5 percent and by 4.3 percent in 2000. Silica fell as well by 28.7 percent in 2000.

However, gypsum and limestone have been on the rise; in 2000, limestone exports rose by 3.6 percent, and gypsum exports skyrocketed with a 40.1 percent increase.

From 1993 to 1997, manufacturing produced $2 billion in exports, mostly to the United States. The industry accounts for 13 percent of GDP, employs 9.4 percent of the work force, and is of increasing importance to the economy. The government has begun granting concessions to industrialization, such as with duty-free imports and tax relief to stimulate industrial growth. New plants are being built for everything from printed fabrics and footwear to agricultural machinery and fertilizer.

Other revenues generated in this area have come from the breaking up of the Government Telecom for $200 million, privatizing the power and public service companies and adding a levy to bauxite sales. Since the signing of NAFTA by President Clinton, the textile industry has shrunk due to competition with Mexico.

Agriculture

Although agricultural exports account for 7 percent of the GDP, the agriculture industry employs 21 percent of the Jamaican workforce. Sugarcane is still the chief crop. In 2001, 2.4 metric tons were exported. Bananas follow at a distant second with 42,000 tons exported in 2000, down 20 percent from the previous year. Jamaica is also the world's largest supplier of pimento, also called allspice.

Blue Mountain Coffee, one of the world's finest and most expensive coffees, is grown in the Blue Mountains of Jamaica. In 2000, 1,721 tons of Blue Mountain coffee was exported, up 18.2 percent from the previous year. In 2009, Blue Mountain coffee exports brought Jamaica $32 million, up 25 percent from the previous year. Other agricultural products include arrowroot, cacao, citrus, corn, ginger, mango, potatoes, and tobacco. As with many other islands, in the Caribbean, rum, distilled from sugarcane, is also a significant export and is considered a byproduct of agricultural production.

Future Outlook

For a successful economic future, Jamaica must overcome many obstacles. The economy has had its ups and downs since 1995. Improvements in private capital are being made and industries are starting to diversify, which could make Jamaica more resilient against natural fluctuations in the global market in the future. Imports are up to about $4.6 billion a year, but exports overall have been down in recent years. 2009 saw exports down to about $1.422 billion. That number is not expected to see much improvement immediately, as Jamaica's main export partner is the United States (accounting for 40 percent of exports), who is also experiencing an economic downturn.

One of the most pressing obstacles for Jamaica in the coming years is to keep its status as a popular tourist destination. Political trouble has injured the tourist industry in the past, and may well do so again. Fortunately, an unnamable mystique of this beautiful island keeps visitors coming back year after year.

Events & Festivals

Jamaica's Events and Festivals

Find music, food, and dance at the many events and festivals that make Jamaica famous

Planning a vacation around an event in Jamaica is a great idea, but it can be a bit tricky. Although many festivals are held annually, situations like extreme weather and sales problems can often lead to rescheduling or a change in location.

Cultural Celebrations

Accompong Maroon Festival
This festival takes place each year on Jan. 6, the birthday of Captain Cudjoe, the man who defeated the English army. The festival celebrates the Maroons, featuring traditional dancing and singing, a fantastic feast, the blowing of the Abeng horn, and playing of the

Maroon war drums. The Accompong celebrates a fun and exciting aspect of the cultural and historical heritage of Jamaica.

Fi Wi Sinting

In February Jamaica hosts a celebration of African culture and traditions.

Misty Bliss

Another February cultural celebration, this is for the communities in the Blue and John Crow Mountaines National Park.

Trelawny Yam Festival

A festival celebrating the cultural heritage of Albert Town in Trelawny, this event takes place in April and features a lot of great food.

Jamaican Coffee Festival

Held each fall in Kingston to celebrate the rich, agricultural tradition of coffee in Jamaica, java lovers will find themselves on a caffeine high like no other at this festival. Farmers and merchants provide visitors with free samples of a wide array of coffees, hot beverages, and other related foods.

Heritage Fest

Also held each fall, this is an annual festival in Kingston that celebrates and uses food, dance and music to explore the diversity of Jamaica's population. From Indian curry to Lebanese dancing to Chinese fortune telling, Heritage Fest pays homage to all of the diverse ethnicitiesfound in Jamaica.

Seville Emancipation Jubilee

This even is a celebration of Jamaica's African ancestors and features food, folk art, music, and more. It takes place in the Seville Heritage Park.

Cultural Extravaganza

If the arts are involved, you'll find it all together at this celebration of Jamaican culture. Drama, culinary arts, music, dance, and crafts all have a place here.

Carnival is held all over the island...

Carnival

One of the most renowned Caribbean festivals, Carnival, spreads across the entire island in one huge party, featuring popular musical entertainment as well as parades. Carnival is held all over the island in the week before Easter and is one of the island's most popular festivals.

Jonkanoo

Called Junkanoo on other Caribbean islands, this is Jamaica's Christmas celebration. Party-goers dressed in masquerade parade through streets in celebration of their West African and slave heritage.

Musical Festivals

Back to the Island
This destination concert is a unique experience where attendees will experience fresh music at world-class resorts.

Heineken Startime

This musical celebration takes place each winter in Kingston and promises to be the most significant musical event of the season. The concert features one of the strongest line-ups in each area of Jamaican music, from ska to rock steady to hip hop, and, of course, reggae.

Africa Jamfest

African music is honored each year in Montego Bay during this Jamfest. Traditional African music, arts and crafts, clothing, and food are present during the Jamfest.

Rebel Salute Music Festival

Also in Kingston, this festival has been held in January for the past 12 years. The festival highlights cultural roots music and focuses more on the folk tradition than other shows. No drugs, alcohol, or meat are allowed at the event. Don't expect any less of a crowd, though, as patrons of this event include locals as well as international guests who show up each year for this amazing concert.

Air Jamaica Jazz and Blues Festival

This amazing festival features a diverse range of musical genres but pulls all their influences toward the blues and jazz lover. From African to Cuban and reggae, this festival gives a great international flavor to the age-old tradition of jazz and blues.

SKAZZ

Bringing jazz and ska music lovers together in one venue, this musical event also showcases local culture and food.

Jazz Month

In Jamaica June is Jazz Month. Jazz fans have numerous options, from the Ocho Rio Jazz Festival to the Jamaica International Jazz Festival; Over 30 jazz events take place throughout the island.

International Reggae Day

This is a blowout musical festival in Jamaica. Usually celebrated in July, this festival hosts not only musical talent shows, but a talent search, workshops and a lecture on the life of reggae icon, Bob Marley. This concert is broadcast live all over the world via satellite television and the Internet.

Reggae Sumfest

Here we have a popular event that takes place the first week in August each year in Montego Bay. The best in reggae are brought together for a week of sonic celebration. Visitors can purchase tickets for just one night of partying or can spend a little more and get weekend passes, or even a pass for the whole week. Some tickets even include backstage passes. Without a doubt, Reggae Sumfest is a great way to enjoy a week of music.

Stir It Up Film and Music Festival

In September, up-and-coming musicians and film makers gather with industry professionals. There are concerts, film screenings, and workshops during the days-long event.

Caribbean Music Expo

More live music will rock the island during this expo at the end of September through the beginning of October. This event takes place in Ocho Rios, and features concerts on the beach and an industry trade show.

Come Celebrate Jesus

A music festival with an international following that promotes gospel and spiritual music, this even includes local and international artists, cocktails, hors d'oeuvres, prizes, and giveaways.

Jamaica Reggae Wine Festival

The first event in the region to combine a wine festival with a reggae music festival, this is a high-class event that draws crowds from around the world.

Dream Weekend

Also known as Independence Weekend, this annual week-long party in Negril, this music festival fuses popular DJ's with an electric vibe.

Sporting Events

Fishing

Jamaica is home to two of the largest fishing tournaments that run in September and October each year. The Falmouth Blue Marlin Tournament and Port Antonio International Fishing Tournamentare popular, and the Port Antonio Tournament is one of the most prestigious in the Caribbean. The Montego Bay Yacht Club holds a fishing tournament in September, as well and in Treasure Beach you'll encounter the Hook N'Line Canoe Tournament.

Sailing

Sailing events are plentiful throughout Jamaica, including the Pineapple Cup in Montego Bay each February, and the Montego Bay Race.

Golfing

Golfing events are also popular in Jamaica. Some of the top LGPA golfers compete each May at the Mojo 6 Golf Tournament. August is when the celebrities come out to play for a good ause at the Ocean Style Celebrity Gof Weekend. For over 12 years in a row, Montego Bay has hosted Annies Revenge Golf which has been described as the best pro-am in the Caribbean. In December, the Jamaica Invitational Pro-Am hosts PGA pros as well as amateurs who take on the courses at Montego Bay's Ritz-Carlton Golf and Spa Resort Rose Hall.
Races: Jamaica's longest running road race takes place on the last Sunday of January. The High Mountain Coffee Road Race includes both a 5K and 10K race. You can also walk, jog, or run to the beat of reggae music during the Reggae Marathon and Half Marathon.

Biking

The Jamaica Fat Tyre Festival, a biking event to promote local trails is in February, Jake's Off-Road Triathalon is in April.

Other Sports

For a special treat, check out the Jamaica Cricket Festival. Teams from around the world meet in Jamaica to compete against one another in over 50 games at various venues throughout the island. Volleyball isn't left out in Jamaica. In March the island' hosts the Venus International Invitational Volleyball Tournament, which is open for men and women. Other unique events include the World Championship of Dominoes in June and Makka Pro Surf Contest in

July. Come July, the International Taekwondo Federation World Cup is held at the Montego Bay Convention Center, bringing martial artists from around the world together to respectfully fight it out.

Other Events and Festivals

Bob Marley Celebrations

A week-long celebration of the life and achievments of Bob Marley, this festival is a local cherished tradition filled with music, food, and exhibitions.

Expo Jamaica

Taking place in April, this expo showcases world-class products and services every year. People from all over come to check out Jamaica's new and exciting innovations.

All Jamaican Grill-Off

A top food centered celebration is the All Jamaican Grill-Off, at which teams of local grill masters compete to cook the best large piece of meet. The event takes place in June at Kingston's Hope Gardens.

Portland Jerk Festival

Don't forget about this favored event in July, where visitors can sample Jamaican jerk and enjoy live music and carnival rides.

Little Ochie Seafood Festival

If seafood is your favorite, you won't want to miss this festival in St. Elizabeth Perish each July. Live music plays during this event as attendees eat all the seafood they can handle.

Calabach International Literary Festival

Book lovers unite each May in Treasure Beach. The event is typified by readings, workshops, and music.

Caribbean Fashion Week

If clothing is your passion, check out this event, which brings top designers from around the world to Kingston's National Indoor Sports Centre in June for fashion shows featuring their latest designs.

Reggae Film Festival

Movie lovers won't want to miss the showings at this event in Montego Bay. Independent films from around the world are screened, and guests can sit in on seminars and gala events. The Reggae Film Festival is typified by live reggae concerts before each screening.

National Festival of the Arts

This runs through the summer, ending on Jamaican Independence Day. Aside from sales of arts and crafts, local competitions showcase the work of indigenous artists in dance, song, drama, speech, painting, sculpture, crafts, culinary arts, and photography, to name just a few. The wide variety of artistic media makes this festival a sure hit.

Kingston on the Edge of Urban Arts Festival

Another great arts festival at which artists of all medias, including performance arts, share their skills with attendees. This festival is held in June.

Kingston Restaurant Week

Some of the city's top restaurants offer discounts to guests in order to introduce their food to a broader audience.

Ocho Rios Seafood Festival

The largest culinary and family event on the island, all forms of seafood can be sampled here. Plus there is live entertainment throughout the day.

Jamaica Bridal Expo

Calling all brides and grooms! If you're getting married soon, this is a great way to learn about all of your options. Fashion, flowers, cakes, limousines, and make up can all be reviewed during this event.

Oktoberfest

For over 30 years this event has been teaching locals and visitors everything they need to know about German spirits and food.

Tastee Talent Contest

Get to know the local talent in December, where young hopefuls compete and big-name entertainers keep things interesting.

Whatever your interest, be it art, music, or just a great party atmosphere, one thing is certain: locals know how to turn events and culture into something spectacular and memorable--a special occasion with the distinct feel of Jamaica that you won't want to miss.

History

History of Jamaica

The history of Jamaica includes both hardships and amazing accomplishments

Understanding a little bit more about the history of Jamaica can help travelers to appreciate its beauty, culture, and unique spirit. However, this island's history has been complicated, with many troubles since Columbus' arrival.

This article provides a brief overview of some of Jamaica's most important historic events, however, if you're looking for more detailed information about any particular historic event, you don't have far to go. More detailed history articles are available chronologically, and a timeline can help you find any event you're looking for. Jamaica's complex history of sugar and warfare has been important to island development.

Changes of Power

The first known inhabitants of Jamaica were the Tainos, an Arawak-speaking tribe that traveled throughout the Caribbean after leaving South America. The Tainos left very little evidence of their time on the island, but their influence was profound. The Tainos' Arawak name for the island was "Xaymaca," which means "land of wood and water." This was later written phonetically by Spanish explorers, who substituted a J for the X at the beginning of the word.

This was not the only name given to the island. During Columbus' second voyage to the Caribbean in 1494, he "discovered" Jamaica and named it for a saint, the way he named many other islands. In this case, St. Jago, but only the Arawak name of Xaymaca stuck to this beautiful island.

Before the arrival of the Spaniards, the Tainos farmed and fished and were even the creators of the hammock. Unlike many other islands in the area, they were never at war with the Carib tribes that peppered the region. After the arrival of the Spanish, Jamaica's history was no longer as peaceful; the Tainos' new enemy was the Spanish, who began enslaving the natives around the time they established their first settlement in 1510.

This settlement was Sevilla Nueva, "New Seville." By the late 16th century, the Tainos had been almost completely wiped out, whether from the hard farm labor, European disease, or by their own hand—committing suicide to escape slavery. There were almost none left, and many Africans were imported to replace the Tainos as slaves.

British Colonialism

Later many settlers moved to Villa de la Vega, "City on the Plains," now called Spanish Town. Spanish Town became the center for the Spanish colonists and was often attacked by the British. In both 1596 and 1643, the British sacked Spanish Town, and in 1655 captured it after failing an assault on Hispaniola (Haiti and the Dominican Republic). It took five years to defeat the Spanish, who eventually fled to Cuba.

However, before fleeing, the Spanish freed and armed their slaves. Most of these freed slaves ran to the interior of the island and formed the Maroons, a group which still exists today. The Maroons waged guerrilla war against the British colonists and are respected for their ability to defeat the British in battles throughout the early colonial period.

The British encouraged new settlers to come to the island through gifts of land, and soon the economy was booming through the business of the vast sugarcane plantations. Jamaica was the world's largest producer of sugar, yielding 22 percent of the world's supply during the 1700s. Sugarcane wasn't the only cash crop grown on the islands, the British also produced cocoa and coffee plants for trade. However, many Africans were brought into slavery to help the British rise to this caliber of economic power on the island.

Slaves were treated poorly, especially after the American colonies split from England and the French Revolution, when feelings of freedom were stronger than before. In fact, Jamaica had more slave revolts than any other West Indian island. With frequent resistance and uprisings, anti-slavery feelings grew in Britain especially after the 1831 Christmas Rebellion, in which 20,000 slaves killed planters and ruined crops. The British owners convinced them to lay down their revolt with promises of abolition, which were never kept. Afterward, 400 slaves were hung, and many more were whipped.

Freeing the Slaves

In 1834, after several more slave revolts, the British made into law theEmancipation Act. This act allowed all slaves under the age of 6 to be immediately freed; all other slaves would serve an apprenticeship to learn helpful skills for several years. This was not a pleasing announcement to the many British landowners who relied on slave labor to produce huge cash crops. Planters imported 35,000 indentured servants from India and later China to fill this gap.

In 1830 the mulattoes or mixed-race people of the island were allowed political power and began fighting for the poor ex-slaves in the 1860s. Again the American political situation affected Jamaica, and the naval blockade during the American Civil War brought economic strife to the island. The Morant Bay Rebellion in 1865 by many blacks was put down aggressively by Jamaica's Governor Edward Eyre. However, the violence of his response was not well-received in England, and the next series of governors chosen was much more liberal.

The production of sugar was no longer the island's most useful export by 1838, and the colonists soon realized that bananas and coffee were more economically sound alternatives. However, the biggest hit Jamaica's economy took was in 1846 with the Sugar Duties Act, which forced Jamaica to compete with other sugar producers in price. The advent of beet sugar in Europe further hurt the island's sugar trade. Bananas bolstered the island until the Great Depression of the 1930s.

Entering the 20th Century

It was just before the Great Depression that Marcus Garvey began his worldwide campaign for Black Nationalism. Born in Jamaica, he was a publisher and journalist as well as a crusader. He left Jamaica and began to travel the world, championing the Back-to-Africa movement. He founded the Universal Negro Improvement Association which spread across the Caribbean and on to several other countries. He also founded Jamaica's first modern political party in 1929, the People's Political Party. After his death he was declared one of Jamaica's first national heroes.

During the Great Depression there was another period of civil unrest on the island, and riots were common. A strike in 1938 resulted in a clash between police and workers and ended with several people dead at a West Indies Sugar Company factory. The strike's leader, Alexander Bustamante founded the first trade union, the Bustamante Industrial Trade Union. The Union also spawned the creation of a political party, and the People's National Party (PNP) was founded by lawyer Norman

Manley. This, following the work of Marcus Garvey in the 1920s and early 1930s, spurred Jamaican nationalism.

During World War II, Jamaica served as an Allied base, however it was the advent of tourism and the first bauxite exports that drove the island to economic success in the 1940s, which in turn helped to stabilize the island's political situation. 1944 saw Jamaica's first election with universal adult voting rights, and Bustamante's Jamaica Labor Party (JLP) won the election. Over time, the JLP adopted a capitalist philosophy while the PNP eventually began leaning toward democratic socialism. The JLP stayed in power until 1955 when the PNP came into power.

Moving to Independence

Jamaica joined the Federation of the West Indies in 1958 but left in 1961 when voters rejected membership and, on Aug. 6, 1962, Jamaica gained independence. Bustamante as a part of the JLP became the island's first prime minister. This was a period of prosperity for the islands, and foreign investment increased in many industries. The JLP stayed in power until 1972, when Manley's son Michael Manley came into power as the country's first biracial prime minister. He improved relations with Cuba, set a minimum wage and helped the poorer classes in many ways. However, this help came at a price, and the internationally owned bauxite industry was hit hard with taxes.

The bauxite industry immediately declined, as company owners lowered their production. This caused an economic slump that was made worse by the oil crisis during 1973 and 1974. In an attempt to make the country more self-sufficient, Manley proposed breaking alliances with the United States and allying with socialist Cuba. This angered America, which quickly imposed economic sanctions. The JLP, now led by Edward Seaga, began attacking the PNP's administration, calling it "communist" but, despite these attacks and the political violence of the time, the PNP won the 1976 elections.

Power switched between the JLP and the PNP during the 1980s, but Manley was forced to resign in 1992 due to failing health. His successor was P.J. Patterson, Jamaica's first black Prime Minister. Patterson won the 1993 election with a less radical platform than Manley's had been. There were again riots in 1999 due to a 30 percent tax increase on gasoline, and after three days of rioting, the government repealed the tax. Jamaica now suffers from international debt, a relic from its early days of independence, but its bauxite and tourism trades are flourishing, as well as its dynamic culture.

Religion

Religion in Jamaica

Religion plays a large role in Jamaica's every day culture

Historical events in Jamaica have influenced every aspect of island life, including religion. Jamaica allowed settlers far more religious freedom than England did. In fact, one of the first Jewish synagogues in the region was built on the island.

While European settlers tolerated most European religions, they were less accepting of African religions. The plantation owners believed that these African religions would help to unite the slaves, allowing them to rise up in revolt. Although there was some basis for this fear, these African beliefs simply stayed out of sight for much of the period.

Since Jamaica's independence, a number of U.S.-based churches have made their way to this Caribbean island. Although the Church of England was the main religion of the plantation owners, Baptists and members of the Church of God have grown to make up a much larger portion of the population in more recent years.

A combination of Christian and African beliefs has created a number of smaller fusion religions. The most important of these combined the African religion of Myal with Christianity to form Revivalism. This religion then split into two smaller groups as well.

After the emancipation of the slaves, Jamaica attempted to survive on indentured servitude. Migrant workers from China and India made their way to the island and often stayed after their term of servitude ended. These new settlers played an important role in the island's religious history.

Rastafari is the most prominent non-Christian religion on the island. It came into prominence as a grass-roots religion in the 1930s and was promoted as an alternative to white-oriented religions. Rastafarians worship the Ethiopian emperor Haile Selassie, or Ras Tafari. Rastafarians also believe in reincarnation and that males should not cut or comb their hair or beards. The emphasis of the belief is on nurturing the inner spirit in each person, which has affected the language with its addition of "I" as a prefix for many words. Marijuana may also be used by Rastafarians as a sacrament and a medicinal aid despite the fact that its use is illegal on the island. It is an evolving religion and culture, and not every member believes in all of these things. Its popularity, however, has spread to many other countries in the region and around the world.

Jamaica's 2001 census data breaks down religious groups as follows:

Religious Type	Specific Denomination	Percent (%)
Protestant	--	61.3%
--	Church of God	24%
--	Seventh-Day Adventist	11%
--	Baptist	7%
--	Pentecostal	10%
--	Anglican	4%
--	Methodist	2%
--	United Church	2%
--	Jehovah's Witness	2%
--	Brethren	1%
--	Moravian	1%

Roman Catholic	--	2%
Other (including spiritual cults)	N/A	10%

The population of Jamaica is strongly Christian, but a large number of islanders adhere to other faiths. Although Rastafarianism contains elements of Christianity, it is not considered a standard Christian denomination.

There is a great deal of variety in Jamaica's religion. While Protestantism from Europe and the U.S. has the strongest hold on the island, the faiths of slaves and indentured servants certainly made their mark here.

Creole Religions in Jamaica

Jamaica's population largely consists of the descendants of African slaves who were brought to the island by the Spanish and the British. The Maroons, freed slaves living in their own communities, had little to do with the religious experiences of the nearby slaves.

Oppositional Involvement

Elements of African religions remained important to the African slaves, and two seemingly opposing religions came to light in Jamaica. Obeah and Myal posed as opposing forces, but they were extremely similar. The British slave owners quickly banned Obeah, condemning it as witchcraft.

In actuality, the practice of Obeah did involve elements of what might be considered witchcraft, including the use of herbal potions, spells, and other forms of mysticism. However, the real danger to the British came from the obeahman's ability to lead the slaves. Their belief in his magical powers increased the possibility of slave uprisings. In fact, obeahmen led Tacky's Rebellion, one of the most important slave rebellions in Jamaica's history.

This gave Obeah an extremely bad reputation on British islands. On the other hand, Myal professed to be the answer to Obeah. The two faiths were not much different, but the myal-men portrayed themselves differently; they claimed to exorcise the bad spirits brought by Obeah.

Practicing Religions

Although the slaveowners viewed Myal as safer than Obeah, they did not respect the religion, which included ritualistic dancing and possessions. Ritualistic possession is an important element in all of the African-based religions in the Caribbean.

According to Myal, positive influences would possess myal-men, allowing them to drive out bad spirits. In this way they were both healers and spiritual leaders. They were much like medicine men, knowing the best curative (or not-so-curative) properties of local plants.

Many other British Caribbean islands did not have the experience of a second, opposing belief system. As an opposing religion to Obeah, Myal was unique to Jamaica. Overall, the practices of both Myal and Obeah were extremely similar, but Myal did incorporate a baptismal practice.

None of the African-based religions is particularly widespread in modern times. Myal joined with Protestant Christianity to form a new creole religion known as Revivalism. This was a strongly Christian religion, but included the spiritual possession found in African religions. It has since been absorbed almost entirely into mainstream Pentecostal churches on Jamaica.

The different cultures on Jamaica's shaped the island's religion, both limiting and encouraging distinct branches of African faiths. The result is a rich religious background and a more cohesive sense of religion in modern times.

Protestantism in Jamaica

As anyone in a predominantly Protestant country probably knows, the number of different Protestant faiths can be staggering. More than half of Jamaica's population claims ties to one of these denominations.

Jamaica's modern history played an important role in the religious diversification of this island's population. Though many British settlers were Anglican, they were part of the smaller, plantation-owning class. Missionaries taught a number of other Protestant beliefs to the slaves, who also held tightly to their own African beliefs.

Baptist and Methodist pastors led groups of former slaves after they had been emancipated. These groups combined African beliefs and spiritualism with the beliefs of the Protestant church to create the Revivalist church. In Revivalist ceremonies, spiritual possession is not far from the regular church activities.

Revivalist churches have since split into two categories: Zion and Pukkumina. Zion bands, as they call themselves, deal primarily with heavenly spirits (God, archangels, and saints) and earth bound spirits (prophets and apostles).

Ground spirits (which are not earth bound spirits), including fallen angels, are considered evil and are not dealt with by the Zion bands. Pukkumina bands deal almost exclusively with such spirits, including the human dead, excluding those from the Bible, and do not regard them as evil.

In more modern times, these Revivalist bands have made their homes among Pentecostal churches. Although they are not a major part of current religious culture, they have strongly influenced the music and singing styles found in churches throughout the island, as well as in popular music such as reggae and dancehall.

More religious changes came to Jamaica when a number of groups from the U.S. entered the island. Encouraged to send missionaries to the island, the Church of God and the Brethren each sent believers, further expanding the number of religious groups on Jamaica.

Throughout history, the dominant religious groups on the island have gone through a number of changes. Today, the people of Jamaica remain very religious, with most of them adhering to Protestant denominations.

Rastafarianism in Jamaica

Jamaica is the home of Rastafarianism, a religious movement spurred by the beliefs of famous Jamaican Marcus Garvey and inspired by an Ethiopianist reading of the King James Bible. Rastafarian beliefs are Christian, with a Jamaican twist.

Ethiopian Prince (Ras) Tafari is at the center of the religion; Rastafarians believe him to be the messiah. In 1932 Tafari was crowned emperor Haile Selassie. Selassie himself claimed lineage from the biblical Solomon and the Queen of Sheba.

Garvey's followers proclaimed him to be a prophet, as he had spoken of an Ethiopian leader who would take control and who would be the messiah. Selassie became their messiah, having ascended to the throne as Garvey predicted.

Ethiopia is associated with heaven on earth, and souls are said to return there after death. Rastafarianism also includes beliefs about the worlds of the living and the dead associating; these stem particularly from beliefs of the now-creolized Obeah and Myal religions on Jamaica.

Beliefs and Believers

Rastafarianism relies most heavily on certain passages from the King James Bible. These texts are read alongside the Kebra Nagast (Glory of the Kings) of Ethiopia and focus on the child born of the Queen of Sheba and King Solomon. This son is said to have founded the Ethiopian dynasty.

In more recent years, Robert Rogers, an Anguillan, developed the Holy Piby. Some Rastafarians use this compiled text as their main text, but not all Rastafarians accept this newer version of the Bible.

Without a distinct dogma, most of Rastafarianism is based on each Rasta's own interpretation. To aid in this, informal gatherings, known as "reasonings," can be called. At these gathers, Rastas, who are usually men, get together and discuss the text. "Reasonings" usually include smoking ganja (marijuana) as a sacrament.

Ritualistic possession is found in creole and Hindu religions, both of which were present on Jamaica and influenced Rastafarianism. Rastas see prophets as incarnations of God, and, though they believe in no other deities, Moses, Elijah, Jesus, and Selassie are seen as avatars of God.

Politics and Religion

Jamaica is known for its strong political leanings, and the Rastafarian movement added to the political firepower common on the island. Before Jamaica's independence, Rastas occasionally refused to pay taxes to England, claiming that the island was Ethiopian and thus owed no loyalty to the British crown. Many of these rebellious men were sentenced to years of labor, but others were committed to asylums.

Others made efforts to return to Ethiopia. Emmanuel Edwards "took" Kingston in 1958 in order to wait for ships that would bring them back across the Atlantic. However, Edwards and his followers were disappointed. Other Rastafarians began preparations for guerrilla warfare, even planning to invite Fidel Castro to take over the island from Cuba.

The so-called "yard" Rastas are considered to be the more radical set, and developed after Garvey's lifetime. Dreadlocked hair and red, green, black, and gold clothing make these Rastas easy to identify. Red symbolizes the blood to be shed for their redemption; black represents their race; and green stands for the lands of the motherland. Ganja, sometimes called "wisdomweed," is an important part of yard Rastas' lives. This group also practices I-talk, a distinct manner of speech. Reggae began its association with Rastafarianism at this stage in the religion's development.

Controversial Beliefs

The word "dreadlocks" comes from the feeling that this hairstyle inspired in others. Rastas grow dreadlocks as a symbol of their beliefs, in part following the biblical prohibition of shaving or cutting your hair. Rastas who follow this tradition can easily tell how long another Rasta has worn his hair in such a manner.

Though it is against the law, the rebellious practitioners of this religion may smoke marijuana. Those who do consider it to be the Bible's "holy herb" and take it as sacrament. It is understood to be the key to understanding the universe and God. Indentured servants from East Indian originally brought marijuana to Jamaica.

Some Rastas believe in eating organic food and follow strict dietary requirements which prohibit alcohol and tobacco consumption as well as salt, meat (particularly pork), and most seafood. This strict organic dietary regimen is called Ital. Many Rastafarians prefer to keep their own gardens to ensure that they can adhere to this diet.

Rastafarianism allows its believers the freedom to make their own choices, particularly in how they worship. This means that many do not agree with any of these three activities (wearing dreadlocks, smoking ganja, and practicing Ital), while some agree with one or two, and a few follow all three. It's important to remember that not every Rastafarian is the same.

Religious Culture

One of the most important aspects of Rastafarianism is its strict belief in the word of the Bible. While some followers refuse to cut their hair and instead grow dreadlocks, more widely accepted tenets are also included.

Womens' rights within the religion are drawn most directly from the Bible. According to Rastafarianism, the husband, or king-man, is the woman's path to divine knowledge, because women are thought to be inferior beings. Rastas practice some Old Testament tenants that are also followed by Orthodox Jews. For example, women must wear ankle-length dresses and cover their hair during ritual events. They must also abstain from cooking during menstruation. In certain circumstances, women may be placed in seclusion. However, since the early 1980s there has been a movement advocating for more women's rights.

While certain factors, most notably age, income, and social status, have no bearing on a person's place in the Rastafarian hierarchy, women are expected to live in a submissive role. While they are not prohibited from performing rituals, they do not have a place in the religion beyond a passive one.

African-influenced social structures that developed within Jamaica's Maroon communities played an important role in the structure of Rastafarian Houses, which are the central meeting areas for Rastafarians. Nyabinghi, or just Binghi, are communal meetings that play an integral part of the culture, and usually include reasonings, drum music, and marijuana smoking. Strong Afro-centric community values include an Assembly of Elders, which leads the Houses.

The name of these meetings comes from the cultural movement calling for the deaths for all oppressors, both black and white. Nyabinghi was particularly important because it recognized black oppression of other blacks. These meetings now commemorate the lives and deaths of important leaders, though Obeah and Myal rituals can be seen in parts of these gatherings.

As in many African rituals, drums are important in Rastafarianism. Three drums, the bass, funde, and akete or kete, are played during ceremonies. Bass drums are played with a covered stick and are struck on the first and third of four beats. Both the funde and akete are improvised and are played with bare hands. This drumming style was adapted from the Zion Revivalist drumming and from Buru and Kumina traditions.

Jamaica is the birthplace of Rastafarianism. As a result, Jamaica's many other religious beliefs have played a part in the growth of this one particular religion. Rastafarianism combines many spiritual aspects and political back-to-Africa sentiments with strong Christian beliefs.

Jamaican Roman Catholicism

The island of Jamaica, known for its distinctive style and culture, has a diverse religious landscape. While the islander's many faiths do include Roman Catholicism, it is far from the most prominent style of worship.

Much of the Caribbean's colonial history contributed to the islands' current religious practices. Jamaica is no exception. Though originally colonized by the Spanish, who were Catholic, the British took control of Jamaica early in the island's history. They brought Protestantism - particularly the Church of England, or Anglican faith - to the islands.

Although many Irish-Catholic servants migrated to the island early in its colonial history, the importation of slaves soon overtook the usefulness of such servants. These European servants were freed after only a few years of service. The slaves were educated in the religion of their masters, which was usually Anglican.

To this day, the majority of the Catholic churches on Jamaica are located in regions near the earliest settlers' homes. Kingston and Mandeville (near Spanish Town) are the two main hubs of Catholicism on the island, but Montego Bay also has a diocese. Kingston is home to the island's Archdiocese and serves as leader of four dioceses, two in Jamaica, one in Belize, and one in the Cayman Islands.

Churches are common around the diocese, but may be harder to find further away from these religious hubs. Hotels can often help vacationers find a church that is right for them.

Jamaica's religious diversity means that many belief systems are represented. If attending a Catholic Mass is an important part of your stay in Jamaica, it's best to take a look around the region and plan accordingly.

Crime

All About Crime in Jamaica

To avoid being the victim of crime while in Jamaica, stay aware of your surroundings

For as long as Jamaica has been a popular vacation spot, the island's reputation for crime and violence has preceded it, often overshadowing the many wonderful aspects Jamaica has to offer its visitors.

While the U.S. State Department has issued travel advisories about crime rates, particularly in Kingston, and Jamaica's own board of tourism offers tips and warnings for keeping you safe while traveling, it's important to keep things in perspective. Jamaica is considered one of the more potentially dangerous places in the Caribbean region, but the region still has one of the lowest crime rates in the world.

As the Jamaican Tourist Board stresses, you are more likely to be mugged in New York than in Montego Bay, so you should not let the reputation deter you from experiencing all the island has to offer. Jamaica is a beautiful island full of friendly, charismatic, and fun-loving people. It has been a favorite vacation spot for years, attracting more than 2 million visitors in 2003, many of whom were repeat visitors who had fallen in love with Jamaica and come back time and again. Simple common sense can make all the difference in ensuring a safe and enjoyable trip, and the precautions suggested for traveling safely in Jamaica are the same that you would take when visiting any large city in the U.S. or Europe.

Jamaicans are extremely passionate about social and political issues and, in the most populous areas these passions can sometimes find destructive outlets. A majority of the violent crimes that occur in Jamaica's metropolitan areas, especially Kingston, is associated with gangs and politics. Impromptu demonstrations have been known to occur and can block roads and interrupt daily business. Sometimes these protests can escalate into riots or shootings and, as a result, curfews and police searches are occasionally conducted in some inner-city neighborhoods. Remember that like any large city, certain areas have worse reputations than others.

It is always advisable to be aware of any current political or social issues that may be a problem at the time of your visit, and travelers to Kingston should check with local Jamaican authorities or the local U.S. Embassy for the most current information available before departing for your trip.

That said, Kingston is still rich with things to see and do. Paul Martin, Executive Editor for National Geographic Traveler Magazine, published a feature article entitled "High on Jamaica" after spending 3 weeks on the island, and wrote, "Today Jamaica's political parties seldom settle their differences Wild West fashion, and, while Kingston has more than its share of big city woes, travelers who bypass the capital miss out on a lot."

The 2010 Jamaica Crime and Safety Report, conducted by the Overseas Advisory Security Council, recorded that violent crimes including murder, shootings, carnal abuse, and robbery are up compared to previous years. The UN stresses, however, that, "Crime statistics are often better indicators of prevalence of law enforcement and willingness to report crime, than actual prevalence."

JAMAICA CRIME STATISTICS FOR THE YEAR 2010:	
Crime	Totals
Larcenies	500
Shootings	1,650
Break-Ins	3,700
Murders	1,700
Rapes	1,650

Robberies	3,000
Total Crimes	39188

While travelers can still find headlines of violence in Kingston, vacationing travelers in Jamaica rarely come in contact with these types of crime. Outside the inner-city areas, theft and other petty crimes are the most prevalent concerns. In most cases, major resorts have plenty of security measures to protect the grounds, so visitors to any of the large-scale resorts have nothing to worry about. If staying in smaller accommodations, or just traveling about on your own, safety is more of a concern, but not so much that seeing Jamaica for yourself isn't warranted or worth the trip. In fact, there's so much to do all over the island of Jamaica that you can't afford not to strike out and see it for yourself.

The U.S. State Department has published a pamphlet called "Tips for Traveling Abroad" for U.S. Citizens planning on traveling outside the country, which is full of useful advice for citizens of any nation planning international travel. It is available by mail from

The Superintendent of Documents
U.S. Government Printing Office
Washington, D.C.
20402

A few of the most significant tips to be found in it are:

- ✓ Make sure you have a signed, valid passport and visa, if required. Make sure that you also fill in the emergency information page of your passport;
- ✓ Familiarize yourself with the local laws and customs of the countries to which you are traveling. Remember, the U.S. Constitution does not follow you beyond American borders. While in a foreign country, you are subject to its laws;
- ✓ Make two copies of your passport identification page. This will serve as a replacement if your passport is lost or stolen. Leave

one copy at home with friends or relatives. Carry the other with you in a separate place from your passport;
- ✓ Leave a copy of your itinerary with family or friends at home so that you can be contacted in case of emergency;
- ✓ Do not leave your luggage unattended in public areas. Do not accept packages from strangers;
- ✓ Prior to departure, you should register with the nearest U.S. Embassy or consulate (or embassy of your home nation, if not a U.S. Citizen). Registration will make your presence and whereabouts known in case it is necessary to contact you in an emergency.

There are also a few precautions to consider specifically for traveling to Jamaica, as vacationers in any city can make popular targets for certain types of crime. Petty theft and pick pocketing can be common in crowded areas. It is particularly a concern on inner-city bus systems and street markets, which can be crowded and jostling. Being particularly careful and aware of your surroundings can help to deter such activity. Holding purses close to your body, keeping wallets in front pockets, and handling large sums of cash discretely are a few simple precautions every traveler can take. Avoid dressing in conspicuously expensive clothes or wearing eye-catching jewelry as well.

If you plan on renting a car, be aware of locals offering to "guard" your car against vandalism in exchange for money. If you encounter that situation, try to find somewhere else to park because the supposed guard can even become your vandal if you refuse their services. Further, only travel in taxis that are clearly marked and beware any drivers offering to show you the "real Jamaica."

Beware of anyone trying to sell you "ganja" (marijuana) because, although it is extremely common, it is still illegal. Being caught with it is a crime that incurs harsh penalties, but not nearly as harsh as if you get caught trying to take it out of the country. There are drug sniffing dogs at the airports and harbors, and if you get imprisoned in Jamaica, you're likely out of reach of U.S., or your home country's, assistance. While Kingston's death tolls will always make headlines, the vast majority of crimes are categorized by petty theft and hustling, which can be avoided with proper precautions. The most vital precaution to remember is simply to use common sense and be aware of your surroundings. You wouldn't leave your bags on a bench in Chicago or Los Angeles, so don't do it in Jamaica.

The most common problem you are likely to encounter in Jamaica isn't actually a crime or danger at all, but rather considered by some to be an inconvenience. Street vendors can be quite persistent, and while some travelers thrill at the exciting and fast-paced experience of bargaining with vendors, others can consider their manner intrusive and uncomfortable. It is important to be firm and, in most cases, you will be left to go on your way. Don't let Jamaica's reputation discolor the fact that it is filled with friendly and helpful people who are eager to help make your trip the best it can be. Of this, Martin wrote:

"Everywhere I went during the three weeks I spent traveling around this Connecticut-size island, I met Jamaicans eager to point out sights that I shouldn't miss. And if I was directed to more than one 'prettiest spot in the country,' well, that was understandable. Any number of places might qualify."

His words also help us not to forget that while Jamaica, as many places, *has* crime, it is important to remember that crime isn't what makes Jamaica, or Jamaicans themselves, for that matter:

"For me, Jamaica is a fragment of Bob Marley heard through the open window of a passing car, and the clean, delicate scent of ginger blossoms after a rain. It's the morning sun boiling up out of the Caribbean like a bright red lobster hoisted dripping from its pot, and a chorus of tree frogs tuning up as another long, slow, velvety night settles in."

Transportation

Transportation Options for Jamaica

Getting to and around Jamaica is simple for visitors, as there are plenty of options

Planning a custom vacation isn't limited to choosing where to stay and what to do; you can also plan how to arrive at your destination. Luckily, getting to Jamaica is relatively easy.

Getting There

As one of the largest and most popular Caribbean islands, it has plenty of travel options, from airports, airlines, cruises, and ports for entry. Jamaica's many visitors are enticed to its shores by this ease of entry as well as its famous beaches and resorts.

Air Travel

Visitors can fly into either of Jamaica's two major international airports in Montego Bay or Kingston. From there, they can travel on by plane to any number of smaller airports across the island, and arrange for transfers to their hotel or resort from any airport. Jamaica is also a regional hub for connecting flights, so it is often the case that international travelers will find themselves with a layover in Jamaica. If this is the case for you, try to plan it so you have a flight landing on the island in the morning and continuing on to another island in the evening, or even the next day. This will give you some time to explore one or two of Jamaica's most famous attractions.

For the more adventurous traveler who has a little extra wiggle room in their budget, chartering a plane can be a great way to see the sites from above, as well as travel quickly from one large city to the next. There are a total of six airports throughout Jamaica, making traveling by plane more feasible than one might imagine.

Sailors who like to travel on their own can also enter through some of the larger ports and gain clearance to sail around the island for as long as they wish. Although Jamaica is not one of the top sailed-to islands in the Caribbean, there is still plenty of reason to do so if you are inclined to take matters into your own hands.

There are eight ports with customs headquarters in Jamaica, making the ease of access greater than most islands, as well as numerous piers and marinas at which to dock. The waters surrounding the island are typically calm enough that even new sailors find them easy to sail, and for those who don't feel comfortable sailing alone there are plenty of chartering options that include crews who know their stuff. Learn more about sailing to Jamaica read from Boating and Sailing page in this book

Cruises

Cruise ship passengers may not stay as long, but the most popular ports offer plenty to explore. In 2011, Falmouth Cruise Terminal in Trelawny opened, bringing the number of cruise ship terminals up to three. The two others are located in Ocho Rios and Montego Bay, two of the largest tourists hubs in the country.

Cruising is a popular option for tourists interested in seeing more than one Caribbean island during their trip. When you make port, you often have the option of participating in a ship sponsored excursion, or you can explore on your own. A day at the beach, doing some duty free shopping, or visiting the childhood home of Bob Marley are all options.

With so many choices and so few hassles, it's easy to see why so many people choose Jamaica as their vacation destination. And with so many great travel options, you're sure to find one that is right for you.

Getting Around

Getting around the Caribbean's third largest island can seem like a task, but knowing which method of transportation is best for you will make touring Jamaica a treat rather than a chore. Adventurous travelers who prefer to take their time, travel on their own schedule, and enjoy independence as they explore have three options: bike, scooter, or car rental.

Rental Cars

Driving a rental car in Jamaica can be a challenge for someone who isn't used to the often unkempt conditions of the roads - but for someone traveling with a group, or who would like to visit a lot of attractions, this can still be the best choice. Driving is done on the left side of the road, as in the United Kingdom, and stop lights are few and far between. Unlike many Caribbean countries, drivers from the United States do not need to obtain a temporary license, making renting a vehicle that much easier. Remember to yield to livestock, which can often be found slowly making their way across country roads.

Bikes and Mopeds

Bicycle rentals are a great option for travelers whose accommodations are within the city and want a quick and efficient way to get around town; perhaps to grab a bite to eat, or do small amount of shopping. Bikes are also great for the athletic traveler who would like to challenge their body as they take in the beautiful scenery of the Blue Mountains.

The perfect candidate for scooter rental is a single traveler, or someone traveling in a small group who would prefer to zip around town on their own. The cost of renting a scooter is significantly lower than renting a car, and may be easier for someone under the age of 25 (the typical age one must be in order to rent a car). Keep in mind that country roads will be difficult to transverse on a scooter, due to pot holes and lack of pavement, so scooter travel is best done in larger cities.

Taxis

If you'd rather leave the driving up to someone who knows their way around, hiring a taxi may be more your style. When choosing a taxi, look for vehicles approved by the Jamaican Union of Travelers Association (JUTA); this will ensure the driver is held to specific safety regulations. You can be sure your driver is JUTA approved if the abbreviation "PP" or "PPV" is displayed on their license plate. Taxis in Jamaica are metered, but drivers will typically negotiate a price, especially if you are interested in using the driver's services as a tour guide.

Buses

Buses in Jamaica are a little different than buses in most places. Generally privately owned, this "public" transportation is not very organized and can be a gamble sometimes. Travelers will find that traveling via bus is the most economical means of transportation on the island - if not the most reliable. Buses rarely run on a set schedule, especially in some of the more remote areas of the island, but mini buses that travel through larger cities can typically be flagged as easily as a taxi cab.

Ferries

Because Jamaica is one large land mass, rather than a series of small islands like some other Caribbean nations, travel by ferry is not as necessary here - but it can make for a great experience and a fun outing. Popular ferry tours include trips to and from Port Royal and Navy Island.

There are many methods of transportation available in Jamaica. Whether you choose a leisurely bike ride between sites, or the unforgettable experience of flying over Jamaica's landscape on a prop plane, the most important thing is to pick the option that is best for you.

Air Travel

How to Reach Jamaica by Airplane
Jamaica's visitors find airline travel to be quick and easy
Jamaica is a regional hub, and has direct service from many countries. A flight from New York to Montego Bay or Kingston takes approximately four hours, while flights from London and Paris take roughly seven hours.

Round-trip tickets are the easiest way to save money on flights, as they're usually much less expensive than one-way flights. Booking well in advance helps both ensure your seating and save money, though sometimes last-minute bargains are well worth the wait, especially for travelers with flexible plans. You may also choose off-peak times to fly in order to save money. Traveling in the off-season will help you find lower prices, and mid-week flights are generally a lower cost as well. Staying over Saturday is another option for lowering the ticket price. Remember that if you find a special rate on your fare, you may be buying a nonrefundable ticket. Fees are often included for altering your ticket after your purchase.

Note that the airports at Montego Bay and Kingston are the two largest, but numerous other Jamaican airports are quite small. Travelers who need to make small hops across the island to reach the airports in Negril and other areas may not be able to deplane directly to the terminal. Vacationers with ailments that cause them trouble walking may want to make special arrangements with the staff at the airline prior to their arrival at their final destination in Jamaica.

Flying to Jamaica from the US

As a major hub for Caribbean air travel, there should be no surprise that flying direct to tennis is pretty easy for residents in the United States. Daily flights are found throughout the United States from as far west as Texas and as far north as Michigan. Even if you do not happen to live in a city that has a direct flights, most airports will have a flight to one that does, meaning the flight to Jamaica will be as short as possible.

NORMAN MANLEY INTERNATIONAL AIRPORT U.S. FLIGHTS

To/From	Airport Code	Airlines
Fort Lauderdale, FL, USA	FLL	Jet Blue
Miami, FL, USA	MIA	American Airlines

SANGSTER INTERNATIONAL AIRPORT U.S. FLIGHTS

To/From	Airport Code	Airlines
Baltimore, MD, USA	BWI	AirTran, Spirit Airlines
Chicago, IL, USA	MDW	AirTran
Detroit, MI, USA	DTW	Delta Airlines
Fort Lauderdale, FL, USA	FLL	Caribbean Airlines, Jet Blue
Los Angeles, CA, USA	LAX	American Airlines
Miami, FL, USA	MIA	American Airlines
Orlando, FL, USA	MCO	AirTran, Jet Blue

Flying to Jamaica from Canada

Jamaica is one of the easiest destinations to reach for Canadian citizens, with direct flights leaving through several cities including Montreal, Winnipeg, and Ottawa. The options might not be as extensive as those from the United States, but considering the distance, it is impressive.

SANGSTER INTERNATIONAL AIRPORT CANADIAN FLIGHTS

To/From	Airport Code	Airlines

Halifax, Canada	YHZ	Air Canada
Montreal, Canada	YUL	Air Canada
Winnipeg, Canada	YWG	Air Canada

Flying to Jamaica from Europe

London and Frankfurt are the main Caribbean gateways for Europe, and it is no different when flying to Jamaica. These cities give travelers the ability to fly straight to Montego Bay. Just keep in mind that it will be a long flight. Making a pit stop in Canada or the United States might not be a bad thing, if only to stretch your legs.

NORMAN MANLEY INTERNATIONAL AIRPORT EUROPEAN FLIGHTS		
To/From	Airport Code	Airlines
London, United Kingdom	LGW	British Airways, Iberia
SANGSTER INTERNATIONAL AIRPORT EUROPEAN FLIGHTS		
To/From	Airport Code	Airlines
London, United Kingdom	LGW	Thomson Airways, Virgin Airlines

Flying to Jamaica from the Caribbean

As mentioned, Jamaica is one of the hubs of air travel in the region, and hosts an impressive assortment of daily flights to other Caribbean islands.

Additionally, there is a strong domestic flight offering available too, called Airlink. If you have to travel from one side of Jamaica to the other, do not dismiss this airline, it can save you time, and in some cases, money.

IAN FLEMING INTERNATIONAL AIRPORT CARIBBEAN FLIGHTS		
To/From	Airport Code	Airlines
Jamaica	POT	AirLink

Caleb Gray

Kingston, Jamaica	KIN	AirLink
Montego Bay, Jamaica	MBJ	AirLink

KEN JONES AERODROME CARIBBEAN FLIGHTS

To/From	Airport Code	Airlines
Jamaica	OCJ	AirLink
Kingston, Jamaica	KIN	AirLink

NORMAN MANLEY INTERNATIONAL AIRPORT CARIBBEAN FLIGHTS

To/From	Airport Code	Airlines
Castries, Saint Lucia	SLU	Caribbean Airlines
Cayman Brac, Cayman Islands	CYB	Cayman Airways
Georgetown, Grand Cayman	GCM	Cayman Airways
Jamaica	OCJ	AirLink
Jamaica	POT	AirLink
Montego Bay, Jamaica	MBJ	AirLink, Caribbean Airlines
Negril, Jamaica	NEG	AirLink
Providenciales, Turks and Caicos Islands	PLS	Intercaribbean Airways
Simpson Bay, The island of St. Martin and Sint Maarten	SXM	Caribbean Airlines
Trinidad, Trinidad and Tobago	POS	Caribbean Airlines
Willemstad, Curacao	CUR	InselAir

SANGSTER INTERNATIONAL AIRPORT CARIBBEAN FLIGHTS

To/From	Airport Code	Airlines
Georgetown, Grand Cayman	GCM	Cayman Airways
Jamaica	OCJ	AirLink
Kingston, Jamaica	KIN	AirLink, Caribbean Airlines
Negril, Jamaica	NEG	AirLink

NEGRIL AERODROME CARIBBEAN FLIGHTS

To/From	Airport Code	Airlines
Kingston, Jamaica	KIN	AirLink

Montego Bay, Jamaica	MBJ	AirLink

TINSON PEN AERODROME CARIBBEAN FLIGHTS		
To/From	Airport Code	Airlines
Antigua, Antigua and Barbuda	ANU	Caribbean Airlines
New Providence Island, Bahamas	NAS	Caribbean Airlines

Air Charters

If you're considering chartering air travel, you can reserve one from the following regional agencies:

CHARTER OPERATORS			
Name	Phone	Location	Island
Intercaribbean Airways at KIN	(800) 572-7628	Norman Manley International Airport - 5.4 mi. (8.7 km) South of Kingston	Jamaica

If after all this you still want to learn more about flying to Jamaica, see our local guides that will explain to you the ins and outs of flying into specific areas within the nation.

Airport Security

Baggage screening procedures and additional security checks have been implemented at airports around the world, including random inspections. It has been recommended by the Transportation Security Administration (TSA) that travelers arrive at the airport at least two hours before their flight.

Following these suggestions can help to reduce your waiting time:

- ✓ Avoid wearing metal objects such as steel-toed boots, heavy jewelry or bulky belt buckles, which can set off the checkpoint detectors. Remove keys, loose change, cell phones, personal data assistants and other metal objects from your pockets.

Plastic bins are provided so that these items, together with shoes, coats and jackets are x-rayed.
- ✓ Metal surgical implants may also set off detectors; bring a note from a doctor to avoid delays due to increased security precautions.
- ✓ Travelers should keep their passport and boarding pass on hand at all times.
- ✓ Remember that only ticketed passengers are allowed to pass through the security checkpoint and to the gate. Non-ticketed people accompanying a child or an elderly or disabled person should check with the airline for proper documentation required.
- ✓ Bring along your ticket or e-ticket confirmation.
- ✓ Check on your flight before leaving for the airport to confirm that it is on schedule.

Arrivals

Upon arrival in Jamaica you'll need to clear customs. You should also consider exchanging your money for Jamaican Dollars, although American dollars are widely accepted. Travelers are encouraged to use airport exchange services to obtain some Jamaican cash at a better exchange rate than is offered by most hotels. As of August 2012, a $20 arrival tax will be assessed to all travelers arriving in Jamaica from abroad. This will typically be included in the cost of your ticket, but you should check with your airline to be sure.

Once you arrive in Jamaica be sure to keep your luggage with you at all times. Though the problem can be worse at Norman Manley International Airport in Kingston, theft is everywhere, making it a good idea to keep a close eye on your luggage.

Buses

Jamaica's buses can take you where you want to go

Jamaica's visitors can choose to ride buses as one of the most economical options for getting around the island and its cities. However, if punctuality and climate control top your list, the savings may not be worth the time you'll spend waiting for the bus to arrive. For the traveler in search of a cultural experience you can't find inside the perimeter of the resort compound, buses are the ideal mode of transit.

Fares on buses and minibuses are extremely low, approximately $1(USD) for 50 miles by bus, and between roughly $1.50 and $2.50(USD) for the same distance on a minibus. A minibus around Negril offers rides across town for $2(USD) all day and into the night. Still, there is more for the intrepid traveler to learn about buses in Jamaica.

Bus Routes

Buses and minibuses throughout the Caribbean are not known for their timeliness, and those in Jamaica are no exception. Outside the city of Kingston travelers may find it difficult to meet buses because the drivers may not follow a strict schedule. Still, the frequency of bus services and their ability to pick up and drop off passengers from just about anywhere around the island makes them very useful. Some buses may pick up passengers literally from the side of the road, though this is not allowed within cities, where buses are restricted to designated stops and terminals.

When traveling by bus in Jamaica, a traveler's cultural journey is usually more interesting than the physical trip around the city or the island. Passengers can delight in the many colorful names that mark the sides of the vehicles. Drivers often allow buses to be packed quite full, and, without air conditioning, you'll be certain to have experienced more than a little local flavor.

BUS ROUTES			
Route	Beginning	Stops Along the Route	End
JUTC Above Rocks	Kingston Bus		Above Rocks Bus

Route	Terminal		Stop
JUTC Constant Spring Route	Kingston Bus Terminal		Constant Spring Bus Stop
JUTC Hellshire Route	Kingston Bus Terminal		Hellshire Bus Stop
JUTC Port Royal Route	Kingston Bus Terminal		Port Royal Bus Terminal
JUTC Portmore Route	Kingston Bus Terminal		Portmore Bus Terminal
JUTC Spanish Town Route	Kingston Bus Terminal		Spanish Town Bus Terminal
Knutsford Express Southern Route	Knutsford Express Kingston Terminal	Savanna la Mar Knutsford Express Bus Terminal, Knutsford Express Mandeville Terminal, Luana Knutsford Express	Knutsford Express Negril Terminal
Montego Bay Metro Eastbound Route	Montego Bay Bus Terminal	Mahee Bay Bus Stop, Rose Hall Bus Stop	Greenwood Bus Stop
Montego Bay Southbound Route	Montego Bay Bus Terminal	Reading Bus Stop, Wiltshire Bus Stop, Mount Carey Bus Stop, Montpeller Bus Stop	Cambridge Bus Stop
Montego Bay Metro Westbound Route	Montego Bay Bus Terminal	Reading Bus Stop, Hopewell Bus Stop	Sandy Bay Bus Stop
Knutsford Express Main Route	Montego Bay Knutsford Express Terminal	Knutsford Express Falmouth Terminal, Knutsford Express Ocho Rios Terminal	Knutsford Express Kingston Terminal

When considering a ride in a bus or minibus in Jamaica, make sure you use a bus operated by the Jamaican Union of Travellers Association, or JUTA. These will be indicated by a red Public Passenger Vehicle (PPV) license plate. Also remember to ask the price before climbing aboard.

In some areas, bus service is better than others. Here are a few guidelines to help you get around Jamaica with ease:

- ✓ In Negril, shuttles at resorts often move their passengers around the city, leaving little need for public transportation;

however, a minibus drives up and down the central Boulevard all day.
- ✓ Public buses in Montego Bay are practically nonexistent, but tourist shuttles are maintained for use by the guests of certain hotels.
- ✓ Kingston's streets are wild, and bus transportation is no better. When using Kingston's buses, watch for pickpockets.
- ✓ Port Antonio's visitors can flag down a minibus for a cheap ride. They operate throughout town, but their schedules are erratic.

Ferries

Ferries offer tours and transportation in Jamaica

Unlike many other island nations in the Caribbean, Jamaica is comprised of just one large land mass. This makes travel by ferry less necessary than it is among nations made up of a group of islands. Still, ferry services are available to and from certain areas of Jamaica.

Visitors to Kingston can take a ferry to Port Royal and catch a glimpse of the colonial history of Jamaica. Although Port Royal was originally an island, the fishing village is now connected to the mainland by the Palisadoes, a series of small cays that have, over time, formed a roadway. While Port Royal may be reached by car, many visitors opt to ride the ferry ride instead. The price is right, and the scenic views are unmatched during the half-hour ride.

Port Antonio also has a ferry; it travels to and from Navy Island 24 hours a day. Reachable only by ferry, Navy Island is notorious for the wild parties Errol Flynn and his Hollywood pals used to throw. Flynn once owned Navy Island and, though it is now slated for development, it is a great picnic spot for vacationers hoping to enjoy the natural scenery of Jamaica. The ferry ride is only a short seven minutes.

Future Plans

Paradise Ferry is an upcoming way to get around, scheduled to launch in July 2019. It will enable passengers to get around Jamaica a bit quicker in a very comfortable way. They will operate between Negril, Montego Bay, Falmouth, and Ocho Rios. The ship will offer free wi-fi, cocktails, live reggae and dance, as well as light food options.

Though ferries are not entirely necessary in Jamaica, they can make for a great and affordable experience when you need to travel from place to place.

Rental Cars

Rental cars provide Jamaica's visitors with the keys to their own destiny

Many travel advisers recommend renting a car in Jamaica. Although it is sometimes pricey, driving your own car will enable your island tour to take off in new directions.

Renting a Car

Several companies throughout the island supply cars, but the best selection is generally in the larger cities of Kingston, Montego Bay and Ocho Rios. Local companies may offer better rates, but larger companies provide more service options, including the ability to pick up the car in one city and drop it off in another.

The Jamaica Tourist Board has also gone out of its way to issue one of the most comprehensive maps of Jamaican roads. Look for the map, titled Discover Jamaica, at tourist board offices and car rental agencies. It can be a big help out on the back roads and in crowded cities.

Check the following table for a list of rental companies.

VEHICLE RENTAL COMPANIES		
Name	Phone	Location

Apex Car Rental	(876) 382-8292	20 Holborn Road - Kingston	
Apex Car Rentals	(876) 953-4595	1341 Providence - The vicinity of Montego Bay	
Aplus Car Rentals	(876) 952-2033	Shop 14 St. James Place - The vicinity of Montego Bay	
Avis Kingston Central	(876) 906-2847	Knutsford Boulevard - Downtown Kingston	
Avis Kingston Uptown	(876) 926-8021	1 Merrick Avenue - Kingston	
Avis Norman Manley	(876) 924-8293	Norman Manley International Airport - 5.4 mi. (8.7 km) South of Kingston	
Avis Sangster International Airport	(876) 952-0762	Sangster International Airport - Montego Bay	
Beaumont's Car Rental & Tours	(876) 940-1494	34 Queens Drive - The vicinity of Montego Bay	
Budget Kingston Airport	(876) 924-8762	Norman Manley International Airport - 5.4 mi. (8.7 km) South of Kingston	
Budget Main Office	(876) 759-1793	53 South Camp Road - 2.4 mi. (3.9 km) South-Southeast of Kingston	
Budget Montego Bay	(876) 952-3838	Sangster International Airport - Montego Bay	
Caribbean Car Rentals Kingston	(877) 801-6767	Kingston	
Caribbean Car Rentals Ocho Rios	(877) 801-6797	Ocho Rios	
Carren Car Rental and Tours	(876) 986-1687	Denbigh Dr - May Pen	
Chalis Car Rentals & Tours	(876) 952-3793	10 Federal Avenue - The vicinity of Montego Bay	
Classique Car Rentals	(876) 632-5874	1 Sunset Boulevard - Montego Bay	
Cole's Car Rental	(876) 952-9156	10 Sunset Boulevard - The vicinity of Montego Bay	
Danjor Car Rentals	(876) 953-9258	34 Queens Drive - Montego Bay	
Demario's Car Rental	(876) 971-	Mt Salem Main Road - The vicinity of Montego Bay	

Caleb Gray

Dhana Car Rental & Tours	(876) 953-4051 9555	Montego Bay
EFAY Rent a Car	(876) 336-7082	3 Churchill Avenue - Montego Bay
Eastern Car Rental, Ltd. Montego Bay	(876) 971-1297	27 Claude Clarke Ave - Montego Bay
Eastern Car Rental, Ltd. Port Antonio	(876) 993-3624	26 Harbour Street - Port Antonio
Escape Car Rental	(876) 962-5895	22 Ward Avenue - Mandeville
Fiesta Car Rentals	(876) 926-0133	14 Waterloo Road - Kingston
Fox Rent-A-Car	(876) 952-3347	25 Gloucester Avenue - The vicinity of Montego Bay
Garmack Car Rentals	(876) 920-1119	1 D Norwood Avenue - 0.9 mi. (1.5 km) Southeast of Kingston
Genesis Tours and Car Rentals Limited	(876) 971-1154	22 Sunset Boulevard - Montego Bay
Genuine Quality Car Rental & Tour	(876) 979-2719	Mable Ewen Drive - The vicinity of Montego Bay
Happy World Car & Bike Rental	(876) 957-4004	Norman Manley Boulevard - 2.1 mi. (3.5 km) North-Northeast of Negril
Hemisphere Car Rental	(876) 962-1921	51 Manchester Road - Mandeville
Hertz Norman Manley	(876) 924-8028	Norman Manley International Airport - 5.4 mi. (8.7 km) South of Kingston
Hertz Sangster International	(876) 979-0438	Sangster International Airport - Montego Bay
Hertz Sunset Boulevard	(876) 952-4250	28 Sunset Boulevard - Montego Bay
Island Car Rental	(876) 979-2426	Sangster International Airport - The vicinity of Montego Bay
Island Car Rentals	(876) 924-8075	Norman Manley International Airport - 5.4 mi. (8.7 km) South of Kingston
Island Cruiser Rentals	(876) 422-2831	Norman Manley Blvd - 0.9 mi. (1.5 km) North-Northeast of Negril

Jaykay's Car Rental	(876) 792-9837	Sangster International Airport - Montego Bay
Liberty Car Rental	(876) 952-4250	The vicinity of Montego Bay
Mack D's Auto Sales & Rentals	(876) 996-9514	Cross Roads Main Street - Annotto Bay
Metro Car Rentals, Ltd.	(876) 978-5468	47F Old Hope Road - 2.8 mi. (4.5 km) East of Kingston
Payless Car Rental	(876) 952-1212	26 Sunset Avenue - The vicinity of Montego Bay
Prospective Rent-a-Car	(876) 952-3524	Sangster International Airport - Montego Bay
Rent-A-Car Caribbean & Tours	(876) 941-8563	Shop 35 94 Red Hills Road - Portmore
Salem Car Rental	(876) 973-4167	Main Street - Runaway Bay
Smart Car Rental	(876) 425-5301	Hopewell Mall, Shop #32 main street, A1 - Orchard
Sun City Car Rental	(876) 952-3207	10 Sunset Boulevard - Downtown Montego Bay
Sun Jam Car Rentals	(876) 979-9355	66 Claude Clarke Avenue - Downtown Montego Bay
Sunsational Car Rental & Tours	(876) 952-1212	26 Sunset Avenue - Downtown Montego Bay
Ucal's Car Rental Tours & Taxi Service	(876) 952-3836	Shop 7c 32 Queens Drive - The vicinity of Montego Bay
Vernon's Car Rental	(876) 957-4354	1.6 mi. (2.6 km) North-Northeast of Negril
Vision Car Rental & Tours	(876) 979-5559	Salt Spring Road - The vicinity of Montego Bay

The Cost of Renting a Car

Rates for car rentals can be steep in the high season, but they can be half the regular rates in the low season. Expect to pay as much as $120 (USD) per day for your rental, including compulsory collision damage waiver coverage. The extra fee covers potential damage to the car. Low season rates can dip as low as $35 (USD) per day. Weekly rentals are generally in the vicinity of $400 (USD).

The following tables provide an indication of what the cost of renting a car will be. The lowest rates shown only apply to the least costly agencies during the slow season. The high end of the range is what you can expect at one of the busiest firms during the peak season.

VEHICLE RENTALS, DAILY RATES

Rental Type	Low Rate	High Rate
Economy Car	$ 23.00	$ 80.00
Compact Car	$ 25.00	$ 81.00
Mid Size Car	$ 28.00	$ 96.00
Full Size Car	$ 38.00	$ 143.00
Light SUV	$ 50.00	$ 125.00
Standard SUV	$ 60.00	$ 210.00
Heavy SUV	$ 64.00	$ 120.00
Full Size Van	$ 75.00	$ 135.00
Pickup Truck	$ 75.00	$ 130.00
Mini Van	$ 80.00	$ 138.00

VEHICLE RENTALS, WEEKLY RATES

Rental Type	Low Rate	High Rate
Economy Car	$ 138.00	$ 470.00
Compact Car	$ 148.00	$ 480.00
Mid Size Car	$ 176.00	$ 600.00
Full Size Car	$ 230.00	$ 790.00
Light SUV	$ 320.00	$ 705.00
Standard SUV	$ 380.00	$ 1400.00
Heavy SUV	$ 385.00	$ 805.00
Full Size Van	$ 435.00	$ 790.00

Mini Van	$ 450.00	$ 770.00
Pickup Truck	$ 485.00	$ 975.00

Travelers should also make sure taxes, fees and surcharges are included in the price they expect to pay, or they should find out what those extra costs are. This will help avoid unwelcome surprises when it comes time to pay for the rental. Speaking of unwelcome surprises, it is not uncommon for rental agencies to run out of vehicles. If you plan to rent a car, make sure to reserve it months in advance.

In order to rent a car in Jamaica, you must be 25-years-of-age or older, have a valid driver's license from your home country, and have a valid credit card.

If you are traveling with a young child, bring his or her safety seat from home, unless you plan on buying a brand new one on the island. Rental companies do not provide child safety seats to customers.

Driving in Jamaica

The road conditions throughout Jamaica vary depending on the type of area you are in. Rural areas have bumpier, less frequently maintained roads that may be difficult to navigate, and are often crowded with livestock. Roads in larger cities and tourist areas are fair to good. You can expect traffic to be manageable no matter where you are driving on the island

It is important to note that Jamaicans drive on the left side of the road, as opposed to the right side like in America, and gas stations only accept cash as payment.

While you shouldn't have any issues locating gas stations, you still may want to check out the listing below for a picture of where some of them are located.

GAS STATIONS		
Name	Phone	Location

Caleb Gray

Alicia's Petcom Service Station	(876) 964-4298	Savoy Cres - Mandeville
Annotto Bay Texaco Service Center	(876) 996-9395	Top Bay - Annotto Bay
Balaclava Full Service Station & Convenience Store	(876) 963-2345	Main Street - Balaclava
Bird George Shell Service Station	(876) 962-2754	Corner Main Street & Caledonia Road - Mandeville
Bo-Mc Ltd Shell Service Station	(876) 974-5340	Dacosta Drive - Ocho Rios
Braeton Texaco	--	4.4 mi. (7.0 km) Southeast of Spanish Town
Braham's Texaco	(876) 993-2706	15 Harbour Street - Port Antonio
Brown's Epping Service Station	(876) 996-1493	Browns Plaza - Portland Parish
Buff Bay Texaco Service Center	(876) 996-1485	9 Thompson Avenue - Portland Parish
Chung Pat Texaco Service Station	(876) 974-2368	26 Main Street - Ocho Rios
Cool Oasis Gas Station	--	Montego Bay
Coore's Texaco Service Station & Star Mart	(876) 984-5164	2 Young Street - Spanish Town
Coral Gardens Shell Service Station	(876) 953-2205	Rose Hall Main Road - The vicinity of Montego Bay
Daniel's Esso Service Center	(876) 982-9811	Golden Grove
Esso Gas Station	--	Downtown Montego Bay
Foster's Shell Service Station	(876) 962-3200	25 Main Street - Mandeville
Fraser's Shell Service Station Lucea	(876) 956-2907	Church Street - Lucea
G & D Texaco	(876) 610-0442	Albert Town
Graham's Service Station	(876) 987-8026	Spaldings
Greg Chung Texaco	(876) 795-	White River - Ocho Rios

Jamaica Travel Guide, Caribbean

		4088	
Gutters Texaco		(876) 607-5524	Peppers - Saint Ann Parish
Haber's Shell Service Station		(876) 992-9632	Main Street - Highgate
Hacker's Service Station		(876) 957-1177	Struie
Heaven's Texaco Service Station		(876) 625-1942	2 Manchester Road - Mandeville
Henry's Texaco		(876) 975-8746	St. Marys
Hopewell Shell Service Station		(876) 956-5543	Orchard
Hudson's Texaco Service Station		(876) 975-8021	Gayle
Jampet Service Station		(876) 981-4062	25 Willowdene Park - St. Johns
Junction Texaco Service Station		(876) 607-9682	Junction
K & W Service Station		(876) 953-8746	669 Half Moon Street - The vicinity of Montego Bay
Kingsland Petcom Service Station		(876) 964-6060	Kingsland Spur Tree - Mandeville
Kinkead's Texaco Service Station		965-0490-1	Pedro Cross - Treasure Beach
Lee Sins Shell Service Station		(876) 975-2327	Main Street - Browns Town
Mac's Texaco Service Station		(876) 963-4079	Williamsfield
Maragh Petro-Central Service Station		(876) 986-0714	Main Road - Hayes
Marco Service Station		(876) 981-2144	36 Featherbed Lane - St. Johns
Marsh's Epping Service Station		(876) 994-2349	Trinity
May Pen Shell		(876) 786-4345	57 Main Street - May Pen

Mclean's Shell Service Station	(876) 617-2189	8 Cornwall Street - Falmouth
Melan Esso Service Station	(876) 984-9227	Spanish Town
Mohan's Texaco Service Station	(876) 902-1559	15 Manchester Avenue - May Pen
Morant Bay Esso Service	(876) 982-2316	2 Red Hills Road - Morant Bay
Multipet Service Station	708-5364-5	9b Church Pen Nightingale Grove - Saint Catherine Parish
Negril Texaco	(876) 957-3024	White Hall
New Hope Service Center	(876) 955-7946	New Hope
Newleigh Texaco Service Station	(876) 962-2045	Manchester Road - Mandeville
Old Harbour Service Station	(876) 983-2220	12 West Street - Old Harbour
Olive's Shell Service Station	(876) 982-2315	12 Church Street - Morant Bay
Oracabessa Shell Service Station	(876) 726-4263	Oracabessa
Persad's Texaco Station	(876) 904-1141	Main Street - Saint Ann Parish
Petcom Service Station	(876) 974-9357	Coconut Grove - Ocho Rios
Petrol Gas Station	--	Montego Bay
Phillips Artie Shell Service Station	(876) 962-2615	Caledonia Road - Mandeville
Port Maria Shell Service Station	(876) 725-0007	Port Maria
Pottinger's Texaco Service Station	(876) 972-2530	23 Main Street - St. Ann's Bay
Pryce Texaco Service Station	(876) 945-8266	Red Hills Square Red Hills Road Top - Portmore
Robbies Gas & Service	(876) 953-4041	Green Pond - The vicinity of Montego Bay

Jamaica Travel Guide, Caribbean

Robinson's Gas Station	--	Linstead
Rory King Texaco Gas Station	--	1.8 mi. (2.9 km) North of Kingston
Rory's Service Station	(876) 905-1116	141 1/2 C Spring Road - Portmore
Russells Esso Service Station	(876) 785-0678	Summerfield
Sanford Esso Service Station	(876) 984-6260	Spanish Town
Scott's Texaco Service Station	(876) 973-9721	Main Street - Discovery Bay
Shell Gas Sation Ocho Rios	(876) 974-7874	Ocho Rios
Shell Gas Station	--	2.8 mi. (4.5 km) West of Spanish Town
Shell Gas Station	(876) 979-7269	Howard Cooke Boulevard - Downtown Montego Bay
Shell Gas Station	--	Tharpe Street - Falmouth
Shell Service Station	941-8454-5	211 C Spring Road - Portmore
Shell Station Negril	--	Sheffield Road - Negril
Shell Station Runaway Bay	--	Main Road - Runaway Bay
Simmonds Texaco Service Station	(876) 942-2979	Long Lane - Stony Hill
Texaco	--	0.7 mi. (1.1 km) East-Southeast of Kingston
Texaco	--	2.0 mi. (3.3 km) West-Southwest of Kingston
Texaco	--	1.7 mi. (2.7 km) North-Northwest of Kingston
Texaco Gas Station	--	Black River
Texaco Station	--	Mandeville
Thompson's Texaco Service center	(876) 926-6200	54 H W T Road - Portmore
Three Miles Texaco	(876) 758-9271	178a Spanish Town Road - Portmore
Total Gas Station	--	4.1 mi. (6.5 km) Southeast of Spanish Town
Total Gas Station	--	2.8 mi. (4.5 km) West of Spanish Town

Total Gas Station	--	1.9 mi. (3.0 km) West of Morant Bay
Total Gas Station	--	1.1 mi. (1.7 km) South-Southeast of Kingston
Total Gas Station	904-2901-2	May Pen
Total Gas Station	(876) 601-5200	Tucker Granville - 2.8 mi. (4.5 km) Southeast of Montego Bay
Total Gas Station	--	Harbour Lane - Falmouth
Total Liguanea Service Station	(876) 977-4039	117 Old Hope Road - Portmore

Requirements and restrictions regarding renting a vehicle in Jamaica can vary. If you are concerned about minimum and maximum age restrictions, insurance requirements and the like, consider contacting each firm directly, before making a final decision.

Jamaica is larger than most Caribbean islands, and the prices, demand, and polcies surrounding rental cars can vary from coast to coast. If you want to learn more about a specific area, read one of the guides below.

Sailing & Boating

Sailing and Boating Near Jamaica
Strike out on your own for a sailing or yachting trip across the Caribbean to visit Jamaica

Jamaica lies within the Caribbean, which is known worldwide for its near-perfect sailing conditions. The water is always warm and there are plenty of beautiful islands to visit. Jamaica itself is not widely regarded as a top sailing spot, however, that should not deter interested travelers.

Although it is far from the most popular way to reach Jamaica, intrepid sailors think nothing of climbing aboard a boat and sailing to and around the island. Chartered and personal boats can certainly be sailed into any number of harbors around Jamaica, and those looking for a day of sailing fun have the option of hopping aboard a party boat or procuring a day rental.

Party Boats

Jamaica is an excellent place to host an event on the water. Everything from weddings to birthday parties to product launches can be hosted aboard a large vessel that will accommodate upwards of 100 people. These types of boats are called Party Boats.

If you simply want to spend a few hours on the water, without the cost and responsibility associated with renting a boat you should take a day sailing excursion. Check out the table that follows to find names and phone numbers for area excursion services.

BOAT EXCURSIONS		
Name	Phone	Location
Barrett Adventures Sailing	(876) 382-6384	Montego Bay Yacht Club - 1.9 mi. (3.1 km) South West of Montego Bay
Buttonwood JA	(876) 374-4266	Downtown Treasure Beach
Captain Dennis Adventures	(876) 435-3779	Downtown Treasure Beach
Cool Runnings Cruises	(876) 974-2446	1 Marvins Park - Port Royal
Dreamer Catamaran Cruises	(876) 979-0102	The vicinity of Montego Bay
Island Charter Co.	(876) 878-2287	Hedonism II - 4.6 mi. (7.4 km) North of Negril
Jamaica Watersports	(876) 381-3229	Montego Bay Yacht Club - 1.9 mi. (3.1 km) South West of Montego Bay
Mike's Glass Bottom Boat	(876) 847-7699	Seven Mile Beach - 2.9 mi. (4.6 km) North of Negril
Sea Shell Charters	(876) 875-4167	Orange Bay
Sunbaby Glass Bottom Boat	(876) 485-4023	Negril

Boat Rentals and Charters

Selecting a crewed charter can be more difficult than some would think, but one possible oversight is crew compatibility. Traveling for weeks with a crew means you'll get to know them very well, and this can be difficult if crew and passengers dislike each other. To help solve this problem, charter brokers step in.

Throughout the Caribbean you'll find plenty of different charter companies. These companies, like any other, come in many sizes. First-time charterers are generally guided toward the larger companies. A smaller company may have a great reputation, but should a boat you requested be unavailable, smaller companies might not have the ability to replace it with an equivalent ship, where larger companies will usually offer a similar or even larger boat at no extra cost. However, some of the smallest companies have purposefully stayed small to maintain their customer service standards.

Another way to divide charter companies is into "tiers." These tiers say nothing about the quality or service of the company, but instead the newness of the yachts being chartered. First tier companies have the best boats, and largest number of extras. Boats older than four or five years are usually sold to second tier companies if they are in good condition. First tier companies will cost more for a charter, but boats may include goodies such as the auto pilot function, GPS systems, stereos and cell phones.

If you're evaluating the option of chartering a boat, you can call one of these area agencies:

CHARTER AND RENTAL SERVICES

Name	Phone	Location
Royal Jamaica Yacht Club	924-8685-6	Palisadoes Park - Portmore
Yamon Red Stripe Catamaran	(876) 443-0178	Norman Manley Boulevard - 1.9 mi. (3.0 km) North-Northeast of Negril

Docking

Private sailing boats to Jamaica must enter the country through an official port of entry. Immigration and customs services are available at the following ports:

- ✓ Kingston
- ✓ Montego Bay
- ✓ Port Antonio
- ✓ Ocho Rios
- ✓ Port Kaiser
- ✓ Port Esquivel
- ✓ Discovery Bay
- ✓ Bowden

Fly your "Q" flag when sailing into port. If you want to spend time cruising around Jamaica, the customs officers can issue you a "Coastwide Clearance" form. This form allows you to sail at will along the coast and must be presented when visiting other ports.

Planning to visit Jamaica using a vessel you own, or a charter from another location? See the chart below to get information on area marinas.

MARINAS		
Name	Phone	Location
Boundbrook Wharf	(876) 832-4765	West Harbour - Port Antonio
Caribatik Marina	--	1.9 mi. (3.1 km) East of Falmouth
Errol Flynn Marina	(876) 832-4765	Port Antonio
Glistening Waters Marina	(876) 954-3229	2.1 mi. (3.4 km) East of Falmouth
Mary's Bay Marina & Fuel Dock	(876) 957-0981	Negril Beach Hotel Zone

Montego Bay Marine Park	(876) 952-5619	Downtown Montego Bay
Montego Bay Yacht Club	(876) 979-8038	Sunset Drive - 1.9 mi. (3.1 km) South West of Montego Bay
Pier One Marina	(876) 952-2452	Pier One - Downtown Montego Bay
Port Antonio Marina and Boatyard	(876) 832-4765	Errol Flynn Marina - Port Antonio
Royal Jamaica Yacht Club	(876) 924-8685	4.8 mi. (7.7 km) South-Southeast of Kingston
Stanley's Marina	(876) 953-2244	The vicinity of Montego Bay
West Indies Yacht Club	(800) 223-1017	Old Harbour
Yacht Harbor Marina	--	Downtown Ocho Rios

You will need to clear customs when you arrive at your first port and also when you depart from Jamaica's territorial waters. Customs officers will indicate to the captain when they have inspected the ship and cleared it through customs. You will need to fill out several forms at customs, including the following:

- ✓ Crew list and declaration
- ✓ Departure permission forms from your last port of call
- ✓ The ship's registrations
- ✓ A list of the ship's stores

There may also be a standard form to be completed in triplicate. This form replaces the crew list and requires details of the ship's flag, registration, last port of call and information about each person on board including full name, date of birth, passport number, nationality, and position on the ship.

The Quarantine Officer will tell you when the "Q" flag may be lowered. He will also require a few items as well. Carry a crew list and a maritime declaration of health provided by a quarantine official, to be signed by the captain and including any bill of health or DE-RAT certificate from the last port of call. Unless travelers have visited countries in which the World Health Organization has reported a communicable disease within the past six weeks, vaccinations are not required.

Immigration officials will need to see a crew list and passports or proof of citizenship. Visitors from countries outside of the US may need 30-day visas before they arrive. Travelers will also need to pass through Immigration for stays longer than six months.

NEARBY ANCHORAGES		
Location	Latitude	Longitude
St. Ann's Bay - St. Ann's Bay	18.4432686349	-77.1972370148
Ocho Rios Bay - Downtown Ocho Rios	18.4114038746	-77.1082627773
Discovery Bay - Discovery Bay	18.4629513234	-77.4032092094
Rio Bueno Bay - 7.7 mi. (12.4 km) West of Runaway Bay	18.4727612933	-77.4533128738
Salt Island	17.8315067582	-77.1400308609
Oracabessa Harbor - Oracabessa	18.4076882579	-76.9479310519
Pigeon Island	17.7984530076	-77.0759153366
Coquar Bay - 10.8 mi. (17.4 km) South of Spanish Town	17.840811513	-76.9920158386
Port Maria Beach - 13.3 mi. (21.4 km) East of Ocho Rios	18.3724981891	-76.8846845417
Manatee Bay - 10.0 mi. (16.2 km) South of Spanish Town	17.8484914492	-76.9715023041
Alligator Reef - 15.8 mi. (25.4 km) East-Southeast of Treasure Beach	17.8084756395	-77.5384998269
Port Kaiser - 10.5 mi. (16.9 km) East of Treasure Beach	17.8624303535	-77.6069498088

Pelican Cays	17.8020198375	-77.0193099976
Salt Bay - 16.4 mi. (26.3 km) East of Ocho Rios	18.3477746194	-76.8429064541
Wreck Bay - 10.4 mi. (16.8 km) South of Spanish Town	17.8420586296	-76.9401740609
Half Moon Cays	17.7363040726	-77.0873736916
Port Royal	17.9376130934	-76.8447518349
Bare Bush Cay	17.7550240822	-77.0345020294
Portland Caye - Portland Cay	17.7102934293	-77.1111273766
Pedro Bay - Treasure Beach	17.8633698238	-77.7418112755
Crab Pond Bay - Crab Pond Bay	18.1053010993	-77.9882311821
Bogue Lagoon - 2.1 mi. (3.4 km) South West of Montego Bay	18.4568763448	-77.9422473907
Bluefields Bay - 14.4 mi. (23.2 km) Northwest of Black River	18.1588819492	-78.0314683914
15.6 mi. (25.1 km) East-Southeast of Negril	18.1972090558	-78.122191471
Mosquito Cove - 12.5 mi. (20.2 km) West of Montego Bay	18.4479910563	-78.1084370823
San San Bay - 3.9 mi. (6.2 km) East of Port Antonio	18.1751660567	-76.3939154148
Tom Pipers Bay - 15.7 mi. (25.2 km) West of Montego Bay	18.4460069985	-78.1562662544
Green Island Bay - Green Island	18.3951928495	-78.2677602768
Bloody Bay - 5.5 mi. (8.9 km) North of Negril	18.3518994212	-78.3381843567

If you're interested in spending at least part of your Jamaican vacation on the open sea, there are multitudes of options available to you.

Whether you choose to sail to the island aboard a chartered yacht, hire a party boat for a night of fun, or spend a day in the Caribbean sea jet skiing and sailing around the island, the opportunity is there.

Even though it is not particularly popular, sailing in Jamaica can be diverse. From urban waters around Kingston to peaceful quiet around Treasure Beach, read our local Jamaica guides to sailing to get a better idea of what to expect in the different areas of the island.

Taxis

Jamaica's taxis are an affordable, reliable form of transportation

Taxis are one of the most popular ways for travelers to get out and see Jamaica. The ease of having someone who knows the area and the country's driving laws will enable you to relax and enjoy your trip. Taxis are typically the best way for vacationers to get around. Still, a little preparation will ensure your taxi trips go off without a hitch.

Taxi Companies

You'll find many types of rides, but all of the official taxis in Jamaica are members of the Jamaican Union of Travellers Association, or JUTA. These are officially licensed cabs and drivers, and their license plates will be red and display "PP" or "PPV," which stand for Public Passenger Vehicle. Rogue or "pirate" taxi services are also available, but visitors are discouraged from using these.

If you'd like to call ahead for a cab to pick you up at a reserved location and time, feel free to get in touch with any of these these taxi services.

TAXI SERVICES		
Name	Phone	Location
Apollo Taxi Service	(876) 929-5153	12 Retirement Cres - 1.0 mi. (1.6 km) South-Southeast of Kingston

Bryon's Taxi Transfers	(876) 391-4914	Falmouth
Confidence Taxi Service	(876) 755-2220	22 Dunrobin Ave - Kingston
Cool Cabs	(876) 930-2012	26 1/2 Giltress Street - Kingston
Cross Jamaica Tours	(876) 362-4906	Negril
Cross Jamaica Tours	(876) 362-4906	1.3 mi. (2.0 km) North-Northeast of Negril
DC Super Shuttle	(876) 845-594	Negril
Dean's Taxi Service	(876) 966-4301	Phillips Plaza - Santa Cruz
Demight Taxi Service	(876) 996-1555	2 Thompson Avenue - Buff Bay
Destiny Travel Service	(876) 949-6367	Portmore Pines Plaza - Portmore
Island Transfer & Tours	(876) 391-4914	Montego Bay
JCAL Tours	(876) 952-7574	Claude Clarke Avenue - Montego Bay
James Bond Tours	(876) 434-1565	Negril
Juta Tours	(876) 952-0309	Sangster International Airport - The vicinity of Montego Bay
Karandas Taxi Services	(876) 974-2063	10 Balivard Avenue - Ocho Rios
Linston's Travel Service	(876) 376-3652	Negril
Luxurious Carib Tours and Taxi	(876) 798-8382	Norman Manley Boulevard, Negril, Jamaica - 3.1 mi. (4.9 km) North of Negril
MCA Taxi Service	(876) 974-2343	Ocho Rios
Michael's On-Time Taxi	(876) 887-9342	Negril
Miracle Taxi Service	(876) 746-	Ceder Palace Plaza - Saint Catherine Parish

		6407	
Nice N Easy Taxi Service	(876) 989-6500	Portmore
No Limit Tours Jamaica	(876) 384-2894	Negril
On Time Taxi Co Limited	(876) 968-4780	12 Burlington Avenue - 0.6 mi. (0.9 km) Northwest of Kingston
Rocky's Taxi and Tours	(876) 648-1877	West End Road - Negril
Safe Travel Taxi Service	(876) 901-5510	Shop 16 27A Seaward Drive - Portmore
Tallman's Jamaica Tours	(876) 439-9076	Negril
Travel Around Jamaica Tours	(876) 287-2180	82 Tryall Gardens, Hopewell - Montego Bay
Turner Taxi and Tours	(876) 461-7452	Norman Manley Boulevard - Negril

Another type of taxi available in Jamaica is the "route taxi" or shared taxi. These taxis are a cross between a taxi and a bus, operating on short, around-town routes with many people. The fares are set between bus and traditional taxi fares.

Rates, Fares, and Fees

Although technically all taxis in Jamaica are metered, drivers rarely, if ever, use them. This means you'll want to negotiate the price, and the currency with which you'll pay, before you get into the cab. Metered fares should be posted inside the taxi. You can ask a driver for a copy if you don't see one. When negotiating the price, begin by offering half the price the driver has asked. Once you get a feeling for the area and the bargaining, you will be better equipped for negotiation.

Fares are rarely cheap—around $20(USD) for every 10 miles—but will almost always be higher if you are using a taxi that is licensed to a hotel. However, tips may be unnecessary once a fare is agreed upon. When tipping for a metered ride, give between 10 percent and 12 percent of the fare. Fares will be 25 percent higher between midnight and 5:00 a.m.

This chart shows some typical cab fares for the area.

TYPICAL FARES AROUND JAMAICA

Typical Cost (USD)	Location A	Location B
$ 65.00 - $ 100.00	Montego Bay	Negril
$ 83.20 - $ 96.00	Downtown Ocho Rios	Falmouth
$ 138.75 - $ 160.00	Negril	Falmouth
$ 46.50 - $ 47.00	Downtown Montego Bay	Falmouth
$ 134.25 - $ 154.50	Negril Beach Hotel Zone	Falmouth
$ 27.90 - $ 28.25	Falmouth	Rio Bueno
$ 9.10 - $ 9.75	Falmouth	Falmouth Cruise Terminal
$ 27.30 - $ 28.60	Falmouth	Braco Airstrip
$ 90.00	Sangster International Airport	Ocho Rios
$ 250.00	Falmouth Cruise Terminal	Black River
$ 60.00	Falmouth Cruise Terminal	Sangster International Airport
$ 50.00	Ocho Rios Cruise Terminal	Hedonism Ii
$ 20.00	Ocho Rios Cruise Terminal	Dunn's River Park
$ 40.00	Ocho Rios Cruise Terminal	Sandals Golf And Country Club
$ 8.00	Ocho Rios Cruise Terminal	Island Village
$ 8.00	Ocho Rios Cruise Terminal	Tajmahal Plaza
$ 50.00	Ocho Rios Cruise Terminal	Beaches Boscobel
$ 55.00	Falmouth Cruise Terminal	Half Moon Club
$ 55.00	Sangster International Airport	Falmouth
$ 35.00	Sangster International Airport	Downtown Montego Bay
$ 79.00	Sangster International Airport	Negril Beach Hotel Zone
$ 150.00	Falmouth Cruise Terminal	Negril
$ 40.00	Falmouth Cruise Terminal	Iberostar Grand Hotel Rose Hall

$ 45.00	Sangster International Airport	Round Hill Hotel & Villas
$ 70.00	Sangster International Airport	West Palm Hotel
$ 60.00	Sangster International Airport	Tryall Club
$ 20.00	Port Zante	St. Pauls
$ 30.00	Ocho Rios Cruise Terminal	Sandals Ochi
$ 90.00	Falmouth Cruise Terminal	Ocho Rios
$ 26.00 - $ 32.00	Douglas-Charles Airport	Newton
$ 70.00	Falmouth Cruise Terminal	Grand Bahia Principe Jamaica
$ 40.00	Ocho Rios Cruise Terminal	San Souci
$ 150.00	Norman Manley International Airport	Ocho Rios
$ 60.00	Norman Manley International Airport	Downtown Kingston
$ 235.00	Norman Manley International Airport	Montego Bay
$ 275.00	Norman Manley International Airport	Negril
$ 5.00	Montego Bay Cruise Terminal	Downtown Montego Bay
$ 90.00	Falmouth Cruise Terminal	Dunn's River Park
$ 8.00	Ocho Rios Cruise Terminal	Downtown Ocho Rios
$ 6.00	Ocho Rios Cruise Terminal	Moon Palace Jamacia Grande
$ 20.00	Ocho Rios Cruise Terminal	Shaw Park Beach
$ 20.00	Ocho Rios Cruise Terminal	New Pineapple Shopping Center
$ 115.00	Sangster International Airport	Jewel Dunn's River Beach Resort & Spa
$ 80.00	Falmouth Cruise Terminal	St. Ann's Bay
$ 50.00	Ocho Rios Cruise Terminal	Couples Sans Souci

Many people call ahead and reserve cabs to take them from the airport to their hotel. Because Jamaica is so large, this can be a pricey endeavor, so it is best to plan ahead.

Below is another table that will give you an idea of taxi policy in some major areas.

ADDITIONAL INFORMATION ON TAXIS IN MAJOR AREAS

Location	Taxi Information
Negril	Fares around town should be approximately $4(USD) or $5(USD). Don't ride with drivers who ask for too much.
Kingston	Fares are per car, not per passenger, and negotiation is a must. Taxis are the most reliable transportation in the city.
Montego Bay	Taxis are the most reliable transportation in the city. Most cabs are found along Gloucester Avenue.
Port Antonio	Fares in the area are approximately $15(USD) to $20(USD). Taxis are often older vehicles.

Touring by Taxi

Travelers can take taxis on sightseeing tours. Remember to negotiate for a fare the same way you would on a regular around-town taxi ride. Fares for an all-day taxi tour can range from $100(USD) to $180(USD), depending on how far the tour takes you. When preparing for an all-day tour, you will want to make sure that you've chosen a driver you like and trust. It may be best to develop a rapport with your driver, even when staying at a hotel that has licensed taxi drivers.

On an island as big as Jamaica, renting a car may be a more effective means of getting around. But, the road conditions are not the best, and it can be a bit confusing trying to get from place to place. This is why many tourists opt for taxis even though the prices can get steep. Buses are another option. Though not the most reliable, they are the most affordable.

For tourists who prefer to leave the driving up to someone who knows their stuff, taxis in Jamaica are the best choice. They are easy to find, they come when you call, and they get you where you need to go.

Jamaica Vacation Planning

Planning Your Vacation in Jamaica

There are many resouces to help you find all the facts you'll need to know before planning a vacation in Jamaica

A vacation in Jamaica can be the perfect getaway. Gorgeous beaches, breathtaking mountain views, and a lively and spirited culture have made the island one of the world's most distinct destinations. Before you get too caught up daydreaming, however, take the time to plan some of the most important aspects of your trip.

Getting the most out of your tropical vacation means evaluating your priorities, researching your destination, and deciding on purchasing methods.

Deciding what sort of trip you will be taking is the first step to planning a successful vacation. Is your time in Jamaica meant to be a romantic retreat for two or a boisterous adventure with friends? Figuring out the ideal atmosphere is essential to finding the perfect island spot and getting the most out of your holiday.

Educating yourself about the regional differences you will encounter on Jamaica will also prove invaluable. Negril, for example, will appeal more to party goers than upscale Ocho Rios, which is a better alternative for honeymooners of all ages. Do as much research as possible before leaving home in order to ensure that you know what to expect once you arrive in Jamaica.

Finally, become familiar with ways to book your vacation. Online vendors have gained popularity in recent years and are now able to offer travelers a few distinct advantages over some of the more conventional methods. No matter what you choose, however, it is essential that you feel comfortable with your decision.

Careful planning beforehand is one of the most important things you can do to help make sure that your vacation in Jamaica is everything you've always dreamed of.

Booking

Booking your Trip to Jamaica

There are a number of great ways to book your getaway in Jamaica
You've done the research, made travel decisions big and small, and now you're ready to purchase your vacation. So, what's the best way to do this? Options abound, but travelers looking to find the best rates and flexible itineraries may find this easier when booking on the Internet.

Some travelers may feel uneasy about arranging their trip online, but if your research and decisions have been guided by this Web site, purchasing your vacation online is the next logical step. Try not to let unfounded fears affect your ability to get the best deals, though. Remember that customer security and protection have come a long way in recent years.

Hotels and airlines are able to offer online customers better prices because they frequently reserve special deals and packages exclusively for those purchasing their vacations on the Internet. Oftentimes if you contact the individual vendors directly, you will find that they may not be aware of the deals available online, so doing your research really helps when comparing rates.

A travel agent is another popular option for booking your trip to Jamaica. Simply visiting your nearby agency can have its disadvantages, however. Chances are that if you have done a lot of research you will already be more knowledgeable about the area you would like to visit than a travel agent that does general worldwide bookings will be. Unless you find a travel agent that specializes in travel to the Caribbean and Jamaica, these agents will need to do some research on the area before being able to make the best recommendations for you.

One way to put your research to use is to take advantage of the growing numbers of Internet travel vendors. By doing this you are able to find a vendor that you are comfortable with, although you should bear in mind that large Web sites that do not focus specifically on the Caribbean (and Jamaica in particular) will present the same problems that generalized travel agents do. Fortunately, it is not difficult to find sellers that cater to vacationers who would like to experience Jamaica. Customers that use these Web sites will benefit from the more detailed descriptions and reviews they provide.

Although the look and style of these Web sites may vary dramatically, you should notice that the prices they offer are often fairly close. This is because most Internet vendors receive similar discounts from hotels and assess a similar mark-up. Any differences should be nominal and any sites that show a large price gap should be examined more closely, as the cause of this discrepancy may simply be one Web site failing to list all the taxes and fees involved in booking your travel or accommodation plans.

Not only can Internet vendors offer discounted rates and special attention to your plans, but they are also in the position to grant travelers unique attention and protection. In the event of trouble or disputes with a lodging provider, for example, third party vendors will be able to take your side and have the leverage of future dealings with the property. By refusing to do business with companies that do not treat their customers well, vacationers who book through Internet travel sellers have the assurance that they'll receive quality customer service.

Finally, selecting a vendor is a good way to let a company know that you appreciated their information or organization. If they were particularly helpful or interesting, using them to book your vacation allows you to support a particular business or Web site.

Knowing that you've done all the required research, made informed decisions, and weighed all your purchasing options carefully will allow you the comfort of mind to enjoy your fabulous vacation once you arrive in Jamaica.

Budgeting

How Much will it Cost to Vacation in Jamaica?

Budgeting before you leave can help you relax and enjoy your time in Jamaica

Beautiful white sand beaches and palm trees await you on the shores of Jamaica. While lounging by the beach is often free, tourists will be expected to pay for any other activity they plan to participate in, and more, over the course of their tropical vacation. Because of this, budgeting is a crucial part of planning for your trip. To ensure you don't forget anything while devising your budget, check off these important items as you make your list.

Accommodations

Jamaica's visitors spend an average of $300(USD) per day for their stay at an all-inclusive resort, but all-inclusives and mega resorts offer guests much more than a room. In addition to food, activities, and entertainment, they also offer travelers more in the way of security. It's possible to find a place to stay for a lesser price, but don't expect to pay much less than $80(USD) per night anywhere you go. Prices for all-inclusives are generally higher because they include meals and activities.

Some of the more chic and attractive areas of Jamaica, such as Montego Bay and Negril, feature hotels and resorts with higher price tags, while visitors staying in out-of-the-way, locally owned inns or guesthouses will find much lower rooming costs. Remember that in Jamaica you almost always get what you pay for, and it is important to carefully research your accommodations before you make a final decision. Negotiation is possible at nearly all places on the island, especially during low season.

Daily Spending

On most vacations, your budget must account for accommodations, food, travel, and activities. If you're an all-inclusive traveler, you've already taken care of most of these in the cost of your hotel. Buying your vacation in one neat, little package may save you money and will definitely cut down on the number of individual items in your budget. Travelers not planning an all-inclusive vacation should consider that a daily budget in Jamaica can run as low as $30(USD) per person, but $40 to $60(USD) is more realistic.

If you're venturing to a restaurant outside your resort or hotel, you can expect to spend from $8 to $30(USD), or more at a top dining establishment. In spite of price and style variations, you should expect to spend a bare minimum of $30(USD) on meals per day. Some hotels that are under the same ownership offer deals to guests who dine at any of these establishments, so be sure to check with the front desk of your hotel to learn how to take advantage of these deals.

Modes of transport can vary, depending on your preferences and how comfortable you feel boarding public transportation in Jamaica. Busesare undoubtedly the least expensive, but the most recommended are JUTA taxis. Buses can take you around town all day for mere dollars, while a day-long taxi tour can cost as much as $180(USD). Most travelers will not spend this much in a day on taxi services. Remember that the normal fares rise 25 percent after midnight, so budget-conscious travelers may want to skip the late-night outings unless they have another way to return to their hotel. Tourists staying at hotels that provide taxi services should be aware that they may be charged a slightly higher rate by the taxi drivers. Without a doubt, the most expensive kind of travel in Jamaica is renting your own vehicle. Rentals can cost more than $100(USD) per day in the high season.

Once arriving in Jamaica, activities will vary by personal preferences, but generally speaking, all-inclusive travelers save more on the cost of activities than travelers buying their vacations piecemeal. Unless your idea of the perfect activity is lounging in the sun, you'll probably want to budget some money for snorkeling, museum entry fees and other activities, such as entertainment at some of Jamaica's lively and popular nightspots. This is, of course, at your own discretion, but it helps to anticipate the type of entertainment you're most likely to pursue.

Tipping and gratuities should also be a consideration in your budget. To avoid tipping more than you planned, always ask at hotels and restaurants if you believe a gratuity may have been added. Typical tips in Jamaica should be between 10 and 20 percent for meals and taxis, though this may vary on unmetered taxi rides.

Taxes

One fee you may not like but you won't want to forget is the departure tax. Currently the departure tax for Jamaica is set at $27(USD), and must be paid in cash. Be careful: You may have already paid the departure tax when you bought your airline ticket, so if you're departing by plane you will want to make sure you don't pay twice.

Another less than welcome expense you'll encounter in Jamaica is an island-wide sales tax, which most visitors forget to budget for. This 16.5 percent VAT on most goods and services is already quoted as part of the price in almost every case. This replaced the room occupancy tax.

Shopping

If you're a shopaholic or just planning to bring home some quirky souvenirs or Jamaican rum, don't forget to add a shopping category to your budget. Souvenirs for family, friends, and yourself can add up before you know it, especially when you take them through customs. Making sure that your items all meet customs regulations can be very helpful. Of course, spending on Jamaican items is up to you because you are the only one who can estimate how much you will want to spend. Remember, negotiation is almost always necessary when shopping in Jamaica and bargaining is an easy way to make your budget go farther.

Getting Info

Getting More Info Concerning Jamaica

Researching information about your upcoming Jamaican adventure is important
The research you do for your vacation in Jamaica can seriously effect how much you enjoy your time on the island. Smart visitors will find out as much as possible before making important travel decisions.

The Internet is an invaluable resource for people who would like to quickly get trustworthy information from a variety of sources. This Web site provides general information for all your Jamaican travel needs, but is most helpful when used alongside VisitJamaica.com, the official Web site for Jamaica. Of course, Internet searches will help you find many other alternatives as well.

One aspect that many people tend to overlook is the information available from Internet travel sellers. Vendors are often able to educate travelers about the amenities and advantages of each individual hotel, helping you to get a better idea of whether or not a certain type of lodging is right for you. These large-scale overviews of accommodation, transportation, and package choices can also help you to find out about options you may have never even known existed.

Additionally, small business directories are frequently included in Web sites for travel vendors, allowing visitors to look up island services such as yacht charter brokers before leaving home. **Vacationers** on a budget will find that many Web sites cater specifically to their interests, as will travelers hoping to spend time in several different locations.

Guidebooks are another indispensable aid when gathering information. Bookstores will frequently carry a wide range of guides and becoming familiar with the different types can help you to find the one that best suits your own personality and vacation style. A lot of the information in the books will be the same; however, money-saving advice, travel tips, and evaluations of restaurants and sitests can differ greatly.

While in the bookstore, make a point of also stopping to peruse travel magazines. Several will be Caribbean-specific and it may be possible to find articles on Jamaica that will have innovative ideas or advice that is relevant to your trip. Online editions may also be available for some of the leading publications and searching the archives can help you find the exact information you're looking for.

People you know are yet another great way to supplement the results of your fact-finding mission. Friends, family, and coworkers who have been to Jamaica can offer real world information and answer any questions you may have. Perhaps your brother-in-law can recommend the perfect roadside stand for getting jerk chicken in Montego Bay or your colleague will advise that you take a certain trail when hiking the Blue Mountains.

If your friends and family haven't had the pleasure of visiting Jamaica, however, message boards and forums on the Internet can allow you the same opportunity to get input from vacationers all over the world. Pose questions, browse the archives, and view vacation photos to help you get a feel for the region that you'll be enjoying on your trip. Bear in mind, however, that you should carefully weigh the trustworthiness of your source before basing an important decision on their advice.

Fortunately, getting information is a very pleasant aspect of vacation planning. Once you feel knowledgeable about the multi-faceted personality of Jamaica, you're all set to enjoy your vacation. After all, the more you know about the island's unique culture, varied terrain, beaches and regional differences the more likely you'll be to make good travel decisions.

Making Decisions

How to Decide What You Want for your Vacation in Jamaica

Making good decisions now will improve your trip to Jamaica
Avid surfers eager to tackle the island's beautiful waves would probably not appreciate arriving on the island to find that their hotel is located high in the Blue Mountains. Nor would many honeymooners like to find themselves booked to stay at a resort that caters to young children. Informed decisions can help prevent unpleasant surprises while visiting Jamaica.

Experiencing the perfect vacation means paying careful attention to detail when making important travel decisions. Once you've determined your priorities and taken the time to learn about Jamaica, you're ready to begin the decision-making process.

Narrow Your Search

If your vacation is strongly guided by a particular activity such as golf, hiking, or water sports, a guidebook or Web site may provide the most useful information for deciding which region of Jamaica is right for you. These guides, as well as other Internet resources can provide some ideas about which areas of the island are best for your visit. Look into this before booking your airfare or accommodations.

Arrivals

The most conventional methods for arriving in Jamaica are via planes and cruise ships. Each offers travelers plenty of options, however, so you should decide how you would like to travel, when you hope to arrive, and how quickly you'd like to get there. Many of the small airports found in Jamaica do not receive direct flights so visitors who are uncomfortable in small planes may want to remain near larger cities that have direct service, such as Montego Bay. Cruise passengers should remember that most ships do not remain in port for very long so they offer a much different experience than the one you might have if you were staying on dry land. For those who believe that getting there is half the fun, experienced sailors are even welcomed to bring their own vessels into certain marinas on the island.

On the Island

Figuring out your itinerary might be the most difficult of all the vacation decisions you'll have to make. First you'll have to settle on a place to stay and determine which activities you're most interested in. If water sports are a top priority, a hotel located on the beach may be essential. Those interested in seeing historic sites might plan to stay in or near colonial structures or plantation homes; luckily, both are easy to find in Jamaica.

Consider which aspect of your visit will be the most meaningful. Do you have your heart set on seeing a specific region or participating in certain activities? Perhaps the style of accommodations tops your list of vacation priorities. If exploring coral reefs are important, you'll want to seek out destinations with nearby marine life and scuba diving or snorkeling facilities. Travelers looking for some solitude will find that out-of-the-way spots outside of the traditional tourist traps offer them the privacy they desire in a more secluded atmosphere.

Your traveling companions will also influence you when making decisions. If planning a family holiday, you will probably find that Caribbean and Jamaica guidebooks that are geared toward family travel will help you to find kid-friendly hotels and activities. On the other hand, if you're traveling with friends you'll need to take everyone's preferences into account before making any major decisions.

Don't be afraid to be picky when you're choosing where you'll stay, how you'll get there and what to see and do while in Jamaica. Once you've done your research you should feel confident about your decision-making ability and prepared to make all the arrangements for a perfect Jamaican vacation.

Packing

Suggestions for Packing for a Vacation in Jamaica

Writing a packing check list will help take a load of stress off your shoulders

There are two types of packers in this world: those that plan for days (if not weeks) in advance, making lists of everything they will pack, and checking that list off as they place items in their luggage; and those that begin tossing random articles of clothing into their suitcases just hours before they are scheduled to leave.

Whatever category you fall into, every vacationer can use a little help determining what is and is not appropriate to pack for their trip to Jamaica especially is this trip is their first to the island.

First and Foremost

In order to travel to Jamaica, you must provide customs officials with a few documents. These include your government-issued identification card (such as a driver's license), your passport, and a $27(USD) fee that will get you a tourist card that is good for up to six months. You will also be required to pay another $27(USD) when you exit the country. Some airlines include these fees in the cost of your ticket, so check with the airlines to determine if you will need the cash on hand. It would also be wise to carry with you photocopies of your identification card and your passport in the event that the originals are lost or stolen. Keep them packed in a location separate from the originals.

You will also want to make sure you have enough money to get you through your trip be it in cash, debit, or credit cards. Expert travelers would recommend you always have cash on hand, in the event that a credit card machine is down. The official currency of Jamaica is the Jamaican Dollar, and you can exchange your money when you arrive at the airport, or at a bank and some hotels. ATMs are also great locations to get local currency, however, these can sometimes be difficult to locate.

Other important documents to have on hand include prescriptions for your medications, notes from your personal physician regarding any health issues you may have, and a list of emergency contacts.

Finally, you certainly won't want to forget your airline tickets, and confirmation of your hotel and rental car, and paperwork regarding and pre-arranged excursions and activities.

Clothing

The great thing about Jamaica is that the typical clothing style of the island is not too formal, or too relaxed, but somewhere in the middle. This means that you won't have to worry about your personal style offending local sensibilities. Still, if you have concerns, check out our guide to Clothes in Jamaica to get a closer look at local style.

When planning what to pack, consider the activities you will be participating in. As you explore the island, you will want to wear comfortable, light weight clothing that is suitable for Jamaican temperatures which is hot. Light-colored, light-weight cottons and linen t-shirts and tank tops are the best choice, with shorts and khaki pants being ideal for your bottom half. Women will likely want to save dresses and skirts for outings that do not require much strenuous activity, for example out to lunch, while shopping, or a short tour through a museum. Again, stick to breathable fabrics.

Additionally, don't forget enough pairs of under garments and socks to get you through your trip. You will also want to bring along at least one pair of pajamas. Where shoes are concerned, you will definitely want to bring along a pair of comfortable athletic shoes for traversing the island on particular tours especially if you are planning to do some hiking and a lot of outdoor exploration. Sandals and flip flops are great secondary shoe choices.

Formal Wear

While you can certainly get away with spending your entire vacation in casual clothing and beach wear, there are some occasions at which you may be required to don something slightly more formal. Collared shirts and slacks for men, and sun dresses, skirts or slacks paired with embellished blouses, or party dresses for women will suffice for dining or nightlife entertainment. Make sure to bring along shoes that fit the occasion, such as dock shoes for men, and heels or strappy sandals for women.

Swim Wear

Depending upon the length of your vacation, you would be smart to pack at least two swimsuits. This will not only give you options, but allow you to leave one to dry in your hotel room while wearing the other. A rash guard may be necessary for you if you plan to participate in watersports like diving because it will protect your skin from the harsh rays of the sun which are amplified in the water.

Also consider bringing along a cover-up such as a sarong or pareo so you can quickly go from the sand into a local eatery or shop, a hat to protect your scalp, face, and neck from the sun, sunglasses, and a pair of sandals to protect your feet from the sometimes scalding hot sand.

Extras to think about packing include your own snorkeling equipment, a dry bag which will float on water and protect your valuables, and a parachute beach blanket. This nifty invention is made of nylon parachute material and remains cool in the hot sun, dries very quickly, and does not build up mildew.

Toiletries and Health Care

Any item that you would use on a daily basis, such as a toothbrush and toothpaste, deodorant, and hair care products should be brought with you to Jamaica, unless you feel comfortable using the items that the hotel provides for you. All of these items can be purchased in small, travel sized containers, and will be less expensive than waiting and buying them in your resort gift shop where the prices of toiletries are often marked up by 20 percent or more. The same goes for sunblock. Remember to pack any medications you will need to take during your stay, as long as you have a prescription slip or note from your doctor in the event you are questioned by customs officials. A first aid kit is a good idea also. Bandages, disinfectant, antiseptic, aspirin, ibuprofen, anti-diarrhea, tweezers, and a thermometer should be included. Make sure you do not forget any of these items.

Jamaica is known to have some pretty nasty sand fleas and mosquitoes, which come out especially strong early in the day and late at night. Bring along insect repellent to apply to your body along with your sun screen before you leave your hotel, and some hydrocortisone cream or Benadryl to relieve you of the itchiness that comes if a bug does end up biting you. Sun block is another must have item, and you'll probably need more than you think you will, plus a lip balm with SPF. In the event you get a sun burn, a soothing aloe vera lotion will be nice to have on hand.

What Else to Pack

In Jamaica, the days are hot, but the nights can be a bit cooler. Packing at least one sweater or wrap would be wise. Additionally, Jamaica is known to experience brief and sporadic **rain** showers on a daily basis. If you fear getting caught out in the rain, an umbrella or rain jacket will keep you dry. If you plan to utilize your resort gym and get in your daily exercise, remember to pack the appropriate clothing for that as well. Extras that might make life easier include zip-lock bags, a collapsible cooler, a small package of laundry detergent, and a bottle opener.

Along with these weather-conscious items, you may also want to consider bringing along a few things to bring you comfort, and keep you occupied when you aren't out exploring the island. A good book or your e-reader, an mp3 player, a portable DVD player, a personal journal, a laptop, and a hand held video game system, are all items that fall into this category. Don't forget to pack enough batteries to get you through your trip. It is also important to be aware that the electrical outlets in Jamaica are different than those in the United States, so you will need to bring along an adapter for your electrical devices. Voltage varies by location, so call your hotel to determine exactly what kind of adapter you will need.

Finally, don't forget to bring your camera and all equipment needed to keep it up and running, plus an extra memory card to store the hundreds of pictures you are likely to take as you try to capture all of your Jamaican vacation memories on film. If you've been considering buying a waterproof camera, now is a great time to do so. .

Packing Concerns

If you are visiting Jamaica for an extended period of time, or you're simply worried about packing too much, consider this trip from travel experts: pack items that are interchangeable, and can be worn a number of ways while still looking fresh. A pair of cloth shorts, for example, will go nicely with a variety of shirts, and a selection of colored shirts can be layered differently each day for a new look.

Some vacationers worry that their luggage will get lost or delayed by the airline when they fly to Jamaica. Although this occurrence is rare, you can arrive prepared for this possibility. Include in your carry-on bag one outfit and a swim suit, along with any small, but valuable items, and medications that are necessary for you to take. This way, you will have a few essential items available to you immediately, and you can shop for the rest when you arrive in Jamaica. Do keep in mind the rules regarding liquid toiletries in a carry-on bag which state that each person may bring one clear, gallon zip-lock bag filled with liquid toiletries that are only three ounces apiece.

Now is a great time to think about the cost of your luggage. Some airlines charge for both your checked and carry-on luggage, while others will only charge for a checked bag, and still others don't charge for luggage at all. To avoid being surprised at the check-in counter, review your airline's policy in advance.

Packing for your Jamaica vacation need not be a daunting task. Just attack your luggage with a plan of action. Determine how long you will be on the island, what activities you will participate in, and try to take into consideration any problems that may arise. Create a list and stick to it, and you are sure to arrive in Jamaica with everything you need.

Best Time to Visit

When is the Best Time to Visit Jamaica?
Low season or high, timing is everything when taking a vacation to Jamaica
For most of Jamaica's visitors, the decision of when to visit the island is based on pre-set vacations from work and school, but if you have the luxury of choosing any time of year to visit, knowing the ebb and flow of seasonal demands will help.

Despite a stable year-round climate, Jamaica has high and low tourist seasons. High season is when tourism is at its peak, and nearly all hotels will be booked. Meanwhile, during the low season, big-ticket items such as accommodations and even airfare can be deeply discounted. This, however, is just the tip of the iceberg.

High Season

The Caribbean provides many vacationers with an escape from the snowy winter climates between mid-December and mid-April. Jamaica is no exception with temperatures averaging between 71 and 88 degrees Fahrenheit year round. Of course, while this may be the perfect time of year for many travelers to see a little sun with easy travel plans around Christmas, New Year's and Easter especially, the popularity also comes with drawbacks.

Booking a room in Jamaica during the high season can be extremely difficult. During holidays and at more popular hotels, rooms may be booked as much as one year in advance. This doesn't mean that you won't be able to get a room, but it may not be your first choice without a little bit of forward thinking. Not only can rooms be hard to come by, rental cars can be almost impossible to procure, and reservations are necessary for things like golf, tours of important landmarks, and dining. Beaches and pools will be more crowded during than in the summer months as well.

Not only is Jamaica a nice change of pace from winter weather, but many festivals also take place. Carnival is one of the Caribbean's best known festivals; it takes place the week following Easter in either March or April and is known to draw a crowd. Junkanoo is Jamaica's traditional Christmas celebration, and several yacht races take place in the early months of the year.

Low Season

Though Jamaica is always a popular destination, the slower summer and fall season from mid-April to mid-December means fewer crowds. May, June, October, and November are Jamaica's rainy seasons, where each day it is likely to rain for a short while in the afternoon. Though it's not likely to spoil your day, it can put a damper on things. Hurricanes are predictable, and visitors often know well ahead of time if there is a threat of danger on Jamaica.

Services on Jamaica tend to be reduced during the low season. Whether you're facing shortened hours at a store or simply one restaurant or bar being closed, you may not feel you're getting the same number of features and services as you might during high season. Further, the best time to renovate is when there are the fewest clients staying in a hotel. To avoid this inconvenience, ask the resort if they have plans to renovate during your stay.

For many travelers, especially families, the benefits of off-season travel can far outweigh these drawbacks. Discounts of up to 50 percent on some hotels are available and there tend to be more options regarding where to stay because so few locations are completely booked. There may be sales on merchandise as well for the souvenir-seeker on each trip. Even top restaurants may not require reservations if you're there during a particularly slow time.

Despite being the low season, there are still plenty of events and festivals that may lure travelers to the area. One of the quintessential Jamaican events is August's Reggae Sumfest which lasts for an entire week, and later in October music lovers will enjoy the Caribbean Music Expo. September and October are filled with fishing and yachtingevents, and art lovers won't want to miss Kingston on the Edge Urban Arts in June.

As always, the choice is yours. Visitors travel during both the low and high seasons regularly, and Jamaica is always popular. For some, the difference between the two seasons may not be as noticeable as it may be for others.

Weather

Learn About the Weather of Jamaica

The weather patterns you'll encounter in Jamaica can vary dramatically around the island

Regardless of when you visit, the tropical climate and warm temperatures of Jamaica essentially guarantee beautiful weather during your vacation.

Average temperatures in Jamaica range between 80 degrees Fahrenheit and 90 degrees Fahrenheit, with July and August being the hottest months and February the coolest. Temperatures in Jamaica generally vary approximately 10 degrees from summer to winter. Nevertheless, you should be prepared for winter in Jamaica to be slightly cooler, especially at the higher altitudes. In the mountains, the thermometer can dip to 40 degrees Fahrenheit (4 degrees Celsius).

The rainiest weather in Jamaica occurs in May and June and again in October and November and can sometimes extend into December. While the average annual rainfall is 50.7 inches, accumulation varies dramatically across the island. In contrast to the southwestern coast of Jamaica, which receives little rain and is often classified as semi barren, the eastern (windward) coast receives considerably more rain than anywhere else on the island. For the most part when it does rain in Jamaica, showers are short, heavy and followed by sunshine.

Jamaica does lie in the hurricane belt, and the official hurricane season runs from June 1 to November 30, with August and September being the peak months. However, the Caribbean region is more vast than most people think, and the chances of any single island being hit directly by a hurricane are very slim. Most often, islands will only receive the heavy rains that come on the outskirts of a hurricane, avoiding the most extreme weather conditions. Direct hits on Jamaica by major storms are so rare, in fact, that many elder Jamaican inhabitants still relate events in history to being before or after "the storm" because they may have only seen one or two of significance in their lifetimes.

Additionally, with today's meteorological technology, advanced warnings for hurricanes will reach you long before you are ever in danger, so keeping an eye on the weather in Jamaica before you leave for your vacation will go a long way toward keeping you prepared. If you hear that a hurricane has hit before you are to arrive, all is not lost. You may not have to alter your vacation at all, but do call ahead to verify current atmospheric conditions and extent of damage to the island; you may also want to get a statement from local business owners as to whether they are conducting business or when they think they will be operational again.

The following statistical weather data is from a weather station in Montego Bay, Jamaica. Keep in mind that on an island the size of Jamaica, the climate will vary slightly across the island. Particularly, it gets noticeably cooler in the evening breeze of the higher altitudes, so when visiting Jamaica's mountainous interior, you'll want to keep a light jacket handy for when the sun goes down. All in all, though, this information should give you a good idea of what to expect on your Jamaica vacation.

Month	Avg. Daily High Temp (Degrees Fahrenheit)	Avg. Daily Low Temp (Degrees Fahrenheit)	Avg. Monthly Precip. (inches)	% Days with Rain
January	82.3	74.2	2.7	36
February	82.3	74.3	1.8	34
March	83.7	75.0	2.3	29
April	85.0	76.4	2.5	31

Jamaica Travel Guide, Caribbean

May	86.5	78.0	5.9	42
June	88.0	78.7	5.5	40
July	88.4	78.2	2.9	30
August	88.5	78.3	5.2	35
September	87.9	77.9	6.1	47
October	86.7	77.6	7.4	47
November	84.9	77.0	5.5	45
December	83.1	75.0	3.6	39

Jamaica Activities

There are a number of great activities and attractions to be found in Jamaica

Jamaican travelers have plenty of options for active (and not so active) adventures. Whether you're interested in a leisurely day on a chartered yacht or roughing it for an afternoon hike through Jamaica's beautiful mountains, there are activities to capture almost anyone's interests.

Bike and Scooter Rental

If you are intrigued by the idea of seeing the sights with the wind in your face, there are a variety of different rental agencies that can help you. Navigate to this page regarding bike and scooter rentals if you need additional information.

Diving

Meanwhile, divers and snorkelers can swim among the colorful coral and sponges. Montego Bay offers the best snorkeling options, while divers can find diverse and exciting sites regardless of which city you take off from. Whether or not you fish or snorkel, you can always sail out on Jamaica's waters with a hired charter or on a cruise tour.

Events and Festivals

Meanwhile, those interested in taking in a bit of culture may enjoy events and festivals, like Carnival and Junkanoo. Both celebrations have people dancing in the streets, wearing elaborate costumes, and really letting loose in masquerade fashion. Festivals aren't the only times parties heat up in Jamaica, however. NightlifeNightlife is as spicy as the ubiquitous jerk seasoning. The most happening nightlife is centered in the tourist driven areas such as Kingston and Negril, and visitors can find everything from dive bars to dance clubs that keep the party going until sun up.

Fishing

Anglers can spend a day out struggling with famous deep sea fish, while snorkelers can come face to face with fish in their own habitat. Deep sea fishing is especially popular in Jamaica, with mahi mahi, wahoo, and barracuda some of the best catches to be found.

If there are some fishing fanatics in your group, they'll be pleased to know 15 charter fishing services operate from this area..

Golf

Avid golfers frequent the area, as indicated by the presence of 10 different golf courses. The area courses include Cinnamon Hill Course, Tryall Golf Course, and Negril Hills Golf Club. Click on the course name for a detailed guide to the course, including contact information, number of holes, location, and more.

Sailing and Boating

Check out the chart below to learn more about local providers that will help you get out on the water.

BOATING OPPORTUNITIES ON JAMAICA		
Name	Phone	Location
Barrett Adventures Sailing	(876) 382-6384	1.9 mi. South West of Central Montego Bay
Buttonwood JA	(876) 374-4266	Downtown Treasure Beach
Captain Dennis Adventures	(876) 435-3779	Downtown Treasure Beach

Cool Runnings Cruises	(876) 974-2446	3.7 mi. Southeast of Central Portmore
Dreamer Catamaran Cruises	(876) 979-0102	The vicinity of Montego Bay, Northwestern part of Jamaica
Garfield Diving Station Boat Tours	(876) 544-4354	Downtown Ocho Rios
Island Charter Co.	(876) 878-2287	4.6 mi. North of Central Negril
Jamaica Watersports	(876) 381-3229	1.9 mi. South West of Central Montego Bay
Mike's Glass Bottom Boat	(876) 847-7699	2.9 mi. North of Central Negril
Sea Shell Charters	(876) 875-4167	0.4 mi. West of Central Orange Bay
Sunbaby Glass Bottom Boat	(876) 485-4023	0.5 mi. North of Central Negril

Shopping

Native goods, from craft work to local Blue Mountain coffee, are popular souvenirs and gifts, and most travelers budget a bit of time for Shoppingshopping. On top of duty free shopping at a lot of shops, travelers can shave between 20 and 30 percent off the price tag of designer goods and brand name products by buying them in Jamaica.

If you have some folks who enjoy shopping traveling with you, they can explore a few of the 90 retail stores in the area. Read on Shopping page to find our guide to shopping on Jamaica.

Sightseeing

Yet another good way to spend some of your vacation is exploring the area's interesting sights. Among other sights, the area has historic sites and a distillery. If you enjoy the great outdoors, you may have a pleasant time visiting the area's waterfalls, outdoor parks, and botanical gardens. For more information about available sightseeing attractions, read on Attraction page.

Jamaica Travel Guide, Caribbean

The chart just below provides you with information on a firm that will guide you to some of the most interesting local sights.

Name	Type	Phone	Location
SIGHTSEEING SERVICES ON JAMAICA			
Barrett Adventures	Excursions and Sightseeing Service	(876) 382-6384	1.9 mi. South West of Central Montego Bay
Blue Mahoe Tours	Excursions and Sightseeing Service	(876) 459-2222	Negril Beach Hotel Zone, Western part of Jamaica
Blue Mountain Tours JA	Nature Tours	(954) 214-9795	0.3 mi. West-Northwest of Central Ocho Rios
Braco Stables	Excursions and Sightseeing Service	(876) 954-0185	1.6 mi. West-Southwest of Central Rio Bueno
Caliche Rainforest Park & Adventure Tours	Excursions and Sightseeing Service	(876) 940-0163	The vicinity of Montego Bay
Champion Tours	Travel and Tour Operators	(876) 377-4793	The vicinity of Negril
Chicken's Magic Bus Tour	Travel and Tour Operators	(876) 378-3348	The vicinity of Negril
Chukka Caribbean Adventures	Excursions and Sightseeing Service	--	2.9 mi. Southeast of Central Bounty Hall
Cruise Shore Excursions Jamaica	Excursions and Sightseeing Service	(877) 767-9993	1.8 mi. South West of Central Montego Bay
De Music Buzz	Travel and Tour Operators	(876) 521-1278	2.4 mi. South of Central Negril Beach Hotel Zone
Dudley's Big Ship Taxi & Tours	Excursions and Sightseeing Service	(876) 772-8759	0.7 mi. North of Central Negril
El Sol Vida Fun Tours Jamaica	Excursions and Sightseeing Service	(877) 839-3924	2.3 mi. East-Northeast of Central Kingston
Explorer Jamaica	Excursions and Sightseeing Service	(877) 767-9993	Downtown Ocho Rios
Explorer Jamaica Transportation & Tours	Excursions and Sightseeing Service	--	Falmouth, Northwestern part of Jamaica
Explorer Jamaica Transportation & Tours	Excursions and Sightseeing Service	(877) 767-9993	1.0 mi. South of Central Negril Beach Hotel Zone
Glamour Luxury Destination Concierge	Excursions and Sightseeing Service	(876) 953-3810	2.7 mi. Northeast of Central Montego Bay

Glistening Waters	Excursions and Sightseeing Service	(876) 954-3229	2.1 mi. East of Central Falmouth
Harmony Tours	Excursions and Sightseeing Service	(876) 953-3937	The vicinity of Montego Bay
Island Routes Caribbean Tours At Sandals Whitehouse	Excursions and Sightseeing Service	(876) 640-3000	1.8 mi. Northwest of Central Whitehouse
Island Routes Caribbean Tours at Grand Pineapple Beach Negril	Excursions and Sightseeing Service	(876) 957-4408	1.7 mi. South of Central Negril Beach Hotel Zone
Island Routes Caribbean Tours at Grande Ocho Rios Sandals	Excursions and Sightseeing Service	(876) 974-5691	Ocho Rios, Northeastern part of Jamaica
Island Routes Caribbean Tours at Sandy Bay	Excursions and Sightseeing Service	(876) 957-5100	1.0 mi. North of Central Negril Beach Hotel Zone
Island Routes Tours at Sandals Royal Plantation	Excursions and Sightseeing Service	(876) 953-2231	3.8 mi. Northeast of Central Montego Bay
J. Charles Swaby's Black River Safari Cruise	Nature Tourism Service	(876) 965-2513	0.9 mi. Southeast of Central Black River
Jamaica Culinary Tours	Excursions and Sightseeing Service	(876) 586-1817	0.4 mi. Northeast of Central Falmouth
Jamaica Tours	Excursions and Sightseeing Service	(876) 953-8865	The vicinity of Montego Bay
Jamaican Cultural Enterprises	Excursions and Sightseeing Service	(876) 374-6370	2.0 mi. North of Central Kingston
Johns Hall Adventure Tours	Excursions and Sightseeing Service	(876) 952-0873	The vicinity of Montego Bay
Juju Tours	Excursions and Sightseeing Service	(876) 789-4309	2.1 mi. North of Central Negril
Karandas Tours	Excursions and Sightseeing Service	(876) 775-8724	1.1 mi. West-Southwest of Central Ocho Rios
Kingsley's Take Care Tours and Transport	Travel and Tour Operators	(876) 885-1383	The vicinity of Negril
Lee's Taxi & Tours	Excursions and Sightseeing Service	(876) 954-9285	0.2 mi. East of Central Falmouth
Liberty Tours Jamaica	Excursions and Sightseeing Service	(876) 448-0473	0.9 mi. South of Central Montego Bay
Lime Tree Farm Hiking	Hiking Tour and Trip Operator	(187) 644-6023 ext. 0	1.7 mi. South of Central Mahs Bank
Little Shaw Park Tours	Excursions and	(876) 974-	Ocho Rios

	Sightseeing Service	2177	
Miracle Tours & Taxi Service	Excursions and Sightseeing Service	(876) 746-6407	The vicinity of Jamaica
Montego Bay Limo & Tours	Excursions and Sightseeing Service	(876) 953-7459	The vicinity of Montego Bay
Ocho Rios Authentic Tours	Excursions and Sightseeing Service	(876) 404-5548	Downtown Ocho Rios
Olympia Tours	Excursions and Sightseeing Service	(876) 953-8656	1.3 mi. East of Central Spot Valley
Patrice Bailey Tours	Excursions and Sightseeing Service	(876) 509-7542	0.8 mi. East of Central Falmouth
Phil Lafayette Tours	Excursions and Sightseeing Service	(876) 427-5829	Downtown Ocho Rios
Prestige Tours	Excursions and Sightseeing Service	(876) 940-6937	The vicinity of Montego Bay
Real Tours Jamaica	Excursions and Sightseeing Service	(876) 335-7922	1.5 mi. West of Central Rose Hall
Reliable Adventures Jamaica	Excursions and Sightseeing Service	(876) 955-8834	1.6 mi. North of Central Belmont
Sexy Rexy's Tours	Travel and Tour Operators	(876) 445-3740	1.7 mi. South West of Central Negril
Sledge Watersports LTD	Excursions and Sightseeing Service	(876) 567-2292	1.8 mi. East of Central Priory
Starlight Chalet & Health Spa Excursions	Excursions and Sightseeing Service	(876) 969-3070	9.0 mi. Northeast of Central Kingston
Sun Valley Plantation Tours & Trails	Excursions and Sightseeing Service	--	4.3 mi. West-Southwest of Central Port Maria
Sun Venture Tours	Excursions and Sightseeing Service	(876) 929-5694	Portmore
Sunshine Watersports & Tours	Excursions and Sightseeing Service	(876) 295-6918	0.9 mi. East-Northeast of Central Ocho Rios
Travel Mania Tours & Services	Excursions and Sightseeing Service	(876) 988-5730	Portmore, Eastern part of Jamaica
Uwi Port Royal Marine Laboratory	Nature Tourism Service	(876) 927-1202	3.7 mi. Southeast of Central Portmore
Wild Crocodile Adventure	Travel and Tour Operators	(876) 881-6917	1.5 mi. Southeast of Central Little London

World Tours & Cruises	Excursions and Sightseeing Service	(876) 974-1152	Ocho Rios
Wynter's Park & Tours	Excursions and Sightseeing Service	(876) 981-9843	Saint Ann Parish

Snorkeling

If you enjoy snorkeling there's good news -- you can easily find places to do so in the waters off the coast of Jamaica. For more details about local snorkeling opportunities, read on Snorkeling page.

Spas

Indulging in a trip to the spa might be one of the highlights of your vacation. Spa-goers will find plenty of options, considering that there are 33 spas in this area. Read on Spas page within this book which is all about spas in the area if you want to find out more specifics.

Sports

Of course, less adventure-seeking travelers have plenty of activities to enjoy as well. Tour the island by renting a bike or hiking the trails, or stay close to the resort and get in some laps at the pool. Hit the links at over a dozen world-class golf courses on the island, and swing that racket for a game of tennis at most large resorts. The Half Moon Resort offers guests both.

Spectator sports attract quite a crowd in Jamaica as well. Football (better known as soccer in the U.S.) and cricket are at the top of the sports food chain, but visitors might also want to check out American football and basketball which are growing in popularity.

Tennis

If you like to play tennis you might want to make your reservations at a hotel that has a tennis court. Fortunately, you can choose from 41 properties in the area that offer tennis.

The table below highlights some key facts. At a glance, you can see the number of tennis courts on-site, whether lighting is available for evening play, and some other helpful details. Click on each name to learn more about the property.

ACCOMMODATIONS WITH TENNIS ON JAMAICA

Property	Location	Tennis Courts	Lit Courts	Tennis Pro
Holiday Inn Resort in Rose Hall	1.4 mi. West of Central Rose Hall	4		
Jamaica Pegasus	1.2 mi. South West of Central Kingston	2		
Couples Swept Away	0.5 mi. South of Central Negril Beach Hotel Zone	10		
Sandals South Coast	0.5 mi. West of Central Crab Pond Bay	4		
Moon Palace Jamacia Grande	Downtown Ocho Rios	2		
Secrets Wild Orchid Montego Bay All Inclusive	1.9 mi. South West of Central Montego Bay	2		
Hotel Riu Montego Bay	3.8 mi. Northeast of Central Montego Bay	2		
Riu Tropical Bay	2.0 mi. North of Central Negril Beach Hotel Zone	2		
Half Moon Club	0.8 mi. West-Northwest of Central Rose Hall	13		
Sandals Montego Bay	2.3 mi. North-Northeast of Central Montego Bay	2		

Other Activities

Information about lots of other activities are displayed here:

OTHER ACTIVITIES ON JAMAICA

Name	Type	Phone	Location
Sun Coast Adventure Park	Amusement/Theme Park	(876) 610-7425	1.4 mi. West-Northwest of Central Grant's Pen

Bamboo Avenue	Scenic Trail	(876) 922-1287 ext. 8	6.4 mi. Northeast of Central Black River
Bull Bay Football Club	Spectator Teams and Clubs	--	1.9 mi. East-Southeast of Central Harbour View
C Jay's Water Sports	Watersports Operator	(876) 940-2327	The vicinity of Montego Bay
Captains Watersports	Watersports Operator	(876) 953-3048	0.8 mi. West-Northwest of Central Rose Hall
Captains Watersports Holiday Inn	Watersports Operator	(876) 538-6225	1.5 mi. West of Central Rose Hall
Captains Watersports at Breathless Resort	Watersports Operator	(876) 538-6225	1.9 mi. South West of Central Montego Bay
Captains Watersports at Round Hill Hotel	Watersports Operator	(876) 538-6225	0.7 mi. Northeast of Central Hopewell
Captains Watersports at Secrets Resorts	Watersports Operator	(876) 538-6225	2.4 mi. South West of Central Montego Bay
Captains Watersports at Zoetry Resort	Watersports Operator	(876) 538-6225	4.2 mi. Northeast of Central Montego Bay
Carib Arcade	Amusement Arcade	--	Ocho Rios, Northern part of Jamaica
Chukka Caribbean Adventures Horseback Ride 'N Swim	Horseback Riding Site	--	2.0 mi. South West of Central Montpelier
Cove Theatre	Movie Theater	(876) 675-8884	Downtown Ocho Rios
Dressel Divers Montego Bay	Watersports Operator	(+34) 963 561 496	1.9 mi. Northeast of Central Spot Valley
Fairfield Theatre	Movie Theater	(876) 952-0182	2.0 mi. South-Southeast of Central Montego Bay
Fern Tree Fitness Centre	Fitness Centers and Instructors	(876) 953-2211 ext. 6871	1.0 mi. West of Central Rose Hall
Harbour View Stadium	Sporting Event Venue	--	Harbour View, Eastern part of Jamaica
Jamaica National Stadium	Sporting Event Venue	--	Kingston, Eastern part of Jamaica
Jamaica Zipline Adventure Tours	Adventure Sports Provider	(876) 912-0936	2.5 mi. West of Central Anchovy

Kool Runnings Waterpark	Amusement/Theme Park	(876) 957-5400	0.9 mi. North of Central Negril Beach Hotel Zone
Materna Wellness Centre	Fitness Centers and Instructors	--	Kingston, Eastern part of Jamaica
Mighty Moves Health Club	Fitness Centers and Instructors	(876) 952-8608	The vicinity of Montego Bay
Mystic Mountain	Amusement/Theme Park	(876) 974-3990	2.8 mi. West of Central Ocho Rios
National Indoor Arena	Sporting Event Venue	--	Kingston, Eastern part of Jamaica
Odeon Cineplex	Movie Theater	(876) 962-1354	Mandeville, Central Jamaica
Palace Multiplex	Movie Theater	(888) 429-5722	1.8 mi. South of Central Montego Bay
Paramount Fitness Center	Fitness Centers and Instructors	(876) 994-9221	Port Maria, Northeastern part of Jamaica
Premium Parasailing	Parasailing Service	(876) 957-3928	0.7 mi. South of Central Negril Beach Hotel Zone
Sligoville Stadium	Sporting Event Venue	--	The vicinity of Kingston, Eastern part of Jamaica
Spartan Health Club	Fitness Centers and Instructors	(876) 927-7575	Kingston, Eastern part of Jamaica
Spot Valley Raceway	Auto Racetracks	--	0.4 mi. South of Central Spot Valley
Trelawny Multi-Purpose Stadium	Sporting Event Venue	--	2.1 mi. Southeast of Central Falmouth
Ultimate Fitness Health Club	Fitness Centers and Instructors	(876) 946-9852	Portmore

Vacationers to Jamaica are encouraged to take advantage of the varied activities found all over the island. No matter what kind of vacation you're looking to have, there are activities to suit your lifestyle. From the most active vacationers to those who want to spend their vacation time relaxing, Jamaica knows how to entertain its visitors.

Bikes & Mopeds

Renting a Bike or Scooter in Jamaica

From motorcycles to bicycles, two wheeled transport abounds in Jamaica

Bikes, motor bikes and scooters can be a great option for vacationers traveling around Jamaica. From the low cost of rental to the easy access to out-of-the-way sites, two-wheeled vehicles are a unique way to travel.

While motor bikes and scooters are a lot of fun, they do require extra measures of caution. In Jamaica, roads can be extremely rough, and the law requiring the use of helmets for all motorcyclists is one to take seriously. Potholes and unusual driving rules can also make two-wheeled travel a challenge. Still, the allure of exploring the beautiful island of Jamaica from the seat of a moped or scooter is understandably strong.

If you like the idea of seeing the sights with the wind in your face, there are a variety of different businesses that can help make it happen.

If you'd like to go riding, you should consider Harley Davidson Falmouth. Although it is illegal to buy and sell motorcycles at 600cc on the island of Jamaica, Harley Davidson has lobbied hard and are able to rent these powerful vehicles out. Many people, tourists and locals alike, turn to Harley Davidson Falmouth to get their motorcycle fix. They are located in Falmouth, in northwestern Jamaica.

Another good option is Harley Davidson Ocho Rios. Harley Davidson has been lobbying the Jamaican government to allow high powered motorcycles on the island since 2006. Although it is still illegal to own them, it is now possible to rent these vehicles and as well as make a purchase from their wide selection of apparel. You can call them at (876) 795-3221.

Still another option is Harley Davidson Whitter Village. Selling highly sought after Harley Davidson apparel as well as renting out bikes for tourists and locals in need of an adrenaline such, this Harley shop is one of three in Montego Bay. located in northwestern Jamaica. They're

The chart directly below enables you to get more details on the 12 rental agencies we are aware of.

BIKE AND MOPED RENTAL ON JAMAICA		
Name	Phone	Location
Elvis Bike Rental	(876) 848-9021	1.1 mi. South of Central Negril Beach Hotel Zone
Gas Bike Rental	(876) 957-4835	Negril, Western part of Jamaica
Harley Davidson Falmouth	(876) 617-2578	0.8 mi. East of Central Falmouth
Harley Davidson Montego Bay	(876) 971-2576	Montego Bay
Harley Davidson Negril	(876) 957-4428	1.2 mi. South of Central Negril Beach Hotel Zone
Harley Davidson Ocho Rios	(876) 795-3221	Downtown Ocho Rios
Harley Davidson Whitter Village	(876) 953-8368	3.5 mi. Northeast of Central Montego Bay
Jah B's Bike Rental	(876) 957-4235	1.6 mi. South of Central Negril Beach Hotel Zone
Jah B's Place	(876) 957-4235	Negril, Western part of Jamaica
Kool Bike Rental	--	Negril, Western part of Jamaica
Prento's Bike Rental	(876) 957-9722	Negril, Western part of Jamaica
Tykes Bike Rental	(876) 957-0388	Negril Beach Hotel Zone

Non-motorized bicycles are a great option for seeing the island while getting plenty of fresh air and exercise, and many rental opportunities make bikes easy to find throughout Jamaica. Resorts offer rentals at reasonable prices, generally around $30 or $40(USD) per day, which can be much lower than the cost of renting a car. Be aware, however, that a driver's license is usually required for rental, and you may need a credit card for the deposit. The cliffs near Negril make a great day trip, but bikes are also ideal for zipping around town once you're in Jamaica.

Diving

Scuba Diving Near Jamaica

The scuba diving and snorkeling opportunities found in Jamaica are not to be missed

The waters of Jamaica offer a unique underwater experience for those travelers interested in scuba diving, enabling vacationers to explore Caribbean aqua life at its very best.

Scuba diving is a sport in which participants are able to explore life underneath the surface of the ocean by utilizing a tank of compressed air strapped to their back in order to breath underwater. Many vacationers make their first dive during a trip to the Caribbean because of the abundance of tropical fish, colorful coral, high visibility, and warm waters.

Negril

Negril and its surrounding areas offer the most peaceful diving found in Jamaica, full of caverns and caves for the underwater explorer. There are several highly recommended diving sites that offer guided tours, such as the reefs found in Negril Marine Park. Negril's truly brave visitors can take a break from scuba diving to cliff jump near Rick's Cafe.

Montego Bay

The Montego Bay area also offers several unique diving opportunities. Most of the diving sites in MoBay are contained within the Montego Bay Marine Park, which was created in 1990 to help preserve the natural underwater beauty of Jamaica's surrounding sea area. The most famous Montego Bay diving site is Widowmaker's Cave. Enter this cave at 80 feet below sea-level and twist and turn your way back up the 10-foot-wide chimney at 35 feet below. If looking for a more large scale tour, the Discovery Bay Marine Laboratory offers outings along the northern coastal area, and those interested should contact the lab when they arrive.

Ocho Rios

The most astonishing of the Ocho Rios sites is the man-made sunken ship reef. This artificial reef site was created recently when Fantasy Divers, the National Resources Conservation Division and the Port Authority worked together to sink a non-working old minesweeper to create a habitat for fish, coral and to protect the local beaches.

Kingston and Surrounding Area

Those wishing to go diving at the sunken city of Port Royal, which sank underwater after the earthquake of 1692, will need to obtain special permission from Jamaican authorities. This is probably best done through local dive operators, who will have the most current and up-to-date information regarding rules about Port Royal.

Low visibility leaves the southern coast of Jamaica largely untouched by divers, particularly surrounding Kingston.

Regardless of where you choose to dive, you will be required to show proof of certification. Resorts often offer training and certification for guests, or you can take dive classes through any local dive shop. Once you have learned the ins and outs of diving, you can expect to pay between $45 and $80(USD) for a one tank dive. On your first dive, your guide will probably take you down about 40 feet below sea level.

Tips

Divers need to keep a few things in mind while they're visiting the creatures under the ocean waves:

- ✓ Be aware of currents and stay watchful of your location. You don't want to end up too far away to return easily.
- ✓ Wear a watch so you don't lose track of time. It is easy to do underwater.
- ✓ Don't feed the fish, and don't touch the animals or coral. This may cause their protective layers to be stripped away.

- ✓ Avoid standing and walking on coral reef, and proceed with caution when in shallow water around reefs. Shuffle your feet to avoid stingrays, and watch out for sea urchins, and spines.
- ✓ Never wear jewelry. Caribbean fish, barracudas especially, seem drawn to shiny objects that look like their natural prey, small silver fish.
- ✓ Avoid jellyfish, fire coral and other stinging creatures.
- ✓ Never reach into holes or crevices; they might be an animal's home, especially moray eels.
- ✓ Shark sightings are rare, and those that are spotted are usually passive. Keep calm, and if necessary, move slowly out of the water.
- ✓ Never remove anything from diving sites and reefs; it is illegal to do so.
- ✓ Consider using a dive flag, which will warn other boaters that you are under water in the area.

There are 27 dive services, some dive shops, and at least 16 good dive sites to choose from.

Dive Operators and Shops

The dive shops you'll be able to find are summarized here:

DIVE SHOPS NEAR JAMAICA

Name	Phone	Location	Island
Fishermen & Divers Paradise	(876) 617-2882	The vicinity of Jamaica	
Sun Divers	(876) 957-4503	Negril, Western part of Jamaica	Jamaica
Waves Aquatic Superstore	(876) 924-6946	Portmore	Jamaica

If you want to go diving, you can check with Kellys Watersports. Through their extensive offering of PADI certification courses, divers at every level can learn a little something about the sport. Daily open water dives are available, and if you're traveling with folks who don't want to dive, they may want to participate in a snorkeling tour or ride on the glass bottom boat. They are found within western Jamaica.

Another good option is Couples San Souci Divers. Find out what exactly goes on underneath the surface of the clear blue waters near this resort when you participate in some of the PADI certified guide hosted scuba tours. Beginners can participate in a free scuba lesson in the pool, while those with experience can choose to sign up for a few dives and continue their training. You can reach them at (876) 994-1206.

A third option is Scubacaribe Ocho Rios. The largest dive operation in the Caribbean, there are more than 20 Scubacaribe locations around the world. This center in particular specializes in scuba diving courses and daily dives despite also offering a great deal of other watersports options. They're found within the vicinity of Ocho Rios, Jamaica.

Some information concerning area dive operators are provided directly below.

DIVE OPERATORS NEAR JAMAICA		
Name	Phone	Location
Beaches Boscobel Diving	(876) 975-7777	2.2 mi. West of Central Oracabessa
Beaches Negril	(876) 957-9270	2.9 mi. North of Central Negril
Couples Negril Divers	(876) 957-5960	4.9 mi. North of Central Negril
Couples San Souci Divers	(876) 994-1206	Ocho Rios, Northeastern part of Jamaica
Couples Swept Away Diving	(876) 957-4061	2.6 mi. North of Central Negril
Dive Seaworld	(876) 953-2180	3.7 mi. Northeast of Central Montego Bay
Dream Team Divers	(876) 957-0054	Negril Beach Hotel Zone
Dressel Divers Montego Bay	(+34) 963 561 496	1.9 mi. Northeast of Central Spot Valley
Garfield Diving Station	(876) 544-4354	Downtown Ocho Rios
Hedonism II Diving	(876) 957-5200	1.5 mi. North of Central Negril Beach Hotel Zone
Jamaica Scuba Divers	(876) 957-4503	Negril Beach Hotel Zone

Jewel Runaway Bay Resort Diving	(876) 633-4000	Runaway Bay, Northern part of Jamaica
Kellys Watersports	(876) 893-2859	1.7 mi. West-Southwest of Central downtown Montego Bay
Lady G'Diver	(876) 715-5957	Port Antonio, Eastern part of Jamaica
Marine Life Divers	(876) 957-3245	1.3 mi. West of Central Negril
Negril Adventure Divers	(876) 487-0002	1.4 mi. North of Central Negril
Negril Fun Diving	(876) 842-3155	1.0 mi. North of Central Negril
Resort Divers Ocho Rios	(876) 973-7866	Ocho Rios
Resort Divers Runaway Bay	(876) 973-7866	Runaway Bay, Northern part of Jamaica
SNUBA Dive Experience	(876) 818-2340	0.7 mi. West-Northwest of Central Montego Bay
Sandals Negril Diving	(876) 957-5216	1.3 mi. North of Central Negril Beach Hotel Zone
Sandals Royal Caribbean Diving	(876) 953-2231	2.3 mi. North-Northeast of Central Montego Bay
Sandals Whitehouse Diving	(876) 640-3000	1.8 mi. Northwest of Central Whitehouse
Scubacaribe Montego Bay	(876) 953-2180	3.8 mi. Northeast of Central Montego Bay
Scubacaribe Negril	(876) 509-0862	2.0 mi. North of Central Negril Beach Hotel Zone
Scubacaribe Ocho Rios	(876) 972-7558	2.3 mi. East of Central St. Ann's Bay
Scubaquatic Jamaica	(876) 973-7000 ext. 500	Runaway Bay, Northern part of Jamaica

Dive Services

Review the chart below for information concerning the approximate cost of typical dive services in this area.

DIVE SERVICES		
Offering Type	Low Rate	High Rate
Discover Scuba	$ 80.0	$ 126.0
Double Tank Dive	$ 70.0	$ 700.0

Night Dive	$ 55.0	$ 95.0
Open Water Certification	$ 350.0	$ 500.0
Single Tank Dive	$ 40.0	$ 70.0

Dive Sites

A few key facts regarding some of the area's major dive sites are shown below.

DIVE SITES NEAR JAMAICA						
Name	Quality	Experience	Max Depth	Current	Latitude	Longitude
Beaches Boscobel	Very Good	All Divers	110.0	--	18.4078287873	-76.97947
Shark Reef	Good	--	70.0	--	18.4603964006	-78.1653213488
Airport Wall	Very Good	Advanced Open Water / CMAS **	150.0	--	18.500368	-77.929583
Alligator Reef	--	--	--	--	17.8072487475	-77.5425124142
Booby Cay	Good	--	60.0	--	18.3377149646	-78.3479328
Breezes Runaway Bay	Good	Open Water / CMAS *	60.0	< 1 knot	18.4649609079	-77.3278713239
Coral Head Reef	Good	--	60.0	--	18.3023806	-78.347625732
Dancing Eel Reef	Very Good	--	35.0	--	18.5154750233	-78.0240402222
Joseph's Cave	Good	All Divers	23.0	< 1 knot	18.2669197637	-78.3678174071
Montego Bay Caverns	Very Good	--	30.0	--	18.5072971021	-77.9352159138
Montego Bay Dive	Good	All Divers	45.3	< 1 knot	18.4669715981	-77.936797142
Runaway Bay Wall	Good	--	--	--	18.4676138668	-77.3315257683

Samuel's Bay Marine Park	--	--	60.0	--	18.381737	-78.313588
Shaw Reef	Good	Open Water / CMAS *	40.0	< 1 knot	18.0879031029	-77.969391346
Tugboat	Good	Advanced Open Water / CMAS **	95.1	< 1 knot	18.2961103866	-78.356552124
Widowmakers Cave	Excellent	Advanced Open Water / CMAS **	90.0	--	18.5369084734	-77.8875732422

Jamaica has plenty of beautiful sights for both snorkeling and diving, but it is always best to keep safety in mind when planning the underwater aspect of your vacation.

Fishing

Jamaica offers sailing and sport fishing options to suit a variety of visitors

Deep-sea fishing is extremely popular among Jamaica's visitors, and the island's annual fishing tournaments are renowned. Travelers visiting Jamaica, however, will need to plan ahead if they intend to set sail during their island adventure in order to make the most of their fishing experiences.

Fishing

The waters that surround the Caribbean islands are home to several types of fishing because of the vast differences in the underwater landscapes of the region. Some fish favor the shallow island edges; others are the bright fish of the coral reefs that have grown over centuries along the edges of some volcanic islands. Jamaica is home to the large sport fish of the deeper waters that sportsmen travel from around the world to capture.

Jamaica's Northern waters are well-known for deep-sea and sport fishing. Anglers can hook an impressive number of fish, including mahi mahi, wahoo, blue and white marlin, sailfish, tarpon, barracuda, and bonito. Jamaica also hosts two international fishing tournaments, the Jamaica International Fishing Tournament and Jamaica International Blue Marlin Team Tournament. Both tournaments take place in the early fall, September and October, so travelers interested in fishing may want to take this into consideration.

Bonefish are the region's shallow water fish and are said to be the best fighters of all fish, pound-for-pound. Their species includes Jamaica's popular tarpon, wahoo and barracuda. Bonefish can be caught from the beach or a small boat in many of the area's shallow waters. Fishing from the shore can be less costly for budget-conscious travelers because there is no need for boat rental.

Jamaica's deep sea and game fishermen will have the most to enjoy with Jamaica's plentiful populations of marlin, wahoo, mahi mahi, and sailfish. There are many varieties of these deep-water fish just off the shores where the sea floor drops down, so visitors may fish as close to a quarter of a mile from the islands.

Although reef fishing is not widespread in Jamaica, live bait such as conch or squid is the best bet for reef fishermen looking to catch some very interesting fish. The most common fish in these areas are grouper, mutton snapper, yellowtail snapper, and jack crevalle.

So, when you're visiting Jamaica, let the urge for adventure take you out to the water's edge to find out if you can hook one of the feisty bonefish, or let it draw you out onto the deep ocean where mighty game fish fight to the end.

Fishing Charters

If you are intrigued by the idea of spending some time on the open water with a rod in your hand, you will find 13 different charter fishing operators that can help make it happen.

If you're ready to get in contact with a fishing charter, you should consider Winter Fresh Fishing and Tours. Winter Fresh Fishing offers you and your family and friends a chance to fish along the beautiful and plentiful coast of Negril, Jamaica. If you don't have your own, fishing equipment is readily available for your excursions. They are located in Negril, in western Jamaica.

Another good option is Marlin Madness. Hunt your prized catch with one of the premier fishing charters on the island, Marlin Madness. Specializing in deep sea fishing and sport fishing, you can be sure that you are in for an adventure as you head out for a day of fishing. You can reach them at (876) 565-5417.

A third good option is Irie Vibes Fishing. Operating out of Di Ole Marina in Port Antonio is Irie Vibes Fishing, a company that offers several water-based activities including spear and deep sea fishing. They are the only service out of Portland to currently offer saltwater fishing, so if this is what you're after, Irie Vibes is who you call. They're located in Port Antonio, in eastern Jamaica.

Be sure to look through the following table if you want more information.

FISHING CHARTERS ON JAMAICA

Name	Phone	Location
Barrett Adventures Fishing	(876) 382-6384	1.9 mi. South West of Central Montego Bay
Deep Drop Fishing	(876) 572-0010	Montego Bay
Fish Jamaica	(876) 965-0743	Treasure Beach
Irie Vibes Fishing	(876) 464-9508	Port Antonio, Eastern part of Jamaica
Jamaica Boats Deep Sea Fishing	(876) 863-7384	Ocho Rios
Lucky Bastard Fishing Charters	(876) 572-0010	Downtown Montego Bay

Marlin Madness	(876) 565-5417	2.0 mi. South West of Central Montego Bay
No Problem Sportfishing	(876) 381-3229	Montego Bay
Reel Magic Charters & Sports Fishing	(876) 563-7699	1.8 mi. South West of Central downtown Montego Bay
Resort Divers Fishing	(876) 973-6131	Ocho Rios
Sea Shell Charters	(876) 875-4167	Negril, Western part of Jamaica
Stanley's Deep Sea Fishing	(876) 957-6341	0.8 mi. West-Northwest of Central Negril
Winter Fresh Fishing and Tours	(876) 440-1119	0.3 mi. South of Central Negril

There are many wonderful sights that can only be seen from aboard a boat. Chartering a boat can grant you unparalleled access to the fishing, diving, and sailing experiences afforded by the gorgeous waters off the coasts of Jamaica.

Golf

Golf in Jamaica is a unique experience

Like most leisure activities on Jamaica, golfing provides another opportunity for the island's unique character and personality to shine through.

You can expect a golfing experience in Jamaica to be a departure from the typical North American links experience. Although only eleven courses serve the entire country, each has its own distinct character.

Local Golf Courses

A trip to Jamaican courses can guarantee, among other things, stellar service. Caddies in Jamaica are expertly trained and very familiar with the nuances of their courses. Each golfer receives individual attention from his or her own caddie, unlike busier golf locations where caddies may be serving one or two golfers at once. It is also important to note that many clubs require that golfers have a caddie. Expect to pay between $15 and $45(USD) for this service.

The main golfing area in Jamaica is the hub of Negril's all-inclusive resorts. Be warned, though, when considering golfing in Negril, that the area's players are predominantly inexperienced golfers. Rather, you'll encounter many first-timers, or once-a-year types.

Tryall Golf Course

One of Jamaica's most serious golf locations is the Tryall Golf Course, about an hour west of Montego Bay. Founded by Texans in the 1950s, the resort is a collection of upscale homes owned by North Americans and Europeans. Tryall is a private resort area, and many golfers are also renters or owners of the resort's villas. If you opt out of staying at Tryall, a visit to their course may be arranged through hotel concierges. Staying at Round Hill Hotel & Villas, a small upscale hotel just east of Tryall, increases the ease with which such a visit can be arranged.

Negril Hills Golf Club

Negril Hills Golf Club is a rare and novel experience, as you travel up and down the elevated tees to the valley fairways, twisting and turning around the guango trees. The course features 18 holes and a "liquormobile" that roams the links, ready to offer players a drink.

Sandals Golf and Country Club

Some of the best golf on the northern coast of Jamaica is at the Sandals Golf and Country Club. This golf area, formerly known as the Upton Country Club, was in a sad state of disrepair until Sandals purchased and revamped the area.

Manchester Country Club

Manchester Country Club is home to the Caribbean's oldest golf course. This golfer's treasure is found in the city of Mandeville on Jamaica's South Coast. Once only nine holes, it recently grew to have

18 holes. It is set in luxurious rolling hills and is worth a visit for aficionados.

Caymanas Golf Club

In the rolling foothills of St. Catherine lies the 18 hole championship golf course, Caymanas. On site golfers will find a driving range, putting greens, a golf pro, and a golf academy.

Half Moon Golf Course

Just east of Montego Bay is the Half Moon Club, which houses an 18-hole course that is home to the Red Stripe Pro Am. Lessons can be obtained at the on-site David Leadbetter Golf Academy in the form of private sessions and week-long retreats.

Cinnamon Hill Course

Cinnamon Hill Course is an 18 hole course that hosts numerous invitational tournaments each year. This course has been previously ranked as one of the top in the world.

GOLF COURSES		
Name	Phone	Location
Caymanas Golf Club	(876) 746-9772 ext. 4	3.1 mi. (5.0 km) Northeast of Spanish Town
Cinnamon Hill Course	(876) 953-2984	Hilton Rose Hall Resort & Spa - 7.7 mi. (12.4 km) East-Northeast of Montego Bay
Constant Spring Golf Club	(876) 755-1729	152 C Spring Road - 3.0 mi. (4.9 km) North of Kingston
Half Moon Golf Course	(888) 830-5974	Half Moon Club - 6.1 mi. (9.9 km) East-Northeast of Montego Bay
Manchester Country Club	(876) 962-2403	Caledonia Road - Mandeville
Negril Hills Golf Club	(876) 957-4638 ext. 3614	1.9 mi. (3.0 km) East of Negril
Runaway Bay Golf Course	(800) 758-2252	Jewel Runaway Bay Resort - Runaway Bay
Sandals Golf and Country Club	(876) 975-0119	2.2 mi. (3.5 km) Southeast of Ocho Rios

Tryall Golf Course	(876) 956-5660	Tryall Club - 9.3 mi. (14.9 km) West of Montego Bay
White Witch Course	(876) 632-7444	White Witch Drive - 6.7 mi. (10.7 km) East of Montego Bay

Golfing on the island of Jamaica is a relaxed activity that generally does not require reservations or advanced booking. Making an impromptu decision to hit the links should be easy and can help open your leisure-activity options.

Nightlife

Locating great nightlife in Jamaica is a breeze!

A country with a cultural heritage as diverse and proud as Jamaica is bound to offer the best in local nightlife and after-dark entertainment. From Hedonism in Negril, to the Centerstage Theatre in Kingston, Jamaica offers visitors enough fun for several nights.

Negril

If spending an evening in Negril, Jamaica, most folks will venture to Rick's about an hour before sunset. The most popular location on the island to view the sun go down, visitors can have a drink and watch adventurous cliff-divers and, if lucky, one might witness the phenomenon of the *green flash* that occurs only when the sun sets on a cloudless night. Scientifically, it happens because the light of the sun is refracted through the earth's atmosphere, but local legend says a couple who witnesses this rara avis will be guaranteed true love.

If you and your significant other hope to nestle in the comfort of a resort, Sandals Negril Beach Resort is for you. One among three locations, which also include Dunn's River and Montego Bay, the resort provides all-inclusive fun for couples looking to get away.

Another famous spot for great nightlife in Negril is Hedonism II, a place famous for its bacchanals and high-end service, but not a place for the weak of heart when it comes to partying. You have to purchase a pass for about $75(USD) if you aren't already a guest, but with unlimited drinks and food, it's well-worth the cost.

If you love listening to live music and discovering new bands, you won't want to miss Alfred's Ocean Place, which features nightly performances right on the beach.

Montego Bay

If you are looking to start off your evening in a fun and novel way, you may want to check out Glistening Waters Restaurant and Marina just outside Montego Bay for dining, disco, and drinks overlooking the glowing river. You will also find the island's most authentic British Pub, the Royal Stocks, in Montego Bay.

In the mood to take a risk? Then you should visit Jackpot Jungle, the premier gaming experience in Jamaica. Whether you are just looking to try your luck, or you are the play-to-win type, this casino's got the game for you. Basics like blackjack and roulette always make for a good time, but the main attractions are the 120+ slot machines available with a wide variety of games, from traditional slots to interactive gaming. Games take US denominations from five cents to $5(USD).

Montego Bay is home to Hip Strip, a section of Gloucester Ave thick with popular bars and clubs. Located in MoBay's favorite hot spot is the Twisted Kilt, the island's first Irish pub, and the very jazzy Blue Beat. Rum Jungle is perhaps the most impressive spot on Hip Street, known for it's theatricality, exotic food, and samples of over 100 different rums. Meanwhile, for true novelty, check out Chillin, a game center with artificial falling snow and an ice bar. Get lucky on Hip Strip by visiting the street's casinos: Caribbean Treasures and Coral Cliff Gaming Room..

For great drinks and good music, there's no place like Margueritaville(also on Hip Strip), and now you can enjoy this great nightlife tradition, Jamaican style. This bar and café has an excellent menu with traditional items, as well as traditional Jamaican drinks and food. During the day, sports events are broadcast on big screen TVs, and after dark, theme nights add to the fun of the laid-back atmosphere.

Kingston

Visitors to Kingston, Jamaica can enjoy a wide variety of nightlife in tourist-centered areas, but without awareness of local trends, you may find yourself lost in the big city. To avoid getting lost or wasting your time, it is probably a good idea to ask your hotel concierge where the local hot spots are (and are not).

Knutsford Blvd in Kingston 5 offers a plethora of after-dark entertainment. Club Asylum offers visitors a sensory taste of genuine Jamaican nightlife. However, if the crowd is at full capacity, nearby Jonkanoo Lounge is a cozy location where patrons can "cool out." Mingles is where to go for a younger crowd, where you can dance to soca, pop, and reggae.

Club Habibi, a Latin nightspot with an Arab name, is a true example of Jamaica's diversity and culture. Habibi hosts theme nights ranging from fashion night, where you show up dressed for the red carpet, to 80s night, a blast from the past. A favorite of locals is Latin night, which features two hours of Latin dance lessons prior to the beginning of a great mix of Latin dance music. Also located on the "hip strip" are Mingles Pub and Pool Bar which grants lovers of Latin music a chance to dance their Saturday night away.

If you crave a more cosmopolitan approach to your nightlife, Redbones Blues Café can provide the perfect backdrop for a beautiful garden setting. This locale is know for smooth jazz and blues music, southern food, and it's art gallery. Carlos' Cafe is another trendy spot in the area.

For more family-oriented entertainment in Jamaica, there is the Centerstage Theatre, a local cast that puts on musical comedies in native tongues. Although you may not understand what's being spoken, it's a great experience to see the culture of the island performed live. The theatre is cozy and comfortable without being too small. Prices will vary depending on when you purchase tickets. The Ward Theater, one of Jamaica's national monuments, is another great spot for live theater in Kingston.

Other Cities

It's the smaller joints that are popular in Port Antonio. The Roof Club, which is located on the second floor of it's building, is a great locale to groove to dancehall hits.

The scene in Ocho Rios is more than a little edgy, and the faint at heart may want to ignore the nightlife in this area. Expect for things to get wild when you visit clubs like Amnesia. If you're in Ocho Rios and want to avoid the crazy club scene, check out Ocean's 11, a bar on the water, or Strawberries, a bar and restaurant featuring local cuisine.

Time 'n' Place, in Falmouth, is an unlikely hot spot. The place is constructed of driftwood and looks slightly delapidated, but it is where locals go for the best mixed drinks in town.

ENTERTAINMENT AND NIGHTLIFE

Name	Type	Phone	Location
Ackee Tree Beer Joint	Bar	(876) 978-1972	Portmore
Alfred's Beach Bar	Bar	--	1.5 mi. North-Northeast of Negril
Amnesia Night Club	Night Club	(876) 974-2633	Ocho Rios
Bar King Frog	Lounge	(876) 953-2650	Rose Hall
Beezy's Reggae Pub	Bar	--	Ocho Rios
Blue Demin Bar Joint	Bar	--	Negril
Boat Bar	Bar	--	1.8 mi. North of Negril
Bowa's Bar & Snack Shop	Bar	(876) 956-9044	Green Island
Carby's Bar	Bar	(876) 983-	Saint Catherine Parish

		8420	
Clarke's Tavern	Bar	(876) 955-2496	The vicinity of Jamaica
Club Nazz Bar	Bar	(876) 615-1571	Falmouth
Collete's Bar	Bar	(876) 429-3636	Negril
Cool N IRIE	Bar	--	Montego Bay
Corner Bar Negril	Bar	--	Negril
Cove Theatre	Movie Theater	(876) 675-8884	Downtown Ocho Rios
D Lagoon Bar	Bar	(876) 786-3465	May Pen
Dancing Lions At The Little Pub	Bar	(876) 974-8537	Ocho Rios
Dashewe Sports Bar & Betting Lounge	Bar	--	2.4 mi. East of Treasure Beach
Dolly's Cafe & Pub	Bar	(876) 979-0045	The vicinity of Montego Bay
Drifter's Bar	Bar	(876) 826-2116	Downtown Ocho Rios
El Negro Y Blanco Bar & Lounge	Lounge	--	0.6 mi. East of Kingston
English Pub	Bar	(876) 952-4420	Saint Ann Parish
Fairfield Theatre	Movie Theater	(876) 952-0182	2.0 mi. South-Southeast of Montego Bay
Fiction Lounge	Lounge	(876) 631-8038	0.8 mi. North of Kingston
Firewater Love Nest	Bar	--	West End
Fridays Sport Bar	Bar	(876) 625-0893	Mandeville
Gee Tees Bar	Bar	(876) 940-1545	The vicinity of Montego Bay
German Bar	Bar	(876) 471-6493	Negril

Jamaica Travel Guide, Caribbean

Name	Type	Phone	Location
Golden Apple	Bar	--	Esher
Hot Shots Pool Bar	Bar	--	Kingston
J & J Lounge & Bar	Lounge	(876) 740-7207	Portmore
Jack's Bar	Bar	(876) 632-8000	Rose Hall
Jasper's Chillin Piano Bar	Bar	--	1.4 mi. East-Northeast of Runaway Bay
John Crow's Tavern	Bar	--	Downtown Ocho Rios
Kelly's Bar	Bar	--	Downtown Montego Bay
Ken's Wildflower Lounge	Lounge	(876) 998-7455	Portmore
Little Ochie Bar	Bar	--	13.1 mi. East of Treasure Beach
Local Bar	Bar	--	Downtown Montego Bay
LTU Pub Bar	Bar	--	1.7 mi. South West of Negril
Margaritaville Montego Bay Bar	Bar	--	Downtown Montego Bay
Margaritaville Negril Bar	Bar	(876) 957-4467	2.2 mi. North of Negril
Marybelle's Pub On The Pier	Bar	(876) 993-9625	Port Antonio
Mattis Sports Bar	Bar	(876) 746-7101	Saint Catherine Parish
May Hotspot Bar	Bar	(876) 943-9966	Spanish Town
Medusa	Night Club	--	Kingston
Mi Yard Bar	Bar	--	Negril
Mike's Supper Club	Lounge	(876) 633-7000	1.9 mi. East of Port Antonio
Mingles Pool Bar	Bar	--	0.8 mi. Southeast of Kingston
Natural Mystic	Bar	(876) 442-0890	The vicinity of Negril
No Limit Bar	Bar	(876) 957-	1.2 mi. West of Negril

		4855	
Oasis Bar & Jerk Center	Bar	(876) 964-9834	Chudleigh
Ocean Eleven Lounge	Lounge	--	Downtown Ocho Rios
Ocean View Bar	Bar	(876) 715-4793	Port Antonio
Odeon Cineplex	Movie Theater	(876) 962-1354	Mandeville
Palace Multiplex	Movie Theater	(888) 429-5722	Montego Bay
Palms Gaming Lounge	Bar	(876) 908-4672	Kingston
Pathfinder Bar	Bar	(876) 949-9410	Saint Ann Parish
Paul's Drinking Saloon	Bar	(876) 708-2400	Saint Ann Parish
Peewee's Bar	Bar	--	1.2 mi. West of Negril
Pelican Bar	Bar	--	5.7 mi. South of Black River
Pennant's Pub	Bar	(876) 987-2833	Pennants
Pier One Bar	Bar	--	Downtown Montego Bay
Pub At Half Moon	Bar	(876) 953-9770	Rose Hall
Pure	Bar	--	0.8 mi. East-Southeast of Kingston
Rainbow Tavern	Bar	(876) 954-2725	Duncans
Rev Nightclub	Night Club	(876) 998-6888	Portmore
Rick's Cafe Bar	Bar	(876) 957-0380	1.7 mi. South West of Negril
Ripples Cocktail Lounge	Lounge	--	5.6 mi. Southeast of Spanish Town
Risky Business Club	Night Club	(876) 957-3008	1.2 mi. North-Northeast of Negril

Roof Club	Night Club	(876) 715-5281	Port Antonio
Roots Bamboo Bar	Bar	--	1.6 mi. North-Northeast of Negril
Rum Shack	Bar	(876) 934-0354	Portmore
Shades Adult Nightclub	Night Club	--	Ocho Rios
Skeeta's Pub	Bar	--	3.7 mi. East of Treasure Beach
Sky Dock	Bar	--	Downtown Ocho Rios
Spot Light	Bar	--	Negril
SunnySide Bar	Bar	--	Negril
Sunset Bar	Bar	--	1.4 mi. East-Northeast of Runaway Bay
Tanya's Sports Bar	Bar	(876) 973-7346	Runaway Bay
Tenesia's Bar	Bar	--	11.9 mi. North-Northeast of Morant Bay
The Cricket Club	Night Club	(876) 953-2650	Rose Hall
The Jungle	Night Club	(876) 957-4005	2.1 mi. North-Northeast of Negril
The Quad	Bar	(876) 754-7823	0.8 mi. East-Southeast of Kingston
Theater Place	Dinner Show and Theater	--	1.0 mi. Southeast of Kingston
Time 'N' Place	Bar	(876) 954-4371	2.9 mi. East of Falmouth
Tony's Bar	Bar	--	1.8 mi. North of Negril
Wayside Sports Bar	Bar	(876) 971-2043	The vicinity of Montego Bay
Wholas Bar	Bar	--	Downtown Montego Bay

A Warning

Certain illicit substances are relatively popular on the party scene in Jamaica, and as a tourist, an offer will more than likely crop up to try them out. Although it may not appear that way, Jamaican law expressly forbids the use of mind-altering substances, and a visit to local jails is the best way to miss out on all the other great nightlife in Jamaica.

Shopping

Great local goods can be discovered when shopping Jamaica's markets

Shopping in Jamaica is an experience in and of itself. The island's vendors peddle wares of all kinds, from local hand-made crafts to imported designer watches and perfumes, all at prices that can seem like a steal.

The key to shopping in Jamaica is to be prepared to bargain. If you are uncomfortable with this idea, stick to duty-free stores, large retailers, and international chains, were prices are fixed and no haggling is allowed. Prices may be slightly higher than marketplace rates, but this policy saves the hassle of bargaining with vendors, and you will likely still end up saving a few bucks.

It is important to note that, as a visitor, you will almost inevitably be approached by local drug dealers offering "something special." The use of marijuana is widespread but strictly forbidden by Jamaican law. A fun Caribbean vacation certainly shouldn't include a visit to local prisons. A firm, "No, thank you," with a stern look should be enough send a drug peddler away.

Bargaining

If you choose to do so, be sure not to approach a vendor regarding an item unless you intend to buy that item. Ask the price, and then act disappointed and begin to walk away. If the vendor wants to lower the price of the item, he may offer a discount as a special treat for you as a visitor to his country. At this time, determine how much you would like to pay for the item and suggest a price lower than that. Eventually, you and your salesperson will compromise somewhere in the middle. Just remember not to give up!

Gifts and Souvenirs

There are definitely items available in Jamaica worth seeking out. Local artists create amazing crafts; from paintings of local scenery to wood relief carvings of local people and sights, local art is unique and will spice up any home.

Exclusive to Jamaica are high-quality woven crafts, available in Montego Bay's Craft Market, or along the street from smaller merchants. Baskets, purses, hats, and other finely handcrafted items are available in a wide variety of colors, but the most commonly found will be the three bright Rastafarian colors, yellow, green, and red, that just shout "Jamaica." One favored souvenir is a hand carved figurine made from lignum vitae wood, which means "tree of life" and is the national tree of Jamaica. It takes a well-trained carver to handle this blonde colored wood, and you can find dolphins, people, and flowers carved into the wood.

Another worthwhile shopping opportunity is the Blue Mountain Coffee for which Jamaica is famous. Locally grown and harvested, this coffee sells in the United States for more than twice its local price. Duty free shops at international airports will sell the coffee in small burlap gift bags for approximately $1(USD) per ounce, but for an even lower price, seek out coffee stands in local markets. Just be wary of street-side coffee vendors; sometimes you'll get coffee that isn't really what you are looking for. Speaking of coffee, Tia Maria, a Jamaican-made coffee liquore can make for a great gift as well.

If you're looking for some gifts or souvenirs you might enjoy a visit to Casa de Oro Time Square, which is located within Negril Beach Hotel Zone, in western Jamaica. In operation since 1932, Casa's is one of the oldest and best established duty free shopping conglomerates in Jamaica. With locations throughout the island, such as this one in

Montego Bay, you'll have multiple chances to shop. If you're looking to call ahead of time, you can do so at (876) 957-3631.

A second possibility is Bijoux Duty Free at the Airport, which is located mi. (km) from Casa de Oro Time Square. Bijoux is a duty free jewelry and accessories shop, selling Luxury watch brands such as Rolex, Breitling, Omega, Hublot, Tag Heuer, Chopard, Movado, Tudor, Raymond Weil, Frederique Constant, Michael Kors, Fossil, Skagen, and Michele watches. In Jewelry they carry Pandora, Roberto Coin, Fope, Endless Diamonds, John Hardy, Marahlago Larimar, and Caribbean Hook Bracelets featuring the "One Love, One Heart" bracelet. Call them at (876) 952-6718.

A third shop you might enjoy is Jamaican Style Gift Shop. Check out Jamaica Style between 9:00 a.m. and 6:00 p.m., daily. If you have questions and want to call ahead of time, you can do so at (876) 957-3060.

Review the following table if you want more information.

GIFTS AND SOUVENIRS ON JAMAICA

Name	Type	Phone	Location
Beach Boyz	Gift and Souvenir Shops	(876) 957-4629	0.5 mi. Northwest of Central Negril
Bijoux Duty Free	Duty Free Store	(876) 953-9530	Downtown Ocho Rios
Bijoux Duty Free Historic Falmouth	Duty Free Store	(876) 953-9530	Falmouth, Northwestern part of Jamaica
Bijoux Duty Free Kingston	Duty Free Store	(876) 953-9530	Kingston
Bijoux Duty Free at the Airport	Duty Free Store	(876) 952-6718	The vicinity of Montego Bay
Bob Marley Experience and Theatre	Gift and Souvenir Shops	(876) 953-3946	The vicinity of Montego Bay
Carby's Gift Shop	Gift and Souvenir Shops	(876) 926-4065	Kingston, Eastern part of Jamaica
Casa de Oro Time Square	Duty Free Store	(876) 957-	2.0 mi. South of Central Negril

			3631	Beach Hotel Zone
Caves Hotel Gift Shop	Gift and Souvenir Shops	(876) 957-0270		1.8 mi. South West of Central Negril
Dis & Dat	Gift and Souvenir Shops	(876) 957-4916		0.5 mi. Northwest of Central Negril
Exquisite Floral & Gift Center	Gift and Souvenir Shops	(876) 734-4311		Morant Bay, Eastern part of Jamaica
Giftland	Gift and Souvenir Shops	(876) 974-6744		Downtown Ocho Rios
Jamaican Style Gift Shop	Gift and Souvenir Shops	(876) 957-3060		Negril Beach Hotel Zone, Western part of Jamaica
Jingle's Gift Shop	Gift and Souvenir Shops	(876) 974-0209		St. Ann's Bay, Northern part of Jamaica
Lamcy Gift Shop	Gift and Souvenir Shops	(876) 957-3958		2.0 mi. South of Central Negril Beach Hotel Zone
Legends Sunshine Village	Gift and Souvenir Shops	(876) 957-4534		0.5 mi. Northwest of Central Negril
Neita's Gift Shop	Gift and Souvenir Shops	(876) 963-5801		Whitehouse, Western part of Jamaica
Santastic Gift & Things	Gift and Souvenir Shops	(876) 975-2432		Browns Town, Northern part of Jamaica
Sona Duty Free	Duty Free Store	(876) 957-3151		0.4 mi. North of Central Negril
Tina's Gift Shop	Gift and Souvenir Shops	(876) 957-3684		0.5 mi. Northwest of Central Negril

Specialty Shops

One of the more interesting specialty retailers in this area is Sun Divers. They're located in Negril, in western Jamaica. A top watersports destination in the area, Sun Divers offers PADI certification training, daily open water dives as well as boat rides, jet skiing, deep sea fishing, snorkeling, parasailing, and the best sunset cruises in Jamaica. If you are looking to call in advance, do so at (876) 957-4503.

A second option is Harmony Hall, which is found a very long distance to the east of Sun Divers. Jamaica's leading artists and craftsmen have a home at Harmony Hall. The building, which was a 19th century Methodist manse, came into Annabella Proudlock's possession in 1980 and she worked with a group of friends to create the perfect locale to display some of the most beautiful pieces of artwork. You can contact them at (876) 975-4222.

Studio174: In addition to teaching classes in various mediums of art, the center offers other education such as English classes. The artwork created by students here is on display for anyone who cares to stop by and see it. Guests will find them at 174 Harbour Street.

Many specialty shops in Jamaica are shown here:

SPECIALTY SHOPS ON JAMAICA

Name	Type	Phone	Location
Bolivar Gallery & Antiques	Art Gallery	(876) 926-8799	Kingston, Eastern part of Jamaica
Clonmel Potters Gallery	Art Gallery	(876) 992-4495	2.7 mi. East-Southeast of Central Gayle
Frame Centre Gallery	Art Gallery	(876) 926-4644	Kingston, Eastern part of Jamaica
Gallery Joe James	Art Gallery	(876) 954-0048	Rio Bueno, Northern part of Jamaica
Gallery of West Indian Art	Art Gallery	(876) 952-4547	1.9 mi. South-Southeast of Central Montego Bay
Gem Palace	Jewelry Store	(876) 974-2735	Ocho Rios
Harmony Hall	Art Gallery	(876) 975-4222	0.3 mi. South of Central Tower Isle
House Of Diamonds	Jewelry Store	(876) 795-2921	Downtown Ocho Rios
LS's Arts Gallery & Gift Shop	Art Gallery	(876) 974-2764	Ocho Rios
Maximum Art Gallery	Art Gallery	(876) 957-4560	0.6 mi. South of Central Negril Beach Hotel Zone

Murton Art's	Art Gallery	(876) 965-8501	Mandeville	
Portland Art Gallery	Art Gallery	(876) 882-7732	0.5 mi. West of Central Port Antonio	
Reve Jewellery & Accessories	Jewelry Store	(876) 908-2498	Portmore	
Studio174	Art Gallery	(718) 218-7735	Downtown Kingston	
Sun Divers	Dive Shop	(876) 957-4503	Negril, Western part of Jamaica	
Swiss Stores Kingston	Jewelry Store	(876) 922-8050	Downtown Kingston	
Tropicana Jewelers Falmouth	Jewelry Store	(876) 533-6100	12.3 mi. East of Central Rose Hall	
Tropicana Jewelers Montego	Jewelry Store	(876) 953-2242	1.0 mi. East of Central Rose Hall	
Tropicana Jewelers Negril	Jewelry Store	(876) 957-9530	2.0 mi. South of Central Negril Beach Hotel Zone	
Z Images Art Gallery	Art Gallery	--	0.5 mi. North of Central Negril	

Clothing and Apparel

Enjoy shopping for clothing? Consider dropping by Things Jamaican -- which is located in Kingston, Jamaica. Things Jamaican is open from 9:00 a.m. to 8:00 p.m. Visitors can find them at 26 Hope Road.

A second option is Maxie Department Store Mandeville -- which is located 47 and a half miles (76 and a half kilometers) to the west of Things Jamaican. One of the most popular department stores in Jamaica is Maxie, where growing families can take care of all of their shoe and clothing needs at affordable prices. You'll find them at 14 Ward Avenue.

A third option for clothing is Little Ones Boutique. Little Ones is open daily from 9:00 a.m. to 5:00 p.m. If you want to call in advance, you can do so at (876) 955-9533.

The table directly below shows more details regarding the 20 apparel shops in Jamaica.

CLOTHING AND APPAREL ON JAMAICA

Name	Type	Phone	Location
7 Leaves Boutique	Boutique	--	0.5 mi. North of Central Negril
All Wet Beachwear Showroom	Swimwear, Beachwear and Sportswear Store	(876) 371-1649	Kingston, Eastern part of Jamaica
Conrad's Unique Fashions	Men's Clothing Store	(876) 918-3305	Westmoreland Parish, Western part of Jamaica
Dunrich Fashion	Clothing Store	(876) 966-2638	Santa Cruz, Western part of Jamaica
Eagle Wing Sports & Things	Men's Clothing Store	(876) 965-8201	Portmore, Eastern part of Jamaica
Fancy Feet	Shoe Store	(876) 974-0529	0.4 mi. West-Northwest of Central Ocho Rios
GlamKollectionz	Women's Clothing and Accessories Store	(876) 398-9011	0.9 mi. South of Central Savanna La Mar
JSL Boutique	Boutique	(876) 957-4551	0.5 mi. Northwest of Central Negril
Little Ones Boutique	Boutique	(876) 955-9533	1.0 mi. West-Northwest of Central Johnson Town
Maxie Department Store Mandeville	Department Store	(876) 625-0525	Mandeville, Central Jamaica
Mello Magic Boutique	Boutique	(876) 966-9543	Santa Cruz, Western part of Jamaica
Norma Soas Boutique	Boutique	(876) 953-3429	4.5 mi. West-Northwest of Central Spot Valley
Pablo Palair Fashion	Clothing Store	(876) 979-1255	Downtown Montego Bay
Princess Fashion Boutique	Boutique	(876) 939-6534	Portmore, Eastern part of Jamaica
Sammy's Shoe Store	Shoe Store	(876) 934-1683	Portmore
Stunning Boutique	Boutique	(876) 929-8636	Kingston, Eastern part of Jamaica

Jamaica Travel Guide, Caribbean

T-Shirt Cafe	T-Shirt Shop	(876) 974-4057	Ocho Rios
Things Jamaican	Boutique	(876) 928-5161	0.6 mi. Northeast of Central Kingston
Wilbrom Whol & Dor's Boutique	Boutique	(876) 965-6431	Seaview Gardens
World of Sports	Swimwear, Beachwear and Sportswear Store	(876) 957-9581	0.4 mi. North of Central Negril

Food and Grocery

Need to pick up some food supplies? Mandeville Liquor Store is located in Mandeville. In addition to drinks, Mandeville Liquor also sells snacks, cigarettes, and phone cards. They're at 4 Villa Road.

Another option is Linstead Market, which is located 32 miles (51 and a half kilometers) to the east of Mandeville Liquor Store. Canned and jarred at the peak of freshness, Linstead Market specializes in Ackee, Callaloo, jams, jellies, spices, sauces, peas, and soups. The jams and jellies come in flavors like guava pineapple and mango chutney, while soups are local favorites: pepperpot soup, gungus pea soup, and red peas soup. Visitors can reach them at (876) 982-4318.

Purity Bakery: For over 50 years, this company has been baking breads and buns in a variety of flavors using timeless, fresh ingredients. They keep the island's stores stocked with breads that everyone can agree on. Visitors will be able to find them at 2F Valentine Drive.

You might want to look through the following chart for more information.

FOOD AND GROCERY STORES ON JAMAICA			
Name	Type	Phone	Location
1876 Wines	Beer, Wine, and Liquor Store	(876) 756-1876	Portmore
Book & Nutrition Center	Nutrition and Body Care Store	(876) 924-5227	Ocho Rios

Captain's Bakery	Bakery	--	Downtown Montego Bay
Captain's Bakery	Bakery	(876) 986-2183	May Pen
Flagstaff Bakery	Bakery	(876) 971-4694	The vicinity of Montego Bay
Hammonds Bakery	Bakery	(876) 957-4734	Negril Beach Hotel Zone
Linstead Market	Fruit and Vegetable Market	(876) 982-4318	Linstead, Central Jamaica
Mandeville Liquor Store	Beer, Wine, and Liquor Store	(876) 625-6900	Mandeville
Purity Bakery	Bakery	(876) 924-1151	Kingston
Rituals Coffee House	Coffee and Tea Store	(876) 953-6031	The vicinity of Montego Bay
Salmon Bakery	Bakery	(876) 952-2579	Downtown Montego Bay
Small's Bakery	Bakery	(876) 972-6212	4.4 mi. South West of Central Priory
Sovereign Supermarket	Grocery Store	(876) 927-5955	Portmore
Super Plus Food Stores	Grocery Store	634-3914-5	Black River, Western part of Jamaica
Superplus Food Stores	Grocery Store	(876) 940-4969	Downtown Montego Bay

Duty Free

Items available at duty-free savings are in abundance in the duty-free shops in Jamaica. U.S. visitors can save 25 to 30 percent on popular items such as brand name crystal and china, brand name watches and perfumes, and brand name leather products such as Fendi and Liz Claiborne.

Another important thing to remember is that in order for shopping items to be considered "duty-free," they must be paid for in foreign currency. American dollars will be accepted almost everywhere, and many locations accept major credit cards.

Restricted Items

Certain items, such as coral and turtle products, are illegal under current Jamaican law, given the damage to the environment caused by their popularity. Although these items may still be found, purchasing and carrying them through the airport could cause unnecessary difficulty in going through customs, both in Jamaica and the United States. Additionally, Cuban cigars, though also readily available, will be confiscated during any U.S. customs inspections.

Although shopping is not one of the main reasons tourists visit Jamaica, there are some great deals to be had if you know where to look. Duty free shopping means you may be able to snag a few designer goods on the cheap, and you certainly won't want to miss a chance to bring home a few locally made souvenirs.

Snorkeling

Snorkeling Around Jamaica

Whether you stick close to the beach or head out for an offshore excursion, the waters that surround the island of Jamaica are bursting with a vibrant sea life that is almost unimaginable. The chance to spend some time under the surface in the calm peacefulness while viewing everything from massive coral reef systems to the tiniest of fish is made possible with the use of a simple contraption called a snorkel.

Snorkeling occurs when a person wearing a dive mask and snorkel uses the snorkeling tube to breath in air from above as they float just below the surface of the water. Fins and a floatation device also aid in the process. If you are in a place like Jamaica where the visibility is usually between 70 and 100 feet, the water temperatures usually remain above 80 degrees Fahrenheit, and there are many calm bodies of water, you'll be able to spend hours of uninterrupted time exploring the majestic underwater world.

Sites you can expect to see will vary by location and time of year, but it is not uncommon to spot squirrelfish, angelfish, clownfish, parrotfish, butterflyfish, barjacks, chromis, wrasses, stingrays, eagle rays, turtles, and rock lobsters making homes and hunting for food within elkhorn, bubble, brain, red cauliflower, star, and torch corals, plus sea fans, sea cucumbers, and much more.

Because some of the best snorkeling sites exist a coral reef systems that are too far offshore to swim to, many accommodations offer snorkeling excursions to their guests. If you are not staying at one of these locations, there are still options. There are some companies that specialize specifically in snorkeling tours, many dive shops offer snorkelers the chance to ride out with them when they take scuba divers to explore, and there are regular tour guides that often include a bit of snorkeling as part of a day around the island. You also have the option of renting a snorkeling kit and hitting all of the spots that have intrigued you on your own.

Snorkeling Sites

If you're ready to see what's down below you might want to visit Rockhouse. On CNNs list of the top underwater sites to photograph, this snorkeling destination feature underwater caves and grottoes teeming with silverfish and snake eels. This snorkeling site is situated in the vicinity of Negril, in the western part of Jamaica.

Doctor's Cave Beach is another option. Warm spring water flows into this beach keeping the temperature extra warm and the visibility even clearer than normal for snorkelers. Underwater, the sites include gorgeous coral reef and friendly fish that are so used to tourists in their territory that they'll swim right up to your hand.

A third location to consider is Coyaba Reef. The diverse underwater habitat that exists in this offshore reef includes chromis, parrotfish, wrasse, and more. Snorkelers should monitor conditions on a daily basis because the waters here can sometimes be rough.

A fourth location where you can go snorkeling is Font Hill Beach. A reef just offshore is popular among snorkelers staying in the area for its abundance of friendly, colorful fish darting about. If you're interested, you'll find this site located in Jamaica.

Montego Beach is a fifth location to consider. A popular spot among tourists, this underwater park has everything you could hope to see in the waters that surround Jamaica including shallow reefs and steep vertical dropoffs.

The table just below lists more details regarding 20 of the most popular places to experience snorkeling in this area.

SNORKELING SITES NEAR JAMAICA	
Site	Location
Rockhouse	1.5 mi. West-Southwest of Central Negril
Doctor's Cave Beach	0.9 mi. Northwest of Central Montego Bay
Coyaba Reef	4.3 mi. Northeast of Central Montego Bay
Font Hill Beach	3.6 mi. West of Central Black River
Montego Beach	1.1 mi. North-Northwest of Central Montego Bay
Treasure Beach	2.2 mi. Southeast of Central Treasure Beach
Runaway Beach	0.5 mi. East-Northeast of Central Runaway Bay
San San Beach	1.2 mi. East of Central Drapers
Runaway Beach	0.7 mi. Northeast of Central Runaway Bay
Bogue Lagoon	2.5 mi. South West of Central Montego Bay
Parkers Bay	1.4 mi. South-Southeast of Central New Hope
Pear Tree River	1.4 mi. West of Central Runaway Bay
Rio Bueno Bay	0.7 mi. East of Central Rio Bueno
Boston Bay Beach	1.0 mi. East of Central Fairy Hill
Bluefields Beach	1.5 mi. North of Central Belmont

Booby Cay	4.6 mi. North of Central Negril
Joseph's Cave	1.8 mi. South West of Central Negril
Negril Reef	3.0 mi. North of Central Negril
Frenchman's Bay	Downtown Treasure Beach
Lime Cay	6.6 mi. South of Central Kingston

Snorkeling Boat Trips

Some people believe the most enjoyable snorkeling is located off shore.

If you'd like to go snorkeling during a boating adventure, you can check with Sea Shell Charters. Captain Phil and the rest of the Sea Shell Charters crew welcome you to explore Negril with them aboard one of their 4 vessels where you may enjoy a variety of water activities.

Another option to investigate is Island Charter Co.. There are four customized cruises available, including a couples cruise and a spa getaway. Sunset cruising, snorkeling gear, swimming, and trips to places like Rick's Cafe and Sands Reef are offered. They're located within Negril Beach Hotel Zone, in western Jamaica.

Still another option is Sunbaby Glass Bottom Boat. Tours include snorkeling at Sandy Reef, shoreline sightseeing tours, river rides, sunset cruises, fishing trips, and a picnic at Booby Cay Island. Any snorkeling and safety equipment you need will be provided by Captain Roger and his crew.

Some details about day sails and boat trips that offer snorkeling opportunities can be found in the following table.

DAY SAILS AND BOAT TRIPS ON JAMAICA		
Name	Phone	Location
Barrett Adventures Sailing	(876) 382-6384	1.9 mi. South West of Central Montego Bay
Dreamer Catamaran	(876) 979-	The vicinity of Montego Bay, Northwestern part of

Cruises	0102	Jamaica	
Island Charter Co.	(876) 878-2287	4.6 mi. North of Central Negril	
Mike's Glass Bottom Boat	(876) 847-7699	2.9 mi. North of Central Negril	
Sea Shell Charters	(876) 875-4167	0.4 mi. West of Central Orange Bay	
Sunbaby Glass Bottom Boat	(876) 485-4023	0.5 mi. North of Central Negril	

Snorkeling Services

If you're looking for a business that offers snorkeling excursions, rentals, or other services, you might want to contact Dressel Divers Montego Bay. Dressel Divers Montego Bay offers clear and lively waters. Certain areas in Montego Bay are considered natural parks and are perfect sites for snorkelers and fish to meet. They are found in northwestern Jamaica.

A second place catering to snorkelers is Stingray City Jamaica. This is your chance to swim with the rays. This tour guide offers guests a trip out to one of the most popular sandbars among snorkelers looking to interact with sting rays, and they also take photos of the experience so you'll be able to bring the experience home with you.

A third option is Kelly's Water Sports. The tour lasts for 90 minutes and brings you to one of the most gorgeous reef systems in the area with the help of a friendly and knowledgeable tour guide. They're located in western Jamaica.

Check the following table for more information regarding 6 companies that provide snorkeling related services.

SNORKELING SERVICES ON JAMAICA			
Name	Type	Phone	Location
Barrett Adventures Snorkeling	Snorkeling Tour Operator	(876) 382-6384	1.9 mi. South West of Central Montego Bay

Dressel Divers Montego Bay	Snorkeling Tour Operator	(+34) 963 561 496	1.9 mi. Northeast of Central Spot Valley
Juju Tours	Snorkeling Tour Operator	(876) 833-2921	62.7 mi. West of Central Discovery Bay
Kelly's Water Sports	Snorkeling Tour Operator	(876) 893-2859	1.6 mi. West-Southwest of Central downtown Montego Bay
Stingray City Jamaica	Snorkeling Equipment Rental Service	(876) 726-1630	0.9 mi. East of Central Boscobel
Sun Divers Watersports	Snorkeling Tour Operator	(876) 957-4503	Negril, Western part of Jamaica

To learn more concerning snorkeling, including helpful suggestions and tips for both "old pros" and beginners, check out this exhaustive discussion of snorkeling in the Caribbean.

Some of the best snorkeling in the world is said to be found in the waters that surround Jamaica, and with so many ways to get out and see why the sport is so loved, there is no excuse not to give it a try.

Spas

Spas in Jamaica

Whatever you imagine when you think of visiting Jamaica, there is no denying the natural appeal, the peaceful scenery, and the relaxed aura. All three of these combine to make this the perfect destination for a spa getaway. Even if you only plan to book one treatment during your stay, you'll find that there is plenty of opportunity to find healing and pampering all at once.

Spa-goers will find plenty of options, since there are 33 spas that operate in this area.

If you want to relax you might want to check with Jakes Driftwood Spa. Utilizing fresh ingredients right from the garden, Jakes Driftwood Spa believes that homeopathy and holistic treatments are what is best for the body. Treat yourself to the healing way of massage arts when you visit this all-natural facility. They are located within downtown Treasure Beach.

Another good option is Fern Tree Spa. Forget about your outside worries and sink into a world of rest and relaxation. Fern Tree Spa is a place where traditional Japanese massage techniques meet new world practices for the most healing, enriching experience out there. You can reach them at (876) 953-2211.

A third option is Ocean Spa at Jamaica Inn. The award wining spa takes a holistic approach to their treatments, sourcing the ingredients for all of their scrubs, wraps, and oils from local organic farmers. Guests will be able to choose from a variety of treatments including massages such as Carib-Style Thai Massages, Four Handed Massages, On the Rocks stone massages, as well as many others and combinations. They're located in Ocho Rios, Jamaica.

Take a look at the following table for a few quick facts.

SPAS ON JAMAICA		
Name	Phone	Location
Awe Spa	(800) 635-1836	Downtown Ocho Rios
Body Essentials Day Spa	(876) 986-7234	May Pen
Cool Running Day Spa	(876) 940-0368	The vicinity of Montego Bay
Escape to Exhale Day Spa	(876) 953-8316	1.4 mi. West of Central Rose Hall
Fern Tree Spa	(876) 953-2211	4.6 mi. West-Northwest of Central Spot Valley
FieldSpa	(876) 622-9153	1.6 mi. East-Northeast of Central Boscobel
Gaia Day Spa	(876) 962-1756	Mandeville
Jackie's on the Reef Spa	(876) 957-4997	1.1 mi. West of Central Negril
Jakes Driftwood Spa	(877) 526-2428	Downtown Treasure Beach
KiYara Spa	(800) 213-0583	2.1 mi. South of Central Negril
Milk River Spa	(876) 610-7745	Clarendon Parish, Southern part of Jamaica

Nasirah's Spa Salon & Cosmetics	(876) 974-8956	Downtown Ocho Rios
Naturalistic Salon & Spa	(876) 745-0554	Old Harbour, Southeastern part of Jamaica
Oasis Spa at Couples Negril	(876) 957-5960	4.9 mi. North of Central Negril
Ocean Spa at Jamaica Inn	(876) 974-2380	0.5 mi. Northeast of Central Ocho Rios
Ocean View Spa Negril	(876) 352-4027	2.5 mi. North of Central Negril
Radiant Spa	(844) 903-1160 ext. 4018	0.5 mi. East of Central Runaway Bay
Red Lane Spa	(876) 957-9270	2.9 mi. North of Central Negril
Red Lane Spa	(888) 726-3257	4.3 mi. North of Central Negril
Reflections Day Spa & Salon	(876) 953-0542	Downtown Montego Bay
Renova Spa Riu Ocho Rios Club Hotel	187) 697 222 00	5.6 mi. West of Central Ocho Rios
Rockfort Mineral Spa	(876) 938-5055	1.5 mi. Northwest of Central Harbour View
Rockhouse Spa	(876) 618-1533	1.5 mi. West-Southwest of Central Negril
Samsara Spa	(876) 957-4395	1.3 mi. West of Central Negril
Shelly's Day Spa & Beauty Salon	(876) 979-5353	1.9 mi. East-Southeast of Central Falmouth
Shirley's Steam Bath	(876) 965-3820	Treasure Beach
Slick Spa & Beauty	(876) 974-7833	Ocho Rios
Starlight Chalet & Health Spa	(876) 969-3070	9.0 mi. Northeast of Central Kingston
Strawberry Hill Spa	(876) 944-8400	6.4 mi. Northeast of Central Kingston
Tanya's Secret Escape	(876) 887-4918	Negril, Western part of Jamaica
The Caves Spa	(876) 957-0270	1.8 mi. South West of Central Negril
The Spa at SPA Retreat	(876) 399-3772	1.0 mi. West-Northwest of Central Negril
Vassa Spa	--	4.1 mi. North of Central Negril

Sports

Jamaica is an up-and-coming country when it comes to sports competition

Sports have been an important part of Jamaica since the time of the island's native people, the Taínos. Athletics have since been replaced by the sporting customs of the island's British colonizers, and games such as cricket and football (soccer) dominate today. Still, there are plenty of other games to watch and play on this beautiful island.

Cricket

Cricket, long revered in England as a gentleman's sport, was first played in Jamaica by the upper classes. Unlike football, a game for the masses, cricket was reserved for the elite and had a reputation as being a game that exemplified English poise. Over time Jamaicans of all social backgrounds became involved in the game, and today cricket is thriving in the West Indies.

The Rules

The rules are both social and technical. The game is played with a bat and ball, though both are different than those used in baseball. Only three men in the field have gloves. A test match is played over five days each with roughly seven hours of play time.

Social rules are equally as strict. Teams are divided between "gentlemen" and "players," and each even has their own locker room. Gentlemen were, until recently, the only men who could captain a team. Players were paid to play on a team.

In the West Indies, teams were divided by color. But in 1948, Jamaican George Headley became the first black man to captain a test side. Headley is regarded as one of the top batsmen in the game.

Teams

Although cricket is popular in Jamaica, there is only one team to represent all of the West Indies in international competition. The first team played in 1928 against England. And in 1935, the team, known as The Windies, won its first test series a group of five five-day-long matches over a period of two to three months.

The biggest change came from a series victory in 1950, when West Indian teams began traveling the world. From the 1960s to the 1980s, the West Indies team began taking the lead in the world game, and in 1960 sent abroad its first team captained by a black man, Frank Worrell of Barbados.

Football (Soccer)

The game of football was introduced by British troops who were sent to keep the peace in the colony in the mid-to-late-1800s. Matches between regiments became important social events, which helped spread the game's popularity to all corners of the island.

As time passed, the game became ingrained in the culture even high schools competed among each other in the early 1900s. Today, most schools have football teams. By the 1920s, Jamaica was ready to enter the international stage and played against neighboring teams on Haiti, Cuba, and the Dominican Republic.

After World War II, the region began organizing, and Jamaica was eventually recognized by FIFA, the world's federation of soccer organizations. The region eventually widened to include the United States and Canada. This led to Jamaica's first entry into the World Cup finals in 1998.

Jamaica's biggest problem in reaching World Cup competition had been its team. Although Jamaica was filled with stars who could play a great game, they did not work together as a team as well as they worked individually. Therefore, after a great deal of training and help from some of the best in the world, the Reggae Boyz became one of three teams to reach the finals in 1998 alongside Mexico and the

United States. Although they were eliminated after the first round, they did finish the round points ahead of the U.S. team.

Olympic Sports

Perhaps it can be attributed to a competitive streak in the Jamaican spirit, but it's clear the island is here to stay in the Olympics. Jamaica has claimed a large number of medals in track and field events, and who could forget the Jamaican bobsled team's participation in previous Winter Olympics?

Track Traditions

After World War II, Jamaicans began competing in track events. In fact, in the 1996 Olympic games Jamaica was ranked as one of the top-five nations based on number of medals won per capita of the population.

Herb McKenley, Merlene Ottey, Donald Quarrie, and Arthur Wint are among some of Jamaica's famous runners. However, you'll also find Jamaicans who now live in other countries competing for top awards.

During the 2012 Olympics, Usain Bolt won two gold medals for Jamaica in both the 100 meter dash and 200 meter dash and set a new world record. His team mates brought home an additional 16 medals; a total of seven gold, four silver, and seven bronze.

Bobsled

The Jamaican Bobsled (Bobsleigh) Team gained international notice when it set its sights on the 1988 Winter Olympics. The team had trouble in this early competition but was performing well by 1992, when it took 14th place against other teams, including the United States and France, in the four-man team. The two-man team came in 10th place, above the Swedish national champions.

Although the team cannot train in Jamaica, where it never snows, they've worked hard to reach the Olympics every four years. Their struggle inspired the Disney movie *Cool Runnings*. They have also participated in the 2002 Winter Olympics and other competitions.

Other Sports

There are some surprises when it comes to other sports that are played on Jamaica. Horse racing is popular, with all of the action centered at the Caymanas Park race track near Kingston. Tennis and golf are also played, though they are not as widely popular as cricket or football. These sports also tend to be pastimes of wealthier Jamaicans, however, they are also popular among travelers.

American football has some followers in Jamaica as well. Most of these fans are those who have emigrated from the United States or who have spent time there. Although pickup games may start up among fans, the game is not widely followed on the island, and there are no local teams.

Basketball, on the other hand, is growing in popularity. Interestingly, many of Jamaica's Chinese were the first to pick up the game in the 1940s. It wasn't until the 1960s that the rest of Jamaica's population began considering the game. They have been playing internationally in CARICOM (Caribbean Community and Common Market) tournaments, and womens player Simone Edwards has played in Europe, as well as in the United States' WNBA with the Seattle Storms.

Cricket and football are the top games in Jamaica, but athletics are so popular that you can always find a way to play when visiting this island, no matter what kind of sports you're interested in. If playing isn't your thing, there are many fun opportunities to be a spectator.

Tennis

Playing Tennis in Jamaica
Visit Jamaica and find world-class tennis on one of the Caribbean's most popular islands

Although nearly every tennis court in Jamaica is located on resort property, each one offers its own unique style or spectacular tropical view.

A few Jamaican resorts are home to what are undeniably some of the most popular courts in the Caribbean, and often staff their courts with highly skilled tennis pros.

Tryall Club has nine hard-surface courts. These are all extremely well-maintained, and three of them also include lighting for nighttime play. Although guests can play free, using the lights will cost $20(USD) per hour. Non-guests need only pay $30(USD) per hour for court time. Reservations help enthusiasts ensure a spot and professional lessons start at $40(USD) per hour.

Half Moon is home to what are considered the top tennis courts on Jamaica. Here, visitors will find 13 all-weather Laykold courts, seven of which are lighted. Guests can play free any time, day or night, at Half Moon. However, those not making the resort their home away from home will need to obtain a $40(USD) day pass, giving them access to all of Half Moon's tennis facilities. These include a pro shop and lessons starting at $50(USD) per hour.

For a change of pace, visit Sandals Grande Ocho Rios, and play on clay or hard surface courts, all of them lighted. However, there are only three clay and three hard courts, so space is limited. Guests play free at all times and are offered lessons starting at $30(USD) per hour. These courts are also noteworthy because they offer guest tournaments and twice-daily tennis clinics.

While these three resorts don't offer the only top-notch tennis on the island of Jamaica, they are certainly a few of the most well-known. Travelers looking for a date with the courts can stay anywhere they like and almost always find a place to play, whether for an additional fee at another resort or at their own.

Other Activities

From hiking to eco-ventures, interesting activities abound in Jamaica

The diverse terrain of Jamaica offers many active options for island explorers.

Spending time at the beach is one of the most popular outdoor activities for Jamaica's visitors, but hiking isn't far behind. Jamaica also draws in many visitors interested in diverse sporting opportunities such as horseback riding, or swimming with dolphins. One thing in certain, no matter what you choose to do on your Jamaica vacation, adventure awaits.

Cockpit Country

Cockpit Country, located in the central-northwestern portion of the island, is a truly wild region in Jamaica. Here there are few roads and little civilization. Here the descendants of the Maroons have lived for generations, though they are now venturing out into the tourism business. Tours are allowed, and hiking is suggested only with a local guide. Tour-based travelers will not have to make any further stops, but those looking to tour on their own will need to handle formalities with former Colonel Harris Cawley (876-909-9222). He will make hiking arrangements, including guides and food. Keep in mind that this is not an area suggested for those without plenty of hiking experience.

Blue Mountains

For equally intriguing hiking experiences, vacationers enjoy spending time in the famed Blue Mountains of Jamaica. Here travelers can choose between enjoying shorter excursions or hiking all the way to the peak, spending several nights camping along the way. The Blue Mountains offer a tamer experience than Cockpit Country.

Hikers can explore the lower regions of the Blue Mountains, but to truly experience the majesty of the mountains one must travel to Blue Mountain Peak. Interested hikers should check into camping opportunities on the island. Camping permits are necessary and must be obtained from Jamaica Alternative Tourism Camping and Hiking Association (JATCHA) and the Jamaica Forestry Department.

Dolphin Cove

Dolphin Cove in Ocho Rios is a popular spot. The facility allows guest to swim with dolphins in an enclosed and supervised environment. Even those uninterested in swimming with the dolphins will enjoy hours exploring the natural habitats of stingrays, eels, "friendly" sharks, snakes, macaws, and other tropical animals. If sea life doesn't entice you, the surrounding tropical rainforest is reason enough to visit. Advance reservations are necessary.

Check out a game of netball, or take a horseback ride. Jamaica also offers plenty of other hiking and nature options, as well as historic site seeing for visitors.

Jamaica Attractions

Explore all that Jamaica has to offer, from the beaches to the casinos

From a plantation-estate past to a party-filled present, Jamaica's attractions run the gamut. Those in search of a sedate stay can enjoy nature, beaches, and history, while those looking for lively activities can meet lady luck as well.

Vacationers can get lost in history on old sugar plantations and in ancient forests or live on the edge by risking some change at a Jamaican casino. Learn about the mysterious White Witch of Rose Hall or the spot where the James Bond novels were written. For those with more musical inclinations, stop in at any of several spots dedicated to Bob Marley.

Beaches

Pristine beaches are a great place to start. Jamaica is home to so many incredible beaches that travelers can choose nearly any area of the island to stay in if they'd like to spend a lazy day at the beach. With it's pleasantly warm waters year-round and claim of naturally restorative powers, Doctor's Cave Beach in Montego Bay is one of Jamaica's most popular beaches. For the rowdier, more carefree set, Seven Mile Beach in Negril is another well liked stretch. Families beware, this is where nude sun bathers stop to get a line-free tan.

There are several beaches to enjoy on the island. Whether you'd rather be part of a busy beach scene, or you like having more of the beach to yourself, you can find a beach that appeals to you. Click on the name of the beach for a detailed review of that beach.

Doctor's Cave Beach: The waters of Doctor's Cave Beach are fed by crystal clear mineral springs, and these extremely gentle waves stay at about 80 degrees Fahrenheit. The beach's golden sands glimmer in the sultry island sun, and the inviting turquoise waters are perfect for swimming.

Another place worth considering is Treasure Beach. Gray and peppered with boats, this isn't a picturesque locale, but it may still be fun to beach comb. This beach also offers a view of the sunset over the water.

Cornwall Beach: Cornwall Beach boasts gentle blue waters and has an easy sloping ocean floor creating mild swimming conditions, and making it a favorite spot to bring children. Its soft white sand also makes it a favorite for those wanting to take a pleasant stroll down the beach.

Fortunately, you will find plenty of other beaches to choose from on the island. For a more comprehensive look at beaches, read from Beaches page in this book.

Landmark Attractions

The impact Bob Marley had on Jamaica is undeniable, with numerous attractions dedicated to his honor. Learn about the man -- the legend -- at the Bob Marley Museum in Kingston, the Bob Marley Experience and Theatrein Montego Bay, and the Bob Marley's Mausoleumin Ocho Rios. Historic plantation homes, like the Bloomfield Great House in Kingston and Rose Hall Plantation offer a glimpse of Jamaica's agricultural past, as well as a view of the dark days of slavery on the island. Other historical sites include the Coyoba River Garden and Museum in Ocho Rios.

If you are looking to do some sight-seeing, visit National Gallery of Jamaica. It is located within downtown Kingston. If you're looking for the largest public art gallery in the Caribbean, you're in the right place. With a focus on local and regional artists, there is much to see in this gallery.

Another common landmark for vacationers is Jamaica Fun Farm. It is situated in E Lacovia, Jamaica. A property that makes farming fun, the owners have created a place where visitors can learn what it takes to remain agriculturally sound while also participating in a number of entertainment activities to keep guests having a great time.

Outameni Theme Park: Outameni is a history theme park that seeks to present the story of Jamaica from its first settlers, the Taino, up to the modern day. While the park may be geared more towards children than adults anyone with interest in Jamaican history as Jamaicans tell it should find Outameni to be an interesting experience.

Natural Attractions

Nature has plenty to offer up as well. The Blue Mountains are a gorgeous backdrop to a vacation, and also a great place to explore. The Martha Brae River is another example of the beautiful and incredible natural wonders you'll see throughout the island. Jamaica's nature is part of what made it such a popular vacation spot in the 1960s. Take part in one of the numerous nature tours to have a knowledgeable guide show you the spots that can't be missed.

Assuming you enjoy the natural environment will frequently enjoy visiting Green Grotto Caves. Underneath the tropical paradise of Jamaica is a whole underground world waiting to be explored. Heading to Green Grotto Cave will give you the opportunity to see the large caves that exist just under the surface.

Another site to consider visiting is Dunn's River Park. This park features Dunn's River Falls, a recreational center and lush tropical vegetation surrounding a 600 foot waterfall that attracts thousands of people each year.

Fortunately, there are additional choices too. Take advantage of Natural Attraction's page in this book to learn more about natural attractions on the island if you'd like to find some more facts.

Casinos

In the mood for some action? Vacationers hoping to test their luck in some gaming action have quite a few places to go on the island.

Monte Carlo Gaming Lounge offers dining on-site, so you can grab a bite to eat before or after you try your luck. The on-site barroom features a beautiful 20-foot mahogany bar and a collection of wall mounted television screens so guests can watch international horse races and other sporting events.

Treasure Hunt Montego Bay is Montego Bay, in western Jamaica. Treasure Hunt is loved in Jamaica for its clear rules and high pay outs. One of four on the island, this Montego Bay locale is home to some of the most unique computerized games out there.

Treasure Hunt Kingston offers a collection of games for guests to enjoy, including Bingo, Bingo - Spanish-style, Craps, Poker - Video Table, and Roulette. Table games at Treasure Hunt include, among others, baccarat and black jack. For computerized games, you'll find such titles as Splash 2, Sakura Festival, Mysteria, and Emerald Falls.

Historic sites, natural locales, and exciting gaming facilities come together to make Jamaica enjoyable for every type of traveler. With so many attractions, it is easy to see how Jamaica has become one of the world's top vacation destinations.

Beaches

The gorgeous beaches found in Jamaica are legendary
The beaches of Jamaica are so beautiful that even locals can't get enough of them. Whether you prefer lying on the sand soaking up the sun, or crashing through the waves, the perfect beach is just waiting for you to find it.

Kingston Area

Just off the coast of Port Royal is Lime Cay, a small island perfect for both sun bathing and water sports. There is no formal form of transportation to and from the island, so your best bet is to head to Port Royal and hire a local fisherman to transport you.

Ocho Rios

Two of the most popular beaches in Jamaica are Turtle Beach and Mallards Beach. Both are tourist-oriented spots with plenty of food, fun activities, and fellow visitors. Several hotels are located along both of the beaches, so if you are looking for a place to stay on the water, these might be good locations to search for accommodations.

Additionally, travelers should be sure to check out the famous James Bond Beach, which is home to the Golden Eye Hotel. The hotel was the former residence of James Bond writer Ian Fleming. The waterfront is owned by the hotel, and for a small fee of $3(USD), non-guests can enjoy the sand and surf of this famous locale. Rentals for water sports equipment are available, which make for a perfect trip for those James Bond fans who dream of their own exciting ride at the site where the movie Dr. No was filmed.

Don't forget to visit Dunn's River Beach, located under the famous Dunn's River Falls, where the Dunn's River meets the Caribbean Sea in amazing, visual splendor. Visitors can climb the falls, swim in small whirlpools or just admire the natural beauty from the beach not far down from the waterfall.

Negril

Seven Mile Beach, famous for being a favorite hot spot of the 1960's hippie movement, is home to a care-free, laid-back environment that includes nude bathing. Although it was once an idyllic retreat into natural Jamaica, now this area is more of a tourist attraction than a hippie retreat. If you are visiting this beach, expect to see many sun worshipers wearing nothing but their birthday suits. Many of the resorts also host nude beaches as well as bars, hot tubs and swimming pools.

Montego Bay

For the more clothing-conscious, or for visitors with children, Montego Bay offers several appropriate retreats. Cornwall Beach is lively and happening, offering a variety of concessions and water-sport activities. Another a great place to visit is Walter Fletcher Beach, which offers exceptional bathing and swimming opportunities that may not be found elsewhere. Because of it's calmer waters, this beach is recommended for visitors with children.

MoBay's most famous bathing spot, Doctor's Cave Beach, was founded in 1906 when a group of doctors banded together to bathe here. At the time, access to the small cave was limited, and it was later destroyed by a 1932 hurricane. Although the cave is no longer there, the popularity of the bathing spot lived on, especially when Sir Herbert Bake claimed in 1920 that the waters in this location had curative powers. The crystal clear water, almost always between 78 and 84 degrees Fahrenheit, is fed by mineral springs. Admission costs approximately $5(USD), and there are plenty of changing areas, showers, and dining options.

Port Antonio

Boston Bay Beach, an easily missed but beautiful bathing area is perfect for small fishing trips and surfing. Snack stands around the beach serve delicious jerk pork, a tradition in Jamaica. Formerly owned by author Roger Moore (The Happy Hooker and The Greek Berets), he donated this small beach to the Jamaican government.

Frenchman's Bay is said to be among the most beautiful beaches in the world. For the small charge of $3(USD), visitors can sunbathe, swim, body surf, or simply relax in the shaded parts of this gorgeous Jamaican treasure.

Blue Lagoon is famous for hosting Brooke Shields in the movie Blue Lagoon. The deep water is a gorgeous shade of cobalt blue and is excellent for swimming and enjoying the environment.

Beach Choices In The Area

You will discover an abundance of beaches to visit on the island. Regardless of whether you're looking forward to people watching, or you enjoy relaxing in a secluded area, you can find a beach that appeals to you. Just click on the beach names for a detailed review of that section of the coast.

Cornwall Beach: Visit Cornwall beach any day of the week between the hours of 9:00 a.m. and 5:00 p.m.

Another option worth considering is Winnifred Beach. This thin and picturesque beach is in a cove, surrounded by trees and brush. Its a perfect spot for a warm swim or a casual snorkeling exploration.

Dunn's River Beach: The beach is accessible by car, with parking available at the Falls. You'll find it off the road running along coast west from Ocho Rios.

The beaches on Jamaica are summarized directly below.

BEACHES ON JAMAICA

Name	Location	Coast
Alligator Pond	3.1 mi. Southeast of Central Junction	South West
Annotto Bay	0.5 mi. West of Central Annotto Bay	East
Auchindown Beach	0.3 mi. South West of Central Auchindown	West
Belmont Beach	0.2 mi. South West of Central Belmont	West
Belvedere Beach	0.7 mi. West of Central Montego Bay	North West
Bengal Beach	3.7 mi. West of Central Discovery Bay	North West
Billy Bay	1.8 mi. West-Northwest of Central downtown Treasure Beach	South West
Bloody Bay	2.9 mi. South West of Central Orange Bay	West

Jamaica Travel Guide, Caribbean

Blue Lagoon	0.5 mi. Southeast of Central Port Antonio	East
Bluefields Beach	1.8 mi. North of Central Belmont	West
Boston Bay Beach	0.9 mi. East-Southeast of Central Fairy Hill	East
Brooks Pen Beach	1.6 mi. South West of Central Harbour View	East
Bucaneer Beach	Montego Bay, Northwestern part of Jamaica	North West
Buff Bay	Buff Bay, Eastern part of Jamaica	East
Bulls Bay Beach	0.1 mi. North-Northeast of Central Bull's Bay	West
Bulls Bay North	2.4 mi. West of Central Haughton Gardens	West
Burwood Beach	0.4 mi. East-Northeast of Central White Bay	North West
Cable Hut Beach	3.7 mi. East-Southeast of Central Harbour View	East
Cornwall Beach	Montego Bay, Northwestern part of Jamaica	North West
Cousin's Cove	1.3 mi. North of Central Green Island	West
Crab Pond Bay	1.5 mi. Northwest of Central Whitehouse	West
Crane Beach	2.9 mi. Southeast of Central Black River	West
Crusoe's Beach	Port Antonio, Eastern part of Jamaica	East
Dead End Beach	Montego Bay, Northwestern part of Jamaica	North West
Doctor's Cave Beach	Montego Bay, Northwestern part of Jamaica	North West
Dump-Up Beach and Events Park	Downtown Montego Bay	North West
Dunn's River Beach	3.7 mi. West of Central Ocho Rios	North
Errol Flynn Marina Beach	0.1 mi. North-Northwest of Central Port Antonio	North East
Fairy Hill Beach	1.0 mi. Northwest of Central Fairy Hill	East
Farquhar's Beach	1.3 mi. East-Southeast of Central Round Hill	--
Ferris Cross Beach	1.3 mi. South West of Central Ferris Cross	West
Fisherman's Beach	Downtown Ocho Rios	North-Northeast
Folly Ruins Beach	Port Antonio, Eastern part of Jamaica	East
Font Hill Beach	3.6 mi. West of Central Black River	West
Fort Clarence	Hellshire, Southeastern part of Jamaica	South East

Caleb Gray

Frenchman's Bay	Downtown Treasure Beach	South West
Frenchmen's Cove Beach	2.2 mi. West-Northwest of Central Fairy Hill	East
Golden Grove Beach	1.4 mi. East-Southeast of Central Iter Boreale	East
Golf Beach	2.8 mi. Northwest of Central Spot Valley	North West
Grande Beach	Ocho Rios, Northern part of Jamaica	North East
Great River Bay	2.1 mi. East of Central Hopewell	North West
Green Island East Beach	1.2 mi. West of Central Green Island	West
Green Island North Beach	1.2 mi. North of Central Green Island	West
Gunboat Beach	3.7 mi. West-Southwest of Central Harbour View	East
Half Moon Beach	Falmouth, Northwestern part of Jamaica	North West
Hellshire Beach	Hellshire, Southeastern part of Jamaica	South East
Hope Bay	0.1 mi. North of Central Hope Bay	East
Hope Well Beach	0.4 mi. North of Central Hopewell	North West
Hunt Bay	1.6 mi. West of Central Black River	West
Innis Bay Beach	0.5 mi. Southeast of Central Long Road	East
James Bond Beach	0.6 mi. West of Central Oracabessa	North East
Lances Bay	0.8 mi. South West of Central Bull's Bay	West
Lime Cay	The vicinity of Kingston, Eastern part of Jamaica	South East
Little Laughlands Bay	4.7 mi. East of Central Runaway Bay	North
Long Bay Beach	3.6 mi. Northwest of Central Rural Hill	East
Mahee Bay Beach	3.6 mi. Northeast of Central Montego Bay	North West
Maiden Cay Beach	3.9 mi. Southeast of Central Portmore	South East
Malcolm Bay	2.1 mi. West of Central Black River	West
Mallards Beach	Ocho Rios, Northern part of Jamaica	North East
Mollasses Beach	1.5 mi. Northeast of Central Johnson Town	West
Montego Beach	Montego Bay, Northwestern part of Jamaica	North West
Navy Island	Port Antonio, Eastern part of Jamaica	East
Negril North Beach	0.8 mi. West-Northwest of Central Negril	West

Jamaica Travel Guide, Caribbean

New Hope South Beach	2.4 mi. East-Southeast of Central Revival	West
Orange Bay Beach East	0.3 mi. North of Central Orange Bay	East
Orange Bay Beach West	3.4 mi. East of Central Buff Bay	East
Palmetto Bay	1.5 mi. Northwest of Central Hart Hill	East
Parottee Bay	5.0 mi. South of Central Black River	West
Pigeon Island Beach	7.9 mi. South of Central Moores Pen	Northwest
Port Antonio East Harbour	0.8 mi. East of Central Port Antonio	--
Port Maria Beach	Port Maria, Northeastern part of Jamaica	North East
Port Maria North	1.0 mi. North of Central Port Maria	North East
Portland Caye	0.0 mi. Northwest of Central Portland Cay	Northwest
Priory Beach	1.3 mi. West-Northwest of Central St. Ann's Bay	North
Puero Seco Beach	Discovery Bay, Northern part of Jamaica	North
Rhodes Hall Beach	2.4 mi. West of Central Green Island	West
Rio Bueno Beach	0.3 mi. Northwest of Central Rio Bueno	North West
Rio Nuevo Battle Site	1.1 mi. East of Central Tower Isle	North East
RioNuoya Beach	2.2 mi. West of Central Oracabessa	North East
Rose Hall Beach Club	3.9 mi. Northwest of Central Spot Valley	North West
Runaway Beach	Runaway Bay, Northern part of Jamaica	North
Rural Hill Beach	2.3 mi. North of Central Long Road	East
Salem Paradise Beach	2.5 mi. East of Central Runaway Bay	North
San San Beach	1.9 mi. West-Northwest of Central Fairy Hill	East
Sandy Bay	0.5 mi. Northeast of Central Sandy Bay	North West
Sandy Ground	1.9 mi. South-Southeast of Central New Hope	West
Seven Mile Beach	2.5 mi. South of Central Negril Beach Hotel Zone	West
Shaw Park Beach	Ocho Rios, Northeastern part of Jamaica	North East
Silver Sands Beach	1.5 mi. Northeast of Central Duncans	North West
Spring Garden Beach	1.7 mi. East of Central Buff Bay	East
St Bran's Burg Beach	1.9 mi. North-Northwest of Central Spot Valley	North West

St. Ann's Bay	1.0 mi. East-Northeast of Central St. Ann's Bay	North
Starve Gut Bay	3.7 mi. Northwest of Central downtown Treasure Beach	West
Steer Town Beach	4.7 mi. West of Central Ocho Rios	North
Tom Pipers Bay	Johnson Town, Western part of Jamaica	West
Tower Isle West Beach	2.3 mi. East-Northeast of Central Ocho Rios	North East
Treasure Beach	2.2 mi. Southeast of Central Treasure Beach	South West
Tropical Lagoon	1.1 mi. West-Northwest of Central Fairy Hill	East
Turtle Beach	Downtown Ocho Rios	North East
Tyrall Beach	1.3 mi. East of Central Sandy Bay	North West
Walter Fletcher Beach	Montego Bay, Western part of Jamaica	North West
Watson Taylor Beach	1.1 mi. North of Central Johnson Town	West
White River Bay	Ocho Rios, Northeastern part of Jamaica	North East
Whitehouse Beach	0.5 mi. South-Southwest of Central Whitehouse	West
Windsor Castle Beach	2.1 mi. Northwest of Central Buff Bay	East
Winnifred Beach	0.5 mi. Northwest of Central Fairy Hill	East
Yerba Buena Beach	1.4 mi. North of Central Robins Bay	North East
Zion Hill Beach	0.9 mi. East-Southeast of Central Fairy Hill	East

Needless to say, there are plenty of other attraction types available too. For more in formation concerning other attractions for Jamaica, read from Attraction page in this book.

With plenty of beaches you are sure to find one you enjoy. Just remeber that Jamaica is large for a Caribbean nation, and two beaches may be hours away from eachother.

Casinos

Casinos offer a glimpse of island gaming for Jamaica's visitors

Tourists who have dreams of the glitz, glamour and neon lights of Las Vegas but don't want to give up a vacation in the tropics, Jamaica now offers the best of both worlds. Even for the casual gambler, a trip to any of the island's casinos can add spice to any vacationg

For a long time there have been many rules and regulations regarding casinos on the island, and up until recently the only place to play the slots (which was the only type of casino gambling allowed) was at resorts that had received special permission by the government to operate a casino on property.

Making it Legal

In 2010, despite opposition from many church organizations, a bill to expand and regulate casino gaming in Jamaica passed both houses of Parliament. It wasn't until November of 2012, however, that legislatures unanimously passed two bills to allow full scale casino operations on the island. What this means for the island is that it is not officially legal to begin building full scale casinos as opposed to mainly slot driven game centers found in many hotels in Jamaica.

Jamaican Casinos Today

Until the big casinos are officially open, slot machines make up the majority of floor games, but video poker, blackjack, Caribbean Stud Poker, craps, and roulette are also sometimes available.

Due to its origin in Aruba, Caribbean Stud Poker is widespread. It is played by many of the same rules as regular poker but has one big difference: the players, instead of playing against each other, play against the dealer only. Another small difference is that all of the players can see one of the dealer's cards, which he deals face up. With this information, players are free to make bets. This type of poker is extremely popular both in Jamaica and on cruise ships.

Where to Find Gambling

Ready for some action? Those hoping to test their luck in some gaming action will discover lots of places to go. Click on each name for additional details.

Treasure Hunt Montego Bay has a restaurant, so you can grab a bite to eat before or after you try your luck. Treasure Hunt is loved in Jamaica for its clear rules and high pay outs. One of four on the island, this Montego Bay locale is home to some of the most unique computerized games out there.

If you like slot machines, consider giving Treasure Hunt Ocho Rios a try. Open 24 hours a day, seven days a week, Treasure Hunt Ocho Rios features 140 gaming machines for gamblers to circulate amongst. When thirst calls, there is a bar on property.

Acropolis Portmore provides a collection of games for gamers to try out, including Blackjack and Roulette. Acropolis Gaming Center is a relative sports bar and restaurant that also just so happens to allow gambling on site. Not only can you eat and drink at the bar while watching your favorite sporting event, but there are table games and slot machines not far off.

The gaming choices you might be interested in are provided in the chart below.

GAMBLING ON JAMAICA					
Name	Type	Located At		Phone	Location
Acropolis Barbican	Casino	--		(876) 978-1299	Kingston, Eastern part of Jamaica
Acropolis Portmore	Casino	--		(876) 902-4763	Portmore, Eastern part of Jamaica
Caribbean Treasures Gaming Lounge	Gambling Arcade	--		(876) 952-8938	0.7 mi. West-Northwest of Central Montego Bay
Christelle's Gaming	Gambling Arcade	--		(876) 969-6686	Kingston, Eastern part of Jamaica
Coral Cliff Gaming Lounge	Slot Machine Arcade	Coral Cliff Hotel		(876) 952-4131	Montego Bay, Northwestern part of Jamaica
Grand Bahia Principe	Casino	--		(876) 973-7000	Runaway Bay, Northern part of Jamaica
Holiday Inn	Slot Machine	Holiday Inn Resort in		(876) 953-	The vicinity of Montego Bay, Northwestern part of

Sunspree Casino	Arcade	Rose Hall	2485	Jamaica
Jamaica Pegasus Derby Room	Slot Machine Arcade	Jamaica Pegasus	(876) 926-3691-9	1.2 mi. South West of Central Kingston
Jungle Negril	Slot Machine Arcade	--	(876) 957-4005	1.5 mi. South of Central Negril Beach Hotel Zone
Macau Gaming Lounge	Gambling Arcade	--	(876) 925-6395	Kingston, Eastern part of Jamaica
Monte Carlo Gaming Lounge	Casino	Terra Nova All Suite Hotel	(876) 926-2211 ext. 2	Kingston, Eastern part of Jamaica
RIU Ocho Rios Casino	Casino	Riu Ocho Rios	(876) 972-2200	2.3 mi. East of Central St. Ann's Bay
RIU Tropical Bay Game Room	Slot Machine Arcade	Riu Tropical Bay	(876) 957-5900	2.0 mi. North of Central Negril Beach Hotel Zone
Rajmaville Gaming Lounge	Gambling Arcade	Rajmaville Gaming Lounge Sea Food & Sports Bar	(876) 749-0312	Spanish Town, Eastern part of Jamaica
Treasure Hunt Montego Bay	Casino	--	(876) 953-9272	Montego Bay, Western part of Jamaica
Treasure Hunt Ocho Rios	Casino	--	(876) 974-8169	Ocho Rios, Northern part of Jamaica
Vegas Gaming Kingston	Gambling Arcade	--	(876) 977-4927 ext. 8	Kingston, Eastern part of Jamaica

If you want to learn about more points of interest beyond what's offered on this page, you should think about other locations. G to Attraction poage to read our page concerning other interesting attractions for Jamaica.

As construction begins on casinos in Jamaica, it is more important to remember to squirrel away a little extra spending cash for your trip. If Jamaica's current hotel casinos are just a hint of what's to come, you can be sure that the future of gaming in Jamaica is going to be spectacular.

Landmarks

Rich in both heritage and natural beauty, Jamaica provides a plethora of sites and sounds

An island like Jamaica, with a rich natural and social history, inevitably has many fascinating sites to explore. Jamaican history includes Spanish rule, a British takeover and a struggle for independence. This mixture of cultural influences means a wide variety of interesting things to see, from famous architecture and artifacts, to natural scenery and historic sites.

Some specific sites in Jamaica include plantation "Great Houses," museums and cultural attractions. Travelers also enjoy the natural scenery of the Blue Mountains, where they can hike and camp. Popular sites abound on this beautiful island and generally surround three of the larger cities: Montego Bay, Ocho Rios, and Kingston.

Museums

Assuming you like to expand your knowledge of other people and places, you might want to visit a museum while on vacation on Jamaica. To learn more information about each museum, just click on the name.

One popular destination is Bob Marley Museum. It is found in Kingston, Jamaica. This museum is dedicated to the works of Marley, and of reggae music in general. Any music fan, reggae or otherwise, may want to make this musical pilgrimage site to priority.

Another popular destination is Outameni Theme Park. It is Falmouth, in northwestern Jamaica. Outameni is a history theme park that seeks to present the story of Jamaica from its first settlers, the Taino, up to the modern day. While the park may be geared more towards children than adults anyone with interest in Jamaican history as Jamaicans tell it should find Outameni to be an interesting experience.

Jamaica Fun Farm: A property that makes farming fun, the owners have created a place where visitors can learn what it takes to remain agriculturally sound while also participating in a number of entertainment activities to keep guests having a great time.

The following table enables you to learn a few details concerning some museums to consider on the island.

MUSEUMS ON JAMAICA		
Name	Phone	Location
Abba Jahnehoy Place	(876) 578-9578	The vicinity of Negril
Bank of Jamaica Money Museum	(876) 922-0750	Downtown Kingston
Bob Marley Museum	(876) 978-2929	1.3 mi. East-Northeast of Central Kingston
Hanover Museum	--	1.3 mi. East of Central Haughton Court
Jamaica Fun Farm	(876) 296-8669	0.3 mi. West of Central E Lacovia
National Gallery of Jamaica	(876) 922-1561 ext. 3	Downtown Kingston
Outameni Theme Park	(876) 954-4035	0.2 mi. East-Northeast of Central Falmouth
People's Museum of Craft and Technology	(876) 907-0322	1.8 mi. West of Central Spanish Town
Reggae Xplosion	(876) 675-8793	Ocho Rios
Trench Town Culture Yard Museum	(876) 572-4085	1.3 mi. Northwest of Central downtown Kingston

Historical Sites

In case you like to experience the history of a foreign country, you might enjoy visiting one or two of these historical attractions while vacationing in Jamaica.

A landmark that often intrigues visitors is Devon House. It is located in Kingston, Jamaica. Devon House is a unique landmark. On an island filled with historic plantation houses once owned by white slave owners, Devon house was built by Jamaica's first black millionaire, George Stielbel.

Many travelers also choose to visit Bellefield Great House. It is found within Jamaica. The tour is available from between the hours of 11:00 a.m. and 3:00 p.m.

St. Peter's Church: Some of the most unique artifacts at St. Peter's Church include a communion plate donated by Sir Henry Morgan and the tomb of Lewis Galdye, which tells us that he was swallowed up in an earth quake, then spit out of the earth into the ocean, where he swam until he was picked up by a boat.

Take a minute to read the following table for more information on historical sites on the island.

HISTORIC SITES ON JAMAICA

Name	Phone	Location
18 Century Iron Bridge	--	0.3 mi. East of Central Spanish Town
Albert George Market	--	Falmouth, Northwestern part of Jamaica
Annandale Great House	--	3.4 mi. South West of Central downtown Ocho Rios
Barbican Estate	--	1.7 mi. West of Central Sandy Bay
Bellefield Great House	(876) 952-2382	2.4 mi. South-Southeast of Central Montego Bay
Bloomfield Great House	(876) 962-7130	Mandeville, Central Jamaica
Bob Marley's Mausoleum	(876) 995-1763	Central Jamaica
Brimmer Hall Estate	(876) 994-2309	0.9 mi. Northwest of Central Llanrumney
Christ Church	--	0.3 mi. Southeast of Central Port Antonio
Davidson House	--	Falmouth, Northwestern part of Jamaica
Devon House	(876) 929-6602	0.6 mi. Northeast of Central Kingston
Falmouth Court House	--	Falmouth, Northwestern part of Jamaica
Folly Ruins	--	0.9 mi. East-Northeast of Central Port Antonio
Fort Balcarres	--	0.5 mi. East-Northeast of Central Falmouth
Fort Montego	--	0.4 mi. West of Central Montego Bay
Good Hope Great House	(876) 469-3444	Falmouth, Northwestern part of Jamaica
Greenwood Great House	(876) 953-1077	2.6 mi. West of Central Salt Marsh

Martha Brae Waterwheel	--	Falmouth, Northwestern part of Jamaica
Old Baptist Manse	--	Falmouth, Northwestern part of Jamaica
Old Court House	--	0.3 mi. Northwest of Central Spanish Town
Old Pera Windmill	--	1.8 mi. East of Central Leitt Hall
Phoenix Foundry	--	Falmouth, Northwestern part of Jamaica
Port Royal	--	3.8 mi. Southeast of Central Portmore
Rose Hall Plantation	(876) 953-2323	1.1 mi. East of Central Rose Hall
St. Peter's Anglican Church	--	Falmouth, Northwestern part of Jamaica
St. Peter's Church	--	1.3 mi. South-Southeast of Central Kingston
Tharp House	--	Falmouth, Northwestern part of Jamaica

Miscellaneous Landmarks

Guests can explore some other intriguing sites to visit on the island. If the more functional aspects of maritime life intrigue you, you might want to see Lover's Leap Lighthouse. The newest lighthouse on the island, this is actually the highest lighthouse in the western hemisphere. Tourists can hike to the spot and take in the structure as well as enjoy the view.

If you'd like to observe the distillery process, another landmark you might consider visiting is Appleton Estate Rum Distillery. Since 1749, Appleton Estate has been Jamaica's premier fine rum producer. Today, over 20 varieties of rum are produced on site and sold world wide.

The chart directly below has some details regarding other kinds of places of interest to visitors.

MISCELLANEOUS LANDMARKS ON JAMAICA		
Name	Type	Location
Appleton Estate Rum Distillery	Distillery	1.4 mi. West of Central Siloah
Bamboo Alley	Scenic Trail	5.8 mi. North of Central Black River
Folly Lighthouse	Lighthouse	1.7 mi. Northwest of Central Turtle Harbour

Galina Lighthouse	Lighthouse	0.4 mi. Northeast of Central Galina
Lover's Leap Lighthouse	Lighthouse	7.0 mi. East of Central downtown Treasure Beach
Negril Lighthouse	Lighthouse	1.9 mi. South-Southwest of Central Negril
Peter Tosh Monument	Monument	0.5 mi. North-Northwest of Central Belmont
Redstripe Plant	Attraction	Kingston, Eastern part of Jamaica

Needless to say, Jamaica includes other attractions. Go to Attraction page and read the our article concerning other interesting attractions for Jamaica.

Natural Attractions

Jamaica is an excellent location for tourists more interested in nature than beach resorts

Nature lovers looking for more than just a beautiful beach resort should consider Jamaica an excellent opportunity to view the spectacular beauty of Caribbean flora and fauna.

The island offers a great variety of outdoor activities, ranging from hiking in the amazing Blue Mountains to spelunking along the unexplored caves of Cockpit Country. Here are some highly recommended natural attractions that promise to inspire and astonish.

Nature Preserves and Hiking

Do you want to enjoy part of your vacation under the open sky? You might be happy to find out that the island has a few interesting nature preserves on it.

Negril Watershed Protection Area is a popular nature preserve the vicinity of Negril, in western Jamaica. This area of the island was set aside for the preservation of a tropical environment and visitors often hike through for a view of the Great Morass.

Those wanting to locate a another great natural attraction will enjoy exploring sites like The Blue Mountains National Park. The peaks of the Blue Mountains rise to an altitude of 7402 feet above sea level, with dangerous terrain typifying the area. Though camping and hiking are permitted, these activities are best done with a knowledgeable guide.

Review this table for information on more nature preserves.

NATURE PRESERVES AND HIKING ON JAMAICA		
Name	Type	Location
Crocodile Reserve & Bird Sanctuary	Nature Sanctuary/Wildlife Reserve	0.6 mi. Northwest of Central Orange Bay
Mount Zion Sanctuary	Nature Sanctuary/Wildlife Reserve	Ocho Rios
Negril Watershed Protection Area	Nature Sanctuary/Wildlife Reserve	1.7 mi. South-Southwest of Central Negril
The Blue Mountains National Park	Nature Sanctuary/Wildlife Reserve	11.2 mi. Northeast of Central Kingston

Waterfalls and Caves

Although most vacationers come for the beaches, that isn't the only way to enjoy the natural wonders available. Jamaica offers multiple choices, including 10 waterfalls and 3 caves.

You should consider visiting Green Grotto Caves, which is northern Jamaica. As you first pass the deceivingly small cave entrance, you will stumble into the large cavern, full of complex stalagmites, pocketed walls, and a ceiling inhabited by the bats that call the caves home. During your forty-five minute tour, you will learn how the the limestone rocks were, over decades, slowly carved by gently flowing water, until it created the cave that now stands.

A second attraction worth considering is Reach Falls. It is eastern Jamaica. This is a very famous waterfall and is easy to get to. On the east coast of the Island there is the main road, A4.

The following chart enables you to learn more details on waterfalls and caves.

WATERFALLS AND CAVES ON JAMAICA

Name	Type	Location
Croydon Waterfalls	Waterfall	Central Jamaica
Dunn's River Falls	Waterfall	1.9 mi. West of Central downtown Ocho Rios
Green Grotto Caves	Cave	1.8 mi. North of Central Dumbarton
Joseph's Cave	Cave	1.8 mi. South West of Central Negril
Mahoe Falls	Waterfall	1.2 mi. South of Central downtown Ocho Rios
Mayfield Falls	Waterfall	3.3 mi. South-Southeast of Central Cascade
Milford Falls	Waterfall	1.8 mi. West of Central Ocho Rios
Reach Falls	Waterfall	1.8 mi. West of Central Williams Field
Shaw Park Garden Falls	Waterfall	1.8 mi. West of Central Ocho Rios
Somerset Falls	Waterfall	2.4 mi. Northwest of Central Hope Bay
Tacky Falls	Waterfall	3.1 mi. West of Central Hope Bay
Two Sister Cave	Cave	6.7 mi. South of Central Portmore
YS Falls	Waterfall	1.1 mi. Southeast of Central Redgate

Parks and Botanical Gardens

Travelers can experience one of the many parks, or 11 botanical gardens on Jamaica.

Dunn's River Park is found within the vicinity of Ocho Rios, Jamaica. This park features Dunn's River Falls, a recreational center and lush tropical vegetation surrounding a 600 foot waterfall that attracts thousands of people each year.

A second popular attraction in this category is Barney's Hummingbird Garden. Explore a beautifully flourishing and well-maintained tropical garden that promotes all that is naturally beautiful about Jamaica, all the while interacting with friendly and busy hummingbirds.

Jamaica Travel Guide, Caribbean

The parks and gardens worth considering can be seen right below.

PARKS AND GARDENS ON JAMAICA		
Name	Type	Location
Neville Antonio Park	Park	0.1 mi. South of Central Port Antonio
Abeokuta Paradise Nature Park	Park	1.9 mi. North of Central Cave
Addison Park	Park	0.5 mi. East of Central Browns Town
Apple Valley Park	Park	5.9 mi. North of Central E Lacovia
Barney's Hummingbird Garden	Botanical Garden	0.5 mi. Northwest of Central Negril
Blue Hole Mineral Spring	Park	0.8 mi. East of Central Revival
Cave Hill Estate Community Park	Park	5.6 mi. South-Southwest of Central Portmore
College Green Communtiy Park	Park	2.8 mi. East of Central Kingston
Cranbrook Flower Forest and River Head Adventure Trail	Botanical Garden	3.4 mi. North of Central Bamboo
Discovery Falls	Park	3.1 mi. Southeast of Central Negril Beach Hotel Zone
Dovecot Memorial Park	Park	4.4 mi. West of Central Spanish Town
Dunn's River Park	Park	1.9 mi. West of Central downtown Ocho Rios
Dunrobin Acres Private Park	Park	1.3 mi. North-Northwest of Central Kingston
Emancipation Park	Park	0.8 mi. Southeast of Central Kingston
Emmett Park	Park	0.7 mi. Northeast of Central downtown Kingston
Fonthill Beach Park	Park	6.0 mi. West of Central Black River
Founders Park	Park	3.4 mi. East of Central Kingston
Hope Gardens	Botanical Garden	3.3 mi. East of Central Kingston
Hope Pastures Park	Park	3.0 mi. East-Northeast of Central Kingston
Long Bay Beach Park	Park	0.8 mi. North of Central Negril Beach Hotel Zone

Caleb Gray

Mahoe Gardens	Botanical Garden	8.8 mi. Southeast of Central Lionel Town
Mandela Park	Park	0.1 mi. North-Northeast of Central Kingston
Mandeville Park	Park	Mandeville, Central Jamaica
Meadowrest Memorial Gardens	Botanical Garden	4.3 mi. West-Northwest of Central Spanish Town
National Heroes Park	Park	2.0 mi. South of Central Kingston
Oaklawn Memorial Gardens	Botanical Garden	Mandeville, Central Jamaica
Parade Square	Park	0.3 mi. Northwest of Central Spanish Town
Rose Duckan Park	Park	Linstead, Central Jamaica
Sabina Park	Park	0.8 mi. Northeast of Central downtown Kingston
Saint William Grant Park	Park	Downtown Kingston
Sam Sharpe Square	Park	Downtown Montego Bay
Shaw Park Botanical Gardens & Water Falls	Botanical Garden	0.7 mi. South West of Central downtown Ocho Rios
Sonneville Gardens	Botanical Garden	Portmore
Struan Castle Garden	Botanical Garden	4.4 mi. North of Central Kingston
Sunset Burial Park	Park	5.7 mi. East of Central downtown Kingston
Turtle River Falls and Gardens	Botanical Garden	1.9 mi. West-Southwest of Central Ocho Rios
Vin Lawrence Park	Park	1.4 mi. Northwest of Central downtown Kingston
Water Square	Park	2.7 mi. West of Central White Bay
Watson Taylor Park	Park	2.0 mi. East of Central Esher
West Palm Memorial Gardens	Botanical Garden	Westmoreland Parish
Whoopie's Hammock Park	Park	2.0 mi. South-Southwest of Central Negril

Zoos and Aquariums

If the concept of spending some time at the zoo tickles your fancy, you should visit Dolphin Cove Ocho Rios. For many, swimming with Dolphins is a life long dream. At Dolphin Cove Ocho Rios, that dream can become a reality.

Another similar attraction is Rockland Bird Feeding Station. The Rocklands Bird Sanctuary is the perfect place for bird-watchers, children, and anyone interested in something different. The sanctuary is home to various birds including hummingbirds, which you can feed by hand.

Be sure to look through this table to learn more.

ZOOS ON JAMAICA		
Name	Type	Location
Dolphin Cove Ocho Rios	Zoo	1.7 mi. West-Northwest of Central downtown Ocho Rios
Rockland Bird Feeding Station	Zoo	3.9 mi. South-Southwest of Central Montego Bay

Farms and Planations

If the concept of experiencing life on a tropical plantation sounds intriguing, you really should consider visiting Croydon in the Mountains. Tour guides explain about the cultivation of local produce as they take guests around the property, and even go so far as to offer samples of pineapple, citrus, and sugarcane.

Another local site to visit is Rhodes Hall Plantation. A horseback tour around Rhodes Hall Plantation takes you to the interior of the property where there are plants indigenous to the island, a fish pond, a mangrove and crocodile reserve, and ends up on the beach.

The chart directly below provides you with more details on the farms and plantations on the island.

FARMS AND PLANTATIONS ON JAMAICA

Name	Type	Location
Croydon in the Mountains	Plantation	2.9 mi. South-Southeast of Central Cambridge
Rhodes Hall Plantation	Plantation	1.1 mi. North of Central Orange Bay
Terravale Estate	Farm	1.7 mi. Northwest of Central Bethel Town

Land Formations

Another fun idea is to visit some of the more popular area land formations. Other options like these on Jamaica are displayed in the following table.

LAND FORMATIONS ON JAMAICA

Name	Type	Location
Black River Spa	Hot Spring	Black River, Western part of Jamaica
Bogue Lagoon	Lagoon	2.5 mi. South West of Central Montego Bay
Central Range	Mountain	The Blue Mountains, Central Jamaica
Discovery Bay	Bay	3.1 mi. Northwest of Central Dumbarton
Grotto Lake	Lake	1.8 mi. North of Central Dumbarton
Martha Brae River	River	1.7 mi. West of Central White Bay
Ocho Rios Bay	Bay	Downtown Ocho Rios
Oracabessa Harbor	Bay	1.4 mi. East-Northeast of Central Boscobel
Port Esquivel	Harbour	2.4 mi. West-Southwest of Central Moores Pen
Port Henderson	Harbour	2.4 mi. South of Central Portmore
Port Kaiser	Harbour	2.9 mi. South of Central Junction
Port Royal Mountains	Mountain	3.7 mi. North of Central Grant's Pen
Rio Bueno Bay	Bay	1.2 mi. East of Central Rio Bueno
Rio Grande	River	0.9 mi. East of Central St. Margarets Bay
Rio Nuevo	River	1.2 mi. West of Central Nuevo Rio
San San Bay	Bay	1.9 mi. East of Central Turtle Harbour

St. Ann's Bay	Bay	6.6 mi. West-Northwest of Central downtown Ocho Rios
Trelawney Luminous Lagoon	Lagoon	1.1 mi. West of Central White Bay
White River Valley	River	3.7 mi. South-Southeast of Central Ocho Rios
Yallahs Pond	Pond	1.5 mi. West of Central Pomfret

The Blue Mountains

Behind the city of Kingston are the Blue Mountains, aptly named for their appearance. The Blue Mountains are home to some of the world's rarest flora and fauna, as well as some of the best biking, hiking and eco-tourismon the island.

The Blue Mountains themselves actually consist of two ranges, the Central Range and the Port Royal Mountains. One thing that they both share, however, is a stunning variety of rare and unusual nature. The first is home to both the highest point in Jamaica at 7,402 feet, and also to the world's second-largest butterfly, the pterourus homerus, formerly known as the papilio homerus (commonly called the great Jamaican swallowtail). Additionally, Jamaica is home to an unusual tree called chusquea abietifolia which blooms once every 33 years. The next scheduled date for bloom is 2017.

One of the most exciting things to do in Jamaica is cycle down and see the scenic nature surrounding the mountains. Cycle tours start at an elevation of 5,060 feet and head downward, stopping along the way to see coffee plantations and rain forest sights. Local tour guides proudly share information on local wildlife and history. Tours include lunch, snacks and bike rental and generally cost about $89(USD) per person. Additionally, the Blue Mountains offer secure and enjoyable camping, which may be a fantastic way to enjoy your visit to the mountains.

A vacation to Jamaica spent indoors is a vacation wasted. Whether on land or in water, the natural beauty that Jamaica has to offer is astounding. Get out doors, breath in the fresh air, and let the surrounding beauty inspire you.

Jamaica Accommodations

The accommodations in Jamaica offer something for every traveler

Like any major tourist destination, Jamaica's accommodations run the gamut from pricey, high-class resorts to bare-bones guest houses and hotels. However, Jamaica sets itself apart by being known for having the most hotel options in the Caribbean, so you can make your accommodation choice based on a large number of factors including price, location and amenities.

There are many ways to narrow down a hotel search. For some vacationers, learning about the different types of accommodations available is the best way to start their search. Others, however, may want to jump right in.

Location
Negril
Despite being more rural than some of the other locations on the island, Negril is perhaps the most popular location for guests to choose to stay. This is due to the fact that the famed Seven Mile Beach is located in Negril, the multitudes of dining options, the exciting nightlife, and the easy access to well-known natural attractions like the Negril Watershed Protection Area. Accommodations in Negril run the gamut, with everything from small hotels to sprawling all-inclusive resorts, and a number of villas and rental properties to choose from as well.

Montego Bay

Montego Bay is a popular destination due to the fact that the airport is located nearby, and the city-like atmosphere. Vacationers who enjoy having numerous shopping, dining, and nightlife options will find it all in Montego Bay, as well as some like the Martha Brae River. Lodgings around Montego Bay are fewer than Negril, but still plentiful, and are mainly hotels.

Ocho Rios

Ocho Rios has a lot of diversity, if you are one who wants to have plenty of options, or if you are traveling with a group who has a lot of different opinions about what is important to see and do in Jamaica. Ocho Rios is home to beautiful beaches, , and natural must-sees like Dunn's River Park. Most of the accommodations here are hotels and resorts.

Hotels

Jamaica offers accommodation possibilities that will suit almost every kind of visitor. Choose from budget hotels, glitzy resorts, and much more in between. Vacationers hoping to enjoy an entertaining bar scene will find just that at plenty hotels around Jamaica. Click on the links to read additional information.

A great destination for active recreation on-site is Jamaica Pegasus. Located in downtown Kingston, the elite 17-story Jamaica Pegasus is one of the island's most popular hotels. Guests at the Pegasus find themselves in the heart of the business and financial district and within walking distance of everything from tourist sites to shopping. Guests will be able to find them at 81 Knutsford Boulevard.

A destination positioned on the water's edge that travelers often enjoy is Riu Tropical Bay. With more than 400 elegant guestrooms, guests at the Hotel Riu Tropical Bay are sure to find the room that is perfect for them. Suites are also available. If you have questions and want to call ahead, you can do so at (876) 957-5900.

Vacationers who are in search of good on-site dining possibilities should look into Half Moon Club. Set amidst lush tropical gardens on Jamaica's northern coast, the Half Moon resort offers a dizzying array of services and facilities, like a world-class golf course, numerous swimming pools of all shapes and sizes, a dolphin lagoon, more than a dozen tennis and squash courts, an equestrian center, a fully-equipped fitness center, gourmet dining, a shopping village and even its own 24-hour medical center. As one of the most popular resorts on the property, it is no surprise that it was ranked as one of the top properties in the Caribbean by Conde Nast Traveler in 2013. If you are looking for something specific and want to call before making reservations, you can do so at (876) 953-2211.

These are only some of what's available. Make your way to Hotels page regarding to more available hotels if you want to find out better information.

Condos and Villa Complexes

Guests will also find non-hotel booking options on the island, including tons of condos and a large variety of villa complexes. Avid beach-goers can usually expect to enjoy easy access to the beach, as a lot of the villas and other accommodations are located on the water.

Tennis enthusiasts often enjoy staying at Round Hill Hotel & Villas, as they offer some nice tennis facilities. Round Hill Hotel and Villas is known for its allure to celebrities and royalty, a fact that has helped it gain its prestige and well-regarded reputation. This upscale luxury hotel ensures that its guests have an unforgettable stay. To talk to them, call (876) 956-7050.

One property located on the waterfront that travelers often enjoy is Tryall Club. Everything you could want in a Jamaican vacation is available to you at Tryall Club, from spacious and private living quarters offering all the comforts of home, to luxurious amenities like spa services, golf, and gourmet meals. Set on 2,200 acres of tropical paradise, Tryall Club is the type of place you dream about. If you want to call before booking a room, you can do so at (800) 238-5290.

Those who prefer staying at a top-notch accommodation, The Cliff Hotel would be a nice place to begin looking. The Cliff Hotel boasts 33 suites and villas, including two one bedroom villas and a four bedroom and five bedroom villa. A;; accommodations come with views of the Caribbean Sea and beautiful sunsets. You will be able to find them on West End Road.

These examples are only some of what's available. To reach our page about more villa complexes on the island, read from Villa Complexes page in this book.

Camping and Eco-Tourism

Travelers who love the outdoors should consider the selection of eco-tourist options offered to them on Jamaica.

Tennis enthusiasts and their families will enjoy staying at Sea Garden Beach Resort, as they have some good tennis facilities. Holistic spa treatments, personalized fitness programs and meal plans, and fun activities abound at the Sea Garden Beach Resort. The first all-inclusive resort on the island to focus on health and wellness, it allows guests to discover the best of themselves in the best of locations. They can be found at 8 Kent Avenue.

One destination positioned on the coast worth mentioning is Negril Treehouse Resort. Negril Treehouse Resort is a small hide-away in the popular tourist destination of Negril. The Tree House is a highly regarded and popular resort in Jamaica because of its exceptional service, comfortable facilities and fantastic location. You can contact them at (876) 957-4287.

Nature enthusiasts can find a selection of different eco-lodges on the island, including Mocking Bird Hill. The 10 rooms at the Hotel Mocking Bird Hill combine elegance and comfort, at an affordable price. All rooms are decorated with locally handmade furniture comprised of sustainable woods, and the fabrics, art, and shuttered windows give the rooms a very tropical feel. For customers who want to call before you go, you can do so at (876) 993-7267.

Luckily, there are many other choices too. You can find out more about eco-accommodations available by readong on Eco Tourism page.

Individual Villas
Certain people would rather have the privacy offered by one of the many individual rental properties. Go to Vila Rentals page to view our extended discussion of rental properties on Jamaica.

All-Inclusive Accommodations
Some travelers seek the convenience of paying for everything on a single bill. There are several reasons why this pricing method is popular. Among other reasons, they let you indulge yourself without having to think about your budget.

For guests searching to stay somewhere with a good bar and club scene, Grand Bahia Principe Jamaica is one spot you may want to consider. Situated on Jamaica's north shore, the eco-friendly Grand Bahia Principe Jamaica is an idyllic retreat for all those seeking a break from the stresses and strains of daily life. If you would like to call before booking a room, do so at (876) 973-7752.

One property positioned on the water's edge that merits your consideration is Riu Ocho Rios. The Hotel Riu Ocho Rios Hotel has 856 rooms and suites. Double Rooms come with a balcony or terrace, and private bathroom. If you'd like to call before booking a room, you can do so at (876) 972-2200.

All Inclusive

All-inclusive resorts in Jamaica offer worry-free vacations for travelers
Jamaica is the birthplace of the all-inclusive resort, a one-stop vacation spot travelers either love or hate.

All-inclusive resorts are extremely popular among Americans, and are appropriately equipped to satisfy American appetites and expectations for safety and consistency. No matter which side of the all-inclusive debate you are on, you will find the most options among the bevy of big-name resorts with meal, lodging and activity packages.

Some visitors love the comfort of an all-inclusive price. There are many reasons for their appeal. For example, they can be the easiest way to know the full cost of your vacation in advance. Click on each to see and compare dining options, amenities, and activities.

Tennis enthusiasts will enjoy staying at Holiday Inn Resort in Rose Hall, as they have some good tennis facilities. The Holiday Inn SunSpree Montego Bay has more than 500 charming rooms replete with colorful tropical decor. Each of the 3 room types, standard, superior and deluxe, has a private balcony providing gorgeous views of the surrounding natural environment. Guests will find them on Highway A1.

One destination located on the coast that merits consideration is Grand Palladium Jamaica Resort and Spa. There are 540 modern rooms that have been built to blend in with the tropical setting. Each room is fully equipped, luxurious, and large, giving you all the space you need to spread out and enjoy your stay. For customers who want to call before booking a room, do so at (876) 619-0000.

If you are trying to stay at a couples-only destination with that special someone, you may want to think about Couples Swept Away. The guestrooms at Couples Swept Away are all about privacy and romance. All rooms feature a private balcony or terrace with lovely views of either the sea or lush tropical gardens. If you have questions and want to call before you go, do so at (876) 957-4061.

Many of the all-inclusive properties on the island are summarized in the following table.

ALL-INCLUSIVE ACCOMMODATIONS ON JAMAICA				
Name	Type	Phone Number	Star	Location

Caleb Gray

			Rating	
Azul Sensatori Jamaica	Resort	(866) 527-4762		4.1 mi. North of Central Negril
Beaches Boscobel Resort & Golf Club	Resort	(876) 975-7330		0.8 mi. West of Central Boscobel
Beaches Negril Resort and Spa	Resort	(876) 957-9270		0.2 mi. South of Central Negril Beach Hotel Zone
Beaches Sandy Bay	Resort	(876) 957-5100		1.0 mi. North of Central Negril Beach Hotel Zone
Bluefields Bay Villas	Villa complex	(877) 955-8993		2.0 mi. North of Central Belmont
Chateau Margarita	Hotel	(876) 609-6367		1.1 mi. Southeast of Central Great River Bay
Club Ambiance	Resort	876-973-4705/6 or 6167 or 4605		0.4 mi. West of Central Runaway Bay
Coral Seas Garden Resort	Resort	(876) 957-4388		0.8 mi. North of Central Negril
Couples Negril	Resort	(876) 957-5960		1.8 mi. North of Central Negril Beach Hotel Zone
Couples Sans Souci	Resort	(888) 403-2822		1.1 mi. East-Northeast of Central Ocho Rios
Couples Swept Away	Resort	(876) 957-4061		0.5 mi. South of Central Negril Beach Hotel Zone
Cove Villas	Villa complex	(876) 972-1639		5.7 mi. West of Central Ocho Rios
Franklyn D. Resort	Resort	(876) 973-4592		2.2 mi. North of Central Daniel Town
Fun Holiday Beach Resort All Inclusive	Resort	(876) 957-9688		1.5 mi. South of Central Negril Beach Hotel Zone
Grand Bahia Principe Jamaica	Resort	(876) 973-7752		0.9 mi. West of Central Runaway Bay
Grand Palladium Jamaica Resort and Spa	Hotel	(876) 619-0000		1.0 mi. North of Central Elgin Town
Grand Palladium Lady Hamilton Resort & Spa	Resort	(876) 620-0000		1.1 mi. North of Central Elgin Town
Grand Pineapple Beach Resort Negril All	Resort	(876) 957-4408		1.7 mi. South of Central Negril Beach Hotel Zone

Jamaica Travel Guide, Caribbean

Inclusive				
Hedonism II	Resort	(876) 957-5200		1.5 mi. North of Central Negril Beach Hotel Zone
Hilton Rose Hall Resort & Spa	Resort	--		1.6 mi. East of Central Rose Hall
Holiday Inn Resort in Rose Hall	Resort	(876) 953-2485		1.4 mi. West of Central Rose Hall
Hotel Gloriana	Hotel	(876) 979-0669		0.9 mi. North-Northwest of Central Montego Bay
Hotel Riu Montego Bay	Resort	(876) 940-8010		3.8 mi. Northeast of Central Montego Bay
Hyatt Zilara	Resort	(876) 953-2800		0.3 mi. Northeast of Central Rose Hall
Iberostar Grand Hotel Rose Hall	Resort	--		1.8 mi. Northeast of Central Spot Valley
Iberostar Rose Hall Beach	Resort	(888) 923-2722		2.0 mi. North-Northwest of Central Spot Valley
Iberostar Rose Hall Suites	Resort	(876) 680-0000		1.8 mi. Northeast of Central Spot Valley
Jackie's On The Reef	Resort	(876) 957-4997		1.1 mi. West of Central Negril
Jewel Dunn's River Beach Resort & Spa	Resort	--		5.5 mi. West of Central Ocho Rios
Jewel Paradise Cove Beach Resort by Curio	Resort	(876) 973-4520		1.4 mi. East-Northeast of Central Runaway Bay
Jewel Runaway Bay Resort	Resort	(800) 931-0907		0.5 mi. East of Central Runaway Bay
Legends Beach Resort	Resort	(876) 957-4395		1.9 mi. South of Central Negril Beach Hotel Zone
Lost Beach Resort	Villa complex	(734) 930-2225		3.4 mi. West-Southwest of Central Little London
Merril's Beach Resort III	Resort	(876) 957-4751		1.8 mi. South of Central Negril Beach Hotel Zone
Moon Palace Jamaica Grande	Resort	--		Downtown Ocho Rios
Negril Inn	Resort	(876) 957-4209		1.8 mi. South of Central Negril Beach Hotel Zone

Prospect Villas	Villa complex	(876) 994-1373		1.3 mi. South West of Central Ocho Rios
Rhodes Resort	Resort	(876) 957-6422		1.1 mi. North of Central Orange Bay
Rio Vista Resort Villas	Villa complex	(876) 993-5444		0.4 mi. South-Southeast of Central Port Antonio
Riu Negril Club All Inclusive	Resort	(876) 957-5700		1.8 mi. North of Central Negril Beach Hotel Zone
Riu Ocho Rios	Resort	(876) 972-2200		5.6 mi. West of Central Ocho Rios
Royal Decameron Club Caribbean	Resort	(876) 973-4702		0.5 mi. North of Central Salen
Royal Plantation	Resort	(876) 974-5601		0.2 mi. Northeast of Central Ocho Rios
Royalton White Sands	Resort	(800) 780-5733		1.9 mi. North of Central Daniel Town
Samsara Hotel	Resort	(876) 957-4395		1.3 mi. West of Central Negril
SandCastles Resort	Hotel	(876) 974-2255		Downtown Ocho Rios
Sandals Carlyle	Resort	(876) 952-4140		1.0 mi. North-Northwest of Central Montego Bay
Sandals Montego Bay	Resort	(876) 952-5510		2.3 mi. North-Northeast of Central Montego Bay
Sandals Negril	Resort	(876) 957-5216		1.3 mi. North of Central Negril Beach Hotel Zone
Sandals Ochi	Resort	(876) 974-5691		0.1 mi. North-Northwest of Central Ocho Rios
Sandals Royal Caribbean	Resort	(876) 953-2231		3.8 mi. Northeast of Central Montego Bay
Sandals Royal Plantation	Resort	(876) 974-5601		0.2 mi. Northeast of Central Ocho Rios
Sandals South Coast	Resort	(876) 640-3000		0.5 mi. West of Central Crab Pond Bay
Sea Garden Beach Resort	Eco resort	(876) 979-0943		2.1 mi. North-Northeast of Central Montego Bay
Sea Palms	Villa complex	(876) 975-4400		2.7 mi. East-Northeast of Central Ocho Rios

Secrets St James Montego Bay	Resort	(809) 468-2151		1.9 mi. South West of Central Montego Bay
Secrets Wild Orchid Montego Bay All Inclusive	Resort	(809) 468-2151		1.9 mi. South West of Central Montego Bay
Shaw Park Beach Hotel All Inclusive	Hotel	(876) 974-2552		0.7 mi. East-Northeast of Central Ocho Rios
Sunset Beach Resort & Spa	Resort	(888) 774-0040		1.6 mi. West-Southwest of Central downtown Montego Bay
Sunset at the Palms Negril	Resort	(876) 957-5350		2.2 mi. North of Central Negril Beach Hotel Zone
The Cliff Hotel	Villa complex	(800) 213-0583		2.1 mi. South of Central Negril
The Oasis Resort	Hotel	(876) 957-4153		1.3 mi. South West of Central Negril
The Spa Retreat	Cottages	(855) 843-7725		1.0 mi. West-Northwest of Central Negril
Villa Sonaté	Hotel	(876) 973-5944		0.8 mi. Southeast of Central Runaway Bay
Villas Sur Mer	Villa complex	(876) 382-3717		1.7 mi. South West of Central Negril
Whistling Bird Resort	Cottages	(876) 957-4403		1.5 mi. South of Central Negril Beach Hotel Zone

Although the term "all-inclusive" may suggest that you get everything you need in one package, some things may not be covered, depending on where you stay. Be sure to check to see what each place includes.

The Benifits of a Resort

People like all-inclusive resorts for several reasons, but the most common is the billing procedure. Guests receive one simple bill up-front for nearly everything they could want to eat, drink or do during their stay. Most all-inclusives in Jamaica are priced with several restaurant options, top-shelf liquors, and sports already included. Although you may have to sign a check once or twice, say, after a massage or a dinner at an on-site upscale restaurant, in general you can spend your vacation not worrying about how much you're paying for everything. Another perk is being able to leave important documents, such as your bank and credit cards and IDs, hidden in the safety deposit box or safe in your room.

For some, this freedom from budgetary concerns helps coax relaxation. After all, tropical vacationers are often interested in leaving their cares and worries back home, and budgeting for a trip can be stressful. Another relaxing thought is that all-inclusives employ security guards to keep the resort safe and worry-free.

Many resorts also offer other extras to keep their visitors happy. All-inclusives in Jamaica generally provide airport transfers as part of the package, which can save some travelers a hefty sum just in bus or cabfare. They also offer plenty of pre-planned activites and on-site nightlife. So, as a rule, all-inclusives can not only be safe but also more affordable than staying at "just" a hotel.

The Negatives of a Resort

Travelers who savor independence more than airtight security and group activities may feel that all-inclusive resorts take some of the fun and flavor out of international travel. Visitors do not generally feel encouraged to leave the grounds and explore Jamaica or spend their travel budget on local foods, activities and merchandise when staying at an all-inclusive resort.

All-inclusives are notorious for not offering great examples of local Jamaican culture to their guests. Plain and simple, guests will need to venture out on their own to taste local flavor and experience what truly makes Jamaica unique, its people. This kind of exploring is especially appreciated by local restaurateurs, who often feel that all-inclusives inhibit their business. Many intrepid travelers believe that elaborate resort security makes too much of the dangers outside the complexes.

Several Jamaican all-inclusives favor couples over singles and adults over children, making family travel to all-inclusive resorts on the island less than ideal. Though family-oriented all-inclusives are gaining in popularity, they still haven't taken over the top spot from adults-only clubs. Research a few of the popular chain resorts, and you'll find plenty of family-friendly programming to choose from.

Visitors traveling to all-inclusive resorts in Jamaica will need to book their trips ahead of time, especially in the winter high season. Many popular resorts book up to a year in advance for popular holidays such as Christmas and New Years.

Eco Tourism

Camping and eco-tourism are one way to explore Jamaica's famous mountains

Visitors in search of nature's splendors and the great outdoors have found exploring and camping in Jamaica to be an incredible experience.

The Blue Mountains are one of the most popular regions for campers and outdoor enthusiasts, not only because of their famous coffee, but because of the breathtaking vistas. Due to the popularity of camping in Jamaica, the Jamaica Alternative Tourism, Camping and Hiking Association, more commonly called JATCHA, was developed to help travelers with an interest in this type of recreation.

Blue Mountains Camping

Campgrounds are found in areas supervised by the Jamaican Forestry Department. Cabins and dormitories account for most of the accommodations in the Blue Mountains, but few supplies are available at forest camps. You will need to bring your own linens, blankets, and kitchen supplies.

Travelers cannot simply arrive at a campsite and pay to use it, you must have a permit. JATCHA can make reservations and leave permits waiting for you at the sites. Otherwise they must be paid for and picked up in advance at the Kingston office of the Jamaican Forestry Department.

Some of the most popular sites in the Blue Mountains include the following:

Campsite	Description
Hollywell National Recreation Park (also: Holywell National Recreation Area)	- Tent Camping Available - Cabins available with fireplace, small kitchen and full bathroon. - Four hiking trails - Covered gazebos for picnics.
Clydesdale	- Former coffee plantation and pine nursery. - 3,700 feet in the mountains. - Bunk bed dormitory that can sleep 30+ with flush toilets, showers and a fire cooking pit.
Cinchona Botanical Gardens	- One hour walk from Clydesdale. - Tent camping available.
Whitfield Hall Hostel	- Privately owned coffee farm. - Provides linens. - May permit tent camping.
Portland Gap Forestry Hut	- 5,200 feet in the mountains. - One hour or more past Whitfield Hall Hostel. - Sleeping is on the floor. - Has running water, outhouse, and space for 30 tents.
Blue Mountain Peak	- Forest hut; tent camping permitted. - Often used by party groups from Kingston on weekends. - Water may not be readily available. - May be very cold between December and February.

Camping in Other Areas

Camping is available in other areas of Jamaica. It is most often accessed through a hotel or resort that allows on-site camping. The best choice for campers outside the Blue Mountains, including the nearby cities Kingston and Port Antonio, is Negril. Beachfront and even front-lawn camping may be allowed at hotels in this area for as low as $5(USD) per night, though the average is closer to $10(USD) per tent. Generally shower, toilet and laundry facilities are available at these campsites.

Camping and Eco-Tourism On Jamaica

Nature enthusiasts and their families might want to consider the opportunities for eco-tourism offered. Besides the eco-lodges that are available, some unique eco-resorts are an alternative possibility. Click on the link to each accommodation to read additional details.

Those wanting to stay in Jamaica will be interested in choices like Mocking Bird Hill. Situated amidst lush tropical gardens in the verdant hills in the outskirts of Port Antonio, the eco-friendly Hotel Mocking Bird Hill is a great place to get away from it all. Guests can chill-out in their cozy rooms while taking in lovely vistas, go for a walk through the 6.5 acres of botanically diverse gardens, enjoy complimentary tea in the afternoon on the hotel terrace, or venture outside the hotel grounds for a number of activity options. If you'd like to call before making reservations, do so at (876) 993-7267.

Zimbali Mountain Retreats is a nice property in Jamaica. Set on seven and a half acres of organic, rolling, lush farm land in the hills just 25 minutes outside of Negril, Zimbali Mountain Retreat is a real farming community and guests really get to interact with nature and the locals as they discover the real side of Jamaica. There are over 800 fruit trees of many varieties and they grow a lot of their own food on site. If you're looking to call before you go, do so at (876) 252-3232.

Country Country Beach Cottages is another good choice to consider. Experience old Jamaican country charm alongside modern conveniences at Country Country Beach Cottages. Located on famous seven-mile beach in Negril, these individual cottages afford guests both seclusion and the sea in their very own tropical paradise. If you are looking for something specific and want to call ahead, you can do so at (876) 957-4273.

The chart below enables you to get some details regarding the eco-tourism accommodations you can choose from.

ECO-ACCOMMODATIONS ON JAMAICA				
Name	Type	Phone	Star	Location

Caleb Gray

		Number	Rating	
Bay View Eco Resort and Spa	Eco resort	(876) 993-3118		1.9 mi. East of Central Port Antonio
Bourbon Beach Hotel	Eco resort	(876) 374-4982		2.0 mi. South of Central Negril Beach Hotel Zone
Camp Cabarita Eco Lodge	Lodge	(876) 520-7825		6.6 mi. Northeast of Central Georges Plain
Chippewa Village Hotel	Lodge	(876) 957-4676		1.2 mi. South of Central Negril Beach Hotel Zone
Country Country Beach Cottages	Eco resort	(876) 957-4273		0.8 mi. South of Central Negril Beach Hotel Zone
Crystal Ripple Beach Lodge	Lodge	(876) 974-6132		0.8 mi. East-Northeast of Central Ocho Rios
Golden Shore Resort	Eco resort	(876) 982-9657		1.1 mi. Southeast of Central Morant Bay
Great Huts	Lodge	(876) 353-3388		3.0 mi. Southeast of Central Fairy Hill
Mocking Bird Hill	Lodge	(876) 993-7267		0.7 mi. Southeast of Central Turtle Harbour
Negril Treehouse Resort	Eco resort	(876) 957-4287		0.8 mi. South of Central Negril Beach Hotel Zone
Prince Valley Guest House	Lodge	(876) 892-2365		6.8 mi. Northeast of Central Kingston
Satori Resort and Spa	Eco resort	(876) 952-6133		2.9 mi. South West of Central Montego Bay
Sea Garden Beach Resort	Eco resort	(876) 979-0943		2.1 mi. North-Northeast of Central Montego Bay
Tingalaya's Retreat	Eco resort	(202) 741-9720		2.1 mi. South-Southwest of Central Negril
Whispering Bamboo Cove Resort	Eco resort	(876) 982-1788		1.7 mi. West of Central Belvedere
Zimbali Mountain Retreats	Eco resort	(876) 252-3232		3.1 mi. West-Southwest of Central Grange Hill

Hotels

Direct access to detailed information about hotels in Jamaica

Jamaica is known for its great variety of accommodation options, so whether you're looking for upscale digs or a cozy bungalow nestled away from the bustle of popular tourist sites, you can find it in Jamaica. Choose between hot hotels with luxurious amenities, or guesthouses and inns that allow visitors a chance to experience authentic Jamaican culture.

Resorts

Resorts of all kinds are most often found on or near beaches, especially in the popular city of Montego Bay, where beachfront lodging is the specialty. In an upscale hotel or resort you'll generally find plenty of features and security, but you may also have to pay for any extra amenities and services you require. Meals are available at on-site restaurants, but concierge services can also direct you to local favorites. These resorts are very similar to Jamaica's ever-popular all-inclusives because they have everything travelers could want (and more) on site. Resorts, of course, have their own style as much as any other hotel in Jamaica.

Small Hotels

The next step down from the high-priced and amenity-packed resorts are small hotels. These can provide an affordable option for budget-conscious travelers. Most hotels will include hot water and a bar or nearby restaurant, and the majority will include a pool, on-site restaurant, and air conditioning. A rule of thumb when it comes to hotels is that the more money you're willing to spend, the more amenities you'll have.

Guesthouses

To truly experience local culture while in Jamaica, you can choose to stay where Jamaicans themselves stay when they're traveling. Guesthouses throughout Jamaica, like those across the Caribbean, differ tremendously from one another. These are generally the cheapest places for travelers to stay, and may have little in the way of furniture. This is truly an explorer's accommodation, though some measure of security is still provided. Here you will most often find shared bathrooms and fans instead of air conditioning. These accommodations are truly unique. Some resemble motels while other are more like small cottages. The variety means that you may find accommodations to be much nicer than they might seem upon reading a guide. There are plenty of guesthouses throughout Jamaica that are safe even for families and single women.

Hotels On Jamaica

Jamaica offers hotel options that will suit nearly any type of visitor. Pick from budget hotels, luxury resorts, and much more in between. Vacationers wanting to enjoy an entertaining bar scene will encounter precisely that at plenty hotels around Jamaica. Read additional details on each of the properties by using the links.

A great spot with on-site recreation is Holiday Inn Resort in Rose Hall. The Holiday Inn SunSpree Montego Bay has more than 500 charming rooms replete with colorful tropical decor. Each of the 3 room types, standard, superior and deluxe, has a private balcony providing gorgeous views of the surrounding natural environment. They are located on Highway A1.

A place along the waterfront worth considering is Grand Palladium Jamaica Resort and Spa. The Grand Palladium Resort and Spa is a mega-resort on the beach of Jamaica's north coast. This property is fully-equipped with everything you need on your all-inclusive vacation, including a staff ready to handle your every want and desire. If you'd like to call in advance, do so at (876) 619-0000.

Vacationers in search of convenient on-site dining opportunities might want to check out Jamaica Pegasus. Located in downtown Kingston, the elite 17-story Jamaica Pegasus is one of the island's most popular hotels. Guests at the Pegasus find themselves in the heart of the business and financial district and within walking distance of everything from tourist sites to shopping. They're located at 81 Knutsford Boulevard.

Take a minute to read this table for more information.

HOTELS ON JAMAICA					
Name	Type	Phone Number	Star Rating	Location	
Alfred's Seaside Guesthouse	Guest house	(876) 957-4669		1.7 mi. South of Central Negril Beach Hotel Zone	
Alpha & Omega Guesthouse	Guest house	--		0.3 mi. West-Northwest of Central Discovery Bay	
Altamont Court Hotel	Hotel	(876) 620-4530		0.9 mi. Southeast of Central Kingston	
Altamont West Hotel	Hotel	(876) 979-9378		0.6 mi. West of Central Montego Bay	
Ansell's Thatchwalk Cottages	Cottages	(876) 957-3419		0.8 mi. North of Central Negril	
Azul Sensatori Jamaica	Resort	(866) 527-4762		4.1 mi. North of Central Negril	
Banana Shout	Cottages	(876) 957-0384		1.7 mi. South West of Central Negril	
Banana's Garden	Cottages	(876) 957-0909		1.6 mi. South West of Central Negril	
Bar B Barn Hotel	Hotel	(876) 957-9619		1.1 mi. North-Northeast of Central Negril	
Barry's Bold As Love Guest Houses	Guest house	(876) 886-6586		1.0 mi. North-Northeast of Central Negril	
Beach House Villas	Hotel	(876) 957-4731		1.0 mi. North-Northeast of Central Negril	
Beachcomber Club	Hotel	(876) 957-4170		0.9 mi. South of Central Negril Beach Hotel Zone	
Beaches Boscobel Resort & Golf Club	Resort	(876) 975-7330		0.8 mi. West of Central Boscobel	
Beaches Negril Resort and Spa	Resort	(876) 957-9270		0.2 mi. South of Central Negril Beach Hotel Zone	
Beaches Sandy Bay	Resort	(876) 957-5100		1.0 mi. North of Central	

Caleb Gray

				Negril Beach Hotel Zone
Big Apple Hotel	Hotel	(876) 952-7240		0.5 mi. South-Southeast of Central Montego Bay
Blue Cave Castle Hotel	Hotel	(876) 957-4845		1.2 mi. West of Central Negril
Blue Harbour Hotel	Hotel	(876) 952-5445		0.3 mi. West of Central Montego Bay
Bolivar Gallery	B & B	(876) 926-8799		0.4 mi. South of Central Kingston
Brandon Hill Guest House	Hotel	(876) 952-7054		0.9 mi. East-Southeast of Central Montego Bay
Brown's Guest House	Guest house	(876) 982-6205		Central Jamaica
Buccaneer Beach Hotel	Hotel	(876) 952-7658		1.2 mi. North of Central Montego Bay
By the Sea	B & B	(876) 993-5480		1.3 mi. East-Northeast of Central St. Margarets Bay
Caribbean Delight	Hotel	--		1.8 mi. South of Central Negril Beach Hotel Zone
Caribbean Sunset Resort	Resort	(876) 957-4250		1.5 mi. West-Southwest of Central Negril
Caribbean Villa Hotel Restaurant and Bar	Hotel	(876) 938-9547		1.3 mi. South-Southeast of Central Kingston
Cariblue Beach Hotel and Scuba Diving Resort	Hotel	(876) 953-2022		3.7 mi. Northeast of Central Montego Bay
Casa Maria Hotel	Hotel	(876) 725-0157		1.3 mi. North of Central Port Maria
Catcha Falling Star	Cottages	(876) 957-0390		The vicinity of Jamaica
Caves	Hotel	(876) 957-0270		1.8 mi. South West of Central Negril
Charela Inn	Resort	(876) 957-4277		1.2 mi. South of Central Negril Beach Hotel Zone
Chateau Margarita	Hotel	(876) 609-6367		1.1 mi. Southeast of Central Great River Bay
Chelsea Hotel	Motel	(876) 828-1127		0.5 mi. Southeast of Central Kingston

Jamaica Travel Guide, Caribbean

Christar Villas	Hotel	(876) 978-3733		1.8 mi. East-Northeast of Central Kingston
Citronella Cottages	Cottages	(876) 460-8369		1.7 mi. South West of Central Negril
Club Ambiance	Resort	876-973-4705/6 or 6167 or 4605		0.4 mi. West of Central Runaway Bay
Coco La Palm Resort	Resort	(876) 957-4227		1.1 mi. South of Central Negril Beach Hotel Zone
Columbus Inn	Hotel	(876) 972-9322		0.6 mi. North-Northeast of Central Priory
Coral Cliff Hotel	Hotel	--		0.7 mi. West-Northwest of Central Montego Bay
Coral Seas Garden Resort	Resort	(876) 957-4388		0.8 mi. North of Central Negril
Cotton Tree Hotel	Hotel	(876) 957-4450		0.5 mi. North-Northwest of Central Negril
Couples Negril	Resort	(876) 957-5960		1.8 mi. North of Central Negril Beach Hotel Zone
Couples Sans Souci	Resort	(888) 403-2822		1.1 mi. East-Northeast of Central Ocho Rios
Couples Swept Away	Resort	(876) 957-4061		0.5 mi. South of Central Negril Beach Hotel Zone
Couples Tower Isle	Resort	(800) 268-7537		3.0 mi. East of Central Ocho Rios
Courtleigh Hotel and Suites	Hotel	(876) 936-3570		0.8 mi. Southeast of Central Kingston
Courtleigh Hotel and Suites	Hotel	(876) 929-9000		0.8 mi. Southeast of Central Kingston
Courtyard by Marriott	Hotel	(876) 618-9900		0.7 mi. Southeast of Central Kingston
Coyaba Beach Resort & Club	Resort	(876) 953-9150		4.2 mi. Northeast of Central Montego Bay
Crane Ridge Suites	Resort	(876) 974-8050		Downtown Ocho Rios
Demontevin Lodge Hotel	Hotel	(876) 993-2604		0.1 mi. East of Central Port Antonio
Doctor's Cave Beach Hotel	Resort	(876) 952-4355		0.8 mi. Northwest of Central Montego Bay

Donaldson's Inn	Hotel	(876) 957-4377	0.7 mi. South of Central Negril Beach Hotel Zone
Dunn's Villa Resort	Resort	(876) 953-7459	1.3 mi. West of Central Spot Valley
Dynasty Jamaica Hotel	Hotel	(876) 987-1221	0.2 mi. North of Central Enrin
Eddie's Tigress Two	Hotel	(876) 957-4249	0.9 mi. West-Northwest of Central Negril
El Greco Resort	Hotel	(876) 940-6116	0.7 mi. Northwest of Central Montego Bay
Emerald Escape Beach Resort	Resort	(876) 952-6133	2.9 mi. South West of Central Montego Bay
Errol's Guest House	Guest house	(876) 838-2448	0.8 mi. North of Central Negril
Executive Inn	Hotel	(847) 979-0359	0.9 mi. North of Central Montego Bay
Executive Shaw Park Guest House	Hotel	(876) 974-0085	0.8 mi. East-Southeast of Central Ocho Rios
Firefly Beach Cottages	Cottages	(876) 957-4358	1.0 mi. South of Central Negril Beach Hotel Zone
Fisherman's Inn	Hotel	(876) 954-3427	2.1 mi. North-Northwest of Central Daniel Town
Fisherman's Point	Resort	(876) 974-5317	Downtown Ocho Rios
Fleur Flats Resorts	Resort	(876) 962-1053	Mandeville, Central Jamaica
Foote Prints on the Sand Hotel	Resort	(876) 957-4300	0.6 mi. South of Central Negril Beach Hotel Zone
Forres Park	Hotel	(876) 927-8275	1.3 mi. South of Central Kingston
Four Seasons Hotel	Hotel	(876) 929-7655	0.3 mi. Southeast of Central Kingston
Franklyn D. Resort	Resort	(876) 973-4592	2.2 mi. North of Central Daniel Town
Fun Holiday Beach Resort All Inclusive	Resort	(876) 957-9688	1.5 mi. South of Central Negril Beach Hotel Zone
Gardenia Resort	Resort	(876) 957-4394	0.7 mi. South of Central Negril Beach Hotel Zone

Jamaica Travel Guide, Caribbean

Name	Type	Phone	Location
Gatehouse Villas	Guest house	(435) 658-1094	1.3 mi. South of Central Negril Beach Hotel Zone
Geejam	Hotel	(876) 993-7000	3.0 mi. East of Central Port Antonio
Glenrock Hotel	Hotel	(876) 316-0610	Mandeville, Central Jamaica
Golden Sands Beach Cottage	Resort	(876) 965-0167	0.1 mi. South-Southwest of Central Treasure Beach
Golden Seas Beach Resort	Resort	(876) 975-3540	1.0 mi. East of Central Boscobel
Golden Sunset Villas	Guest house	(876) 957-4241	1.7 mi. South of Central Negril Beach Hotel Zone
GoldenEye	Resort	876-6229-007	1.6 mi. East-Northeast of Central Boscobel
Golf View Hotel	Hotel	(876) 962-4477	Mandeville, Central Jamaica
Grand Bahia Principe Jamaica	Resort	(876) 973-7752	0.9 mi. West of Central Runaway Bay
Grand Palladium Jamaica Resort and Spa	Hotel	(876) 619-0000	1.0 mi. North of Central Elgin Town
Grand Palladium Lady Hamilton Resort & Spa	Resort	(876) 620-0000	1.1 mi. North of Central Elgin Town
Grand Pineapple Beach Resort Negril All Inclusive	Resort	(876) 957-4408	1.7 mi. South of Central Negril Beach Hotel Zone
Grand Port Royal Hotel	Hotel	(876) 967-8494	3.7 mi. Southeast of Central Portmore
Grandiosa Hotel	Hotel	(876) 979-3205	0.7 mi. North-Northwest of Central Montego Bay
Greenleaf Cabins	Cottages	(876) 429-6438	1.1 mi. South of Central Negril Beach Hotel Zone
Half Moon Club	Resort	(876) 953-2211	0.8 mi. West-Northwest of Central Rose Hall
Half Moon Royal Villas	Resort	(876) 953-2211	0.3 mi. West-Northwest of Central Rose Hall
Harbour Way	Hotel	(876) 952-4329	Downtown Montego Bay
Harlem Resort	Hotel	(876) 926-7872	1.4 mi. North of Central Portmore
Harmony Hall	Cottages	(876) 974-2870	0.6 mi. West-Northwest of

Name	Type	Phone	Location
			Central Ocho Rios
Heart Beat Resort	Cottages	(876) 957-4329	1.0 mi. West-Northwest of Central Negril
Hedonism II	Resort	(876) 957-5200	1.5 mi. North of Central Negril Beach Hotel Zone
Hibiscus Lodge	Resort	(876) 974-2676	1.1 mi. West of Central Ocho Rios
Hidden Paradise Resort	Hotel	(876) 957-3370	1.1 mi. North-Northeast of Central Negril
Hilton Rose Hall Resort & Spa	Resort	--	1.6 mi. East of Central Rose Hall
Holiday Inn Resort in Rose Hall	Resort	(876) 953-2485	1.4 mi. West of Central Rose Hall
Home Sweet Home Seaside Resort	Resort	(612) 377-6336	1.1 mi. West of Central Negril
Horizon Cottages	Cottages	--	1.3 mi. North-Northeast of Central Belmont
Hotel Casanova	Hotel	(876) 939-6999	1.6 mi. South of Central Portmore
Hotel Commingle	Hotel	(876) 918-1011	0.4 mi. East-Northeast of Central Savanna La Mar
Hotel Gloriana	Hotel	(876) 979-0669	0.9 mi. North-Northwest of Central Montego Bay
Hotel Riu Montego Bay	Resort	(876) 940-8010	3.8 mi. Northeast of Central Montego Bay
Hotel Tim Bamboo	Hotel	(876) 993-2049	0.7 mi. Southeast of Central Port Antonio
Hotel Versalles	Hotel	(876) 986-2775	1.2 mi. Southeast of Central May Pen
Hyatt Zilara	Resort	(876) 953-2800	0.3 mi. Northeast of Central Rose Hall
Iberostar Grand Hotel Rose Hall	Resort	--	1.8 mi. Northeast of Central Spot Valley
Iberostar Rose Hall Beach	Resort	(888) 923-2722	2.0 mi. North-Northwest of Central Spot Valley
Iberostar Rose Hall Suites	Resort	(876) 680-0000	1.8 mi. Northeast of Central Spot Valley

Jamaica Travel Guide, Caribbean

Idle Awhile The Beach	Resort	(877) 243-5352	1.1 mi. South of Central Negril Beach Hotel Zone
Idlers Rest Beach Hotel	Hotel	(876) 965-9000	0.3 mi. East-Southeast of Central Black River
Indies Hotel	Hotel	(876) 926-2952	0.5 mi. East-Southeast of Central Kingston
Invercauld Hotel	Hotel	(867) 965-2750	0.4 mi. South of Central Black River
Ital Rest	Cottages	(876) 421-8909	1.5 mi. Southeast of Central Treasure Beach
Jackie's On The Reef	Resort	(876) 957-4997	1.1 mi. West of Central Negril
Jah B's Cottages	Hotel	(876) 957-4235	1.6 mi. South of Central Negril Beach Hotel Zone
Jake's Resort	Resort	(876) 965-3145	0.3 mi. South of Central Treasure Beach
Jamaica Inn	Hotel	(876) 974-2514	0.4 mi. Northeast of Central Ocho Rios
Jamaica Palace Hotel	Hotel	(876) 993-7720	0.4 mi. East of Central Turtle Harbour
Jamaica Pegasus	Resort	(876) 926-3690	1.2 mi. South West of Central Kingston
Jamaica Tamboo	Resort	(876) 957-4282	1.9 mi. South of Central Negril Beach Hotel Zone
Jewel Dunn's River Beach Resort & Spa	Resort	--	5.5 mi. West of Central Ocho Rios
Jewel Paradise Cove Beach Resort by Curio	Resort	(876) 973-4520	1.4 mi. East-Northeast of Central Runaway Bay
Jewel Runaway Bay Resort	Resort	(800) 931-0907	0.5 mi. East of Central Runaway Bay
Knutsford Court Hotel	Hotel	(876) 929-1000	0.4 mi. Southeast of Central Kingston
Kuyaba	Hotel	(876) 957-4318	2.0 mi. South of Central Negril Beach Hotel Zone
Kyle's Bed & Breakfast	B & B	(876) 964-0762	Spaldings, Central Jamaica
Legends Beach Resort	Resort	(876) 957-4395	1.9 mi. South of Central Negril Beach Hotel Zone

Lighthouse Inn 2	Hotel	(876) 957-4052		1.8 mi. South-Southwest of Central Negril
Little Shaw Park	Guest house	(876) 974-2177		1.5 mi. West of Central Ocho Rios
Lovers Leap Guest House	Guest house	(876) 965-6004		3.2 mi. East of Central Santa Cruz
Mandeview Flats	Hotel	(876) 630-1500		Mandeville, Central Jamaica
Mandeville Hotel	Hotel	(876) 962-9764		Mandeville, Central Jamaica
Mango Ridge Guest Cottages	Cottages	(876) 275-7222		0.4 mi. South of Central Port Antonio
Marine View Hotel	Hotel	(876) 974-5753		1.2 mi. West of Central Ocho Rios
Mariners Negril Beach Club	Resort	(876) 957-4220		0.9 mi. North of Central Negril
Mariposa Hideaway	Hotel	(876) 957-4918		1.4 mi. South of Central Negril Beach Hotel Zone
Match Resort Cottage	Cottages	(876) 993-9629		1.3 mi. South of Central Kingston
Mayfair Hotel	Hotel	(876) 926-1610		1.0 mi. Northeast of Central Kingston
Medallion Hall Hotel	Hotel	(876) 927-5866		1.2 mi. East-Northeast of Central Kingston
Meditation Heights Hotel	Hotel	(876) 975-9180		1.0 mi. Northeast of Central Browns Town
Merril's Beach Resort III	Resort	(876) 957-4751		1.8 mi. South of Central Negril Beach Hotel Zone
Milk River Mineral Bath & Spa	Hotel	(876) 610-7745 ext. 7		1.3 mi. South of Central Rest
Mirabay Resort	Resort	(876) 952-7744		0.5 mi. West-Northwest of Central Montego Bay
Mirage Resort	Resort	(876) 957-0386		1.7 mi. South West of Central Negril
Mom's Place	Cottages	(876) 957-3349		1.0 mi. North of Central Negril
Mona Visitor's Lodge	Hotel	(876) 970-2893		0.8 mi. North-Northwest of Central August Town

Jamaica Travel Guide, Caribbean

Moon Hill	B & B	(876) 294-3615		3.2 mi. Northeast of Central Kingston
Moon Palace Jamacia Grande	Resort	--		Downtown Ocho Rios
Morant Villas Hotel	Hotel	(876) 982-2422		0.7 mi. East of Central Morant Bay
Mountain Edge Guest House	Guest house	(917) 338-4865		6.3 mi. Northeast of Central Kingston
Negril Escape Resort And Spa	Cottages	(876) 851-6506		1.6 mi. South West of Central Negril
Negril Inn	Resort	(876) 957-4209		1.8 mi. South of Central Negril Beach Hotel Zone
Negril Palm Beach Club	Hotel	(876) 957-4218		1.2 mi. South of Central Negril Beach Hotel Zone
Negril Rainbow Arch	Hotel	(876) 957-4745		1.2 mi. South of Central Negril Beach Hotel Zone
New Moon Cottages	Cottages	(876) 957-4305		1.1 mi. West of Central Negril
Nirvana	Cottages	(941) 708-0203		1.3 mi. South of Central Negril Beach Hotel Zone
Ocean View Villa	Guest house	(876) 953-2481		3.5 mi. Northeast of Central Montego Bay
Olympia Crown Hotel	Hotel	(876) 923-5269		0.8 mi. West-Northwest of Central Kingston
Palm Bay Guest House	Guest house	(876) 952-1795		2.7 mi. South of Central Montego Bay
Palm Beach Leisure	Hotel	(876) 957-4218		1.2 mi. South of Central Negril Beach Hotel Zone
Palm Tree Guest House	Hotel	(876) 956-9007		1.4 mi. South West of Central Industry Cove
Paradise Clarridge View	Guest house	(876) 414-0548		3.5 mi. South West of Central Montego Bay
Paradise Inn Resort	Resort	(809) 993-5169		0.5 mi. East-Northeast of Central St. Margarets Bay
Pineapple Court Hotel	Hotel	(876) 974-2727		Downtown Ocho Rios
Piper's Cove Resort	Resort	(876) 973-7156		0.1 mi. East-Northeast of Central Runaway Bay

Name	Type	Phone	Location
Platinum Hotel	Hotel	(876) 386-2165	0.3 mi. East of Central May Pen
Point Village Resort	Resort	(876) 957-4394	1.6 mi. North of Central Negril Beach Hotel Zone
Port Of Call Hotel	Hotel	(876) 965-2360	0.2 mi. North-Northeast of Central Black River
Prestige Hotel	Hotel	(876) 927-7239	1.6 mi. Northeast of Central Kingston
Rafjam's Bed and Breakfast	B & B	(876) 944-8094	6.4 mi. Northeast of Central Kingston
Rayon Hotel	Hotel	(876) 957-9166	1.1 mi. South of Central Negril Beach Hotel Zone
Relax Resort	Hotel	(876) 979-0656	1.2 mi. North-Northeast of Central Montego Bay
Retreat Guesthouse Luxury Suites	Guest house	(876) 954-9858	1.8 mi. North of Central Daniel Town
Rhodes Resort	Resort	(876) 957-6422	1.1 mi. North of Central Orange Bay
Richmond Hill	B & B	(876) 952-3859	0.3 mi. Southeast of Central Montego Bay
Riu Negril Club All Inclusive	Resort	(876) 957-5700	1.8 mi. North of Central Negril Beach Hotel Zone
Riu Ocho Rios	Resort	(876) 972-2200	5.6 mi. West of Central Ocho Rios
Riu Tropical Bay	Resort	(876) 957-5900	2.0 mi. North of Central Negril Beach Hotel Zone
Robin's Bay Village and Beach Resort	Resort	(876) 361-2144	0.7 mi. North of Central Robins Bay
Rock Cliff Hotel	Hotel	(876) 957-4331	1.5 mi. West-Southwest of Central Negril
Rockhouse Hotel	Hotel	(876) 957-4373	1.5 mi. West-Southwest of Central Negril
Rondel Village	Hotel	(876) 957-4413	1.4 mi. South of Central Negril Beach Hotel Zone
Rooms On The Beach	Hotel	(876) 957-3500	1.6 mi. South of Central Negril Beach Hotel Zone
Rooms On The Beach	Hotel	(800) 971-5100	Downtown Ocho Rios

Jamaica Travel Guide, Caribbean

Roosevelt Guest House	Guest house	(876) 978-4803	1.5 mi. East of Central Kingston
Root's Bamboo	Cottages	(876) 957-4479	1.5 mi. South of Central Negril Beach Hotel Zone
Royal Decameron Club Caribbean	Resort	(876) 973-4702	0.5 mi. North of Central Salen
Royal Decameron Montego Beach Hotel	Resort	(876) 952-4340	0.9 mi. Northwest of Central Montego Bay
Royal Plantation	Resort	(876) 974-5601	0.2 mi. Northeast of Central Ocho Rios
Royal Reef Hotel	Hotel	(876) 953-1700	1.3 mi. West of Central Rose Hall
Royalton White Sands	Resort	(800) 780-5733	1.9 mi. North of Central Daniel Town
Runaway Bay H.E.A.R.T. Hotel	Resort	(876) 973-6671 ext. 4	0.8 mi. Southeast of Central Runaway Bay
Runaway Bay Heart Hotel	Hotel	(876) 973-6671	1.2 mi. East of Central Runaway Bay
Samsara Hotel	Resort	(876) 957-4395	1.3 mi. West of Central Negril
San San Tropez	Hotel	(876) 993-7213	0.9 mi. West of Central Port Antonio
SandCastles Resort	Hotel	(876) 974-2255	Downtown Ocho Rios
Sandals Carlyle	Resort	(876) 952-4140	1.0 mi. North-Northwest of Central Montego Bay
Sandals Montego Bay	Resort	(876) 952-5510	2.3 mi. North-Northeast of Central Montego Bay
Sandals Negril	Resort	(876) 957-5216	1.3 mi. North of Central Negril Beach Hotel Zone
Sandals Ochi	Resort	(876) 974-5691	0.1 mi. North-Northwest of Central Ocho Rios
Sandals Royal Caribbean	Resort	(876) 953-2231	3.8 mi. Northeast of Central Montego Bay
Sandals Royal Plantation	Resort	(876) 974-5601	0.2 mi. Northeast of Central Ocho Rios
Sandals South Coast	Resort	(876) 640-3000	0.5 mi. West of Central Crab Pond Bay

Sandy Haven Resort	Resort	(876) 957-3200	1.1 mi. South of Central Negril Beach Hotel Zone
Sea Castles Beach Condos	Resort	(855) 786-6952	1.6 mi. East of Central Rose Hall
Sea Horse Rider Inn	Hotel	(876) 704-6245	1.7 mi. South-Southeast of Central Portmore
Sea Palms	B & B	(888) 790-5264	2.9 mi. East of Central Ocho Rios
Sea Scape Hotel	Hotel	(876) 957-3489	1.8 mi. South of Central Negril Beach Hotel Zone
Sea Splash Resort	Hotel	(876) 957-4041	0.7 mi. South of Central Negril Beach Hotel Zone
Seacrest Beach Hotel	Hotel	(876) 972-8973	0.5 mi. North-Northeast of Central Priory
Seastar Inn	Hotel	(876) 957-0553	1.4 mi. South West of Central Negril
Secrets Cabins	Cottages	(876) 957-4358	1.2 mi. South of Central Negril Beach Hotel Zone
Secrets St James Montego Bay	Resort	(809) 468-2151	1.9 mi. South West of Central Montego Bay
Secrets Wild Orchid Montego Bay All Inclusive	Resort	(809) 468-2151	1.9 mi. South West of Central Montego Bay
Shaw Park Beach Hotel All Inclusive	Hotel	(876) 974-2552	0.7 mi. East-Northeast of Central Ocho Rios
Shields Negril Villas	Hotel	(876) 957-3112	0.9 mi. North of Central Negril
Shirley Retreat Hotel	Hotel	(876) 946-2679	1.1 mi. East-Northeast of Central Kingston
Silver Seas	Hotel	(876) 974-2755	1.1 mi. West of Central Ocho Rios
South Sea View Guest House	Guest house	(876) 963-5172	1.9 mi. South-Southeast of Central Whitehouse
South Shore Guest House	Guest house	(876) 965-2172	1.5 mi. Southeast of Central Black River
Spanish Treasure Hotel	Hotel	(876) 984-2474	0.5 mi. North-Northwest of Central Spanish Town
Springburn House	Guest	(876) 969-7237	2.9 mi. North-Northwest of

Jamaica Travel Guide, Caribbean

		house			Central Kingston
Starlight Chalet & Health Spa		Hotel	(876) 969-3070		9.1 mi. Northeast of Central Kingston
Strawberry Hill		Cottages	(876) 944-8400		6.4 mi. Northeast of Central Kingston
Sumerset Village		Hotel	(876) 957-4409		1.5 mi. West-Southwest of Central Negril
Sunflower Beach Resort		Cottages	(888) 790-5264		0.2 mi. East-Northeast of Central Runaway Bay
Sunquest Cottages		Cottages	(876) 957-4470		2.2 mi. North of Central Negril
Sunrise Club		Cottages	(876) 957-4293		1.1 mi. North-Northeast of Central Negril
Sunset Beach Resort & Spa		Resort	(888) 774-0040		1.6 mi. West-Southwest of Central downtown Montego Bay
Sunset Inn Hotel		Hotel	(876) 929-7283		0.9 mi. Southeast of Central Kingston
Sunset On The Cliffs Resort		Hotel	(876) 957-3147		1.5 mi. West-Southwest of Central Negril
Sunset Resort		Resort	(876) 965-0143		1.1 mi. South-Southwest of Central Plowden
Sunset at the Palms Negril		Resort	(876) 957-5350		2.2 mi. North of Central Negril Beach Hotel Zone
Tamarind Tree Resort Hotel		Resort	(778) 855-1212		1.4 mi. East of Central Runaway Bay
Tensing Pen Hotel		Cottages	(876) 957-0387		1.7 mi. South West of Central Negril
Terra Nova All Suite Hotel		Hotel	(876) 926-2211		0.7 mi. North-Northeast of Central Kingston
The Blue House		B & B	(876) 994-1367		1.3 mi. East of Central Ocho Rios
The Cardiff Hotel and Spa		Resort	(876) 973-6671 ext. 4		0.8 mi. Southeast of Central Runaway Bay
The Oasis Resort		Hotel	(876) 957-4153		1.3 mi. South West of Central Negril
The Palms Resort		Hotel	(876) 957-4375		0.7 mi. South of Central

				Negril Beach Hotel Zone
The Palmyra Resort and Spa	Resort	(876) 632-9000		0.5 mi. East-Northeast of Central Rose Hall
The Spa Retreat	Cottages	(855) 843-7725		1.0 mi. West-Northwest of Central Negril
The Spanish Court Hotel	Hotel	(876) 926-0000		0.9 mi. East of Central Kingston
The Yellow Bird	Hotel	(876) 957-4252		1.9 mi. South of Central Negril Beach Hotel Zone
Tobys Resort	Hotel	(876) 952-4370		0.9 mi. Northwest of Central Montego Bay
Top Beach Cabins	Cottages	(876) 957-3295		0.6 mi. South of Central Negril Beach Hotel Zone
Tranquility Cove	Resort	(876) 999-3147		1.4 mi. West-Northwest of Central downtown Ocho Rios
Travellers Beach Resort	Hotel	(876) 957-3039		0.9 mi. North-Northeast of Central Negril
Treasure Beach Hotel	Resort	(876) 965-0114		0.2 mi. West of Central Treasure Beach
Tropical Court Hotel	Hotel	(876) 979-2075		1.4 mi. North-Northeast of Central Montego Bay
Tropical Gardens	Resort	(305) 468-4637		1.6 mi. South West of Central Negril
Tropical Lagoon	Hotel	(954) 278-7170		1.7 mi. East of Central Drapers
Tropics View Hotel	Hotel	(876) 625-2452		Hatfield, Central Jamaica
Two Seasons Guest House	Guest house	(876) 965-3170		0.6 mi. Northwest of Central Treasure Beach
Verney's Tropical Resort	Hotel	(876) 952-8628		0.7 mi. North of Central Montego Bay
Versalles Hotel	Hotel	(876) 986-2775		1.3 mi. Southeast of Central May Pen
Villa Bella Hotel	Hotel	(876) 964-2243		Sedburgh, Central Jamaica
Villa La Cage	Motel	(876) 957-4114		0.5 mi. South-Southwest of Central Negril

Villa Lilletha	Hotel	(773) 463-6688		1.3 mi. South of Central Kingston
Villa Mora	Cottages	(876) 957-4206		1.6 mi. South of Central Negril Beach Hotel Zone
Villa Royall	Hotel	(876) 953-9252		0.9 mi. South of Central Montego Bay
Villa Sonaté	Hotel	(876) 973-5944		0.8 mi. Southeast of Central Runaway Bay
Village Hotel	Hotel	(876) 974-2645		Downtown Ocho Rios
Waterloo Guest House	Guest house	(876) 965-2278		0.6 mi. South-Southeast of Central Black River
West Indies Yacht Club	Hotel	(800) 223-1017		Old Harbour
West Palm Hotel	Hotel	(876) 956-2321		1.6 mi. West of Central Elgin Town
Westender Inn	Hotel	(876) 957-4991		3.5 mi. South West of Central Sheffield
Wexford Hotel	Hotel	(876) 952-2854		0.8 mi. Northwest of Central Montego Bay
Whistling Bird Resort	Cottages	(876) 957-4403		1.5 mi. South of Central Negril Beach Hotel Zone
White Sands	Hotel	(305) 503-9074		1.2 mi. South of Central Negril Beach Hotel Zone
Xtabi On the Cliffs	Resort	(876) 957-0121		1.4 mi. West of Central Negril
kariba Kariba Guest House	Guest house	(876) 962-8006		Mandeville, Central Jamaica

Jamaica is home to perhaps the most famous all-inclusive resorts in the Caribbean. It's up to you whether you'd like all the little details of your vacation taken care of, or if you'd rather explore the area on your own, looking for unique dining options and attractions near your hotel. Even non-inclusive hotels sometimes offer watersports and activities that families traveling with children will enjoy.

Villa Complexes

Renting a vacation spot in Jamaica is for travelers who want to make their own rules

Rental properties are available as small as studio apartments or as spacious as villas that allow large groups to stretch. Because Jamaica offers so many variations in rental properties, you should be able to find almost anything you desire.

Travelers who like freedom and autonomy on their vacations often enjoy rental properties, not only because of a sense of freedom, but because they can prepare their own meals and usually have more room than hotels offer.

Most rental properties are designed for vacationers staying in Jamaica for more than one week, and during the Christmas season many rentals may only be rented for periods of 10 days or more. Of course, each rental property is different when it comes to rules and amenities.

Condos and Villa Complexes On Jamaica

Guests will find non-hotel accommodations on the island, which include tons of condos and several villa complexes. Beach-goers will generally have easy access to the beach, as many lodgings are situated on the coast. Those looking to enjoy a bit of tennis during their trip will find several condo and villa rentals that house excellent tennis facilities. Read further details regarding each property by clicking the names.

One such destination ideal for poolside loungers is The Cliff Hotel. The Cliff Hotel boasts 33 suites and villas, including two one bedroom villas and a four bedroom and five bedroom villa. A;; accommodations come with views of the Caribbean Sea and beautiful sunsets. You'll find them on West End Road.

A noteworthy location along the coast that is worth considering is Trident Hotel. Set on the lip of the Caribbean Sea, this hotel offers a sensuous vision of contemporary luxury: spectacular views, modernist design and luxurious amenities. If you are looking to call before you go, you can do so at (876) 633-7000.

Another notable option will be Castles by the Sea. Castles on the Sea Resort includes four one-bedroom suites with shared bathroom facilities, as well as four full-bath suites. Each room is air conditioned and features an ocean front terrace and luxurious beds. For customers who want to call before making reservations, you can do so at (876) 953-3250.

The following chart provides you with more details regarding condo and villa complex possibilities.

CONDOS AND VILLA COMPLEXES ON JAMAICA					
Name	Type	Phone Number	Star Rating	Location	
Beachview Apartments	Apartment building	(876) 971-3859		0.6 mi. West-Northwest of Central Montego Bay	
Blue Harbour Guest House and Villas	Villa complex	(876) 725-0289		1.7 mi. North of Central Port Maria	
Bluefields Bay Villas	Villa complex	(877) 955-8993		2.0 mi. North of Central Belmont	
Carib Beach Apartments	Apartment building	(876) 957-4358		1.7 mi. North of Central Negril Beach Hotel Zone	
Castles by the Sea	Villa complex	(876) 953-3250		0.5 mi. North-Northwest of Central Galina	
Catch A Falling Star Resort	Villa complex	(876) 957-0390		1.7 mi. South West of Central Negril	
Catcha Falling Star Gardens	Villa complex	(876) 957-0279		1.7 mi. South West of Central Negril	
Chrisanns Beach Resort	Villa complex	(876) 975-4467		2.8 mi. East-Northeast of Central Ocho Rios	
Columbus Heights Condominiums	Villa complex	(876) 974-2940		1.9 mi. West of Central Ocho Rios	
Coral Cay Villas	Apartment building	(876) 926-0255		2.8 mi. East-Northeast of Central Ocho Rios	
Coral Cove Resort	Villa complex	(876) 412-6914		1.3 mi. East-Southeast of Central Revival	
Cove Villas	Villa complex	(876) 972-1639		5.7 mi. West of Central Ocho Rios	

Crystal Waters Villas	Villa complex	(876) 957-4284	0.9 mi. South of Central Negril Beach Hotel Zone
Emerald View Villas	Villa complex	(876) 465-2054	3.1 mi. West-Northwest of Central Salt Marsh
Frenchman's Cove Resort	Villa complex	(876) 993-7270	1.4 mi. East of Central Turtle Harbour
Goblin Hill Villas at San San	Villa complex	(876) 925-8108	2.0 mi. East of Central Turtle Harbour
Golden Cove Villas	Villa complex	(876) 968-3235	0.4 mi. Northeast of Central Boscobel
Holiday Haven	Apartment building	(876) 973-4893	0.4 mi. East of Central Runaway Bay
Idle Awhile The Cliffs	Villa complex	(877) 243-5352	0.6 mi. Northwest of Central Negril
Idle Awhile The Villas	Villa complex	(877) 243-5352	1.0 mi. South of Central Negril Beach Hotel Zone
Lost Beach Resort	Villa complex	(734) 930-2225	3.4 mi. West-Southwest of Central Little London
Marblue Villa Suites	Villa complex	(876) 965-3408	14.0 mi. West of Central Plowden
Montego Bay Club	Apartment building	--	0.7 mi. Northwest of Central Montego Bay
Moonrise Villas	Apartment building	(876) 957-4344	2.0 mi. North-Northeast of Central Negril
Negril Beach Club Condos	Villa complex	(876) 957-4323	0.9 mi. North-Northeast of Central Negril
Our Past Time Hotel	Apartment building	(876) 631-2752	4.5 mi. North of Central Negril
Pier View Vacations Apartments	Apartment building	876 9 742607	Downtown Ocho Rios
Prospect Villas	Villa complex	(876) 994-1373	1.3 mi. South West of Central Ocho Rios
Rio Vista Resort Villas	Villa complex	(876) 993-5444	0.4 mi. South-Southeast of Central Port Antonio
Round Hill Hotel & Villas	Villa complex	(876) 956-7050	1.5 mi. West-Northwest of Central Great River Bay
Sea Palms	Villa complex	(876) 975-	2.7 mi. East-Northeast of

		4400		Central Ocho Rios
Sea Sand Eco Villas	Villa complex	(876) 957-4376		0.7 mi. South of Central Negril Beach Hotel Zone
Seville Villas and Apartments	Villa complex	(876) 952-3662		1.8 mi. South West of Central Montego Bay
Shields Negril Villas	Apartment building	(876) 957-3112		0.8 mi. North-Northeast of Central Negril
Silver Creek Resort	Villa complex	(876) 973-4949		1.0 mi. Southeast of Central Runaway Bay
Skycastles Condominiums	Villa complex	(876) 973-4810		1.9 mi. West of Central Ocho Rios
Summerset Village	Villa complex	(876) 957-4409		0.2 mi. North of Central Negril
Taino Cove	Apartment building	(876) 965-3893		1.2 mi. Southeast of Central Treasure Beach
The Cliff Hotel	Villa complex	(800) 213-0583		2.1 mi. South of Central Negril
Tigress Two Resort	Apartment building	(876) 957-4249		0.7 mi. West of Central Negril
Tower Cloisters Condominium Resort	Apartment building	(876) 975-4360		2.8 mi. East-Northeast of Central Ocho Rios
Trident Hotel	Villa complex	(876) 633-7000		1.9 mi. East of Central Port Antonio
Tryall Club	Villa complex	(800) 238-5290		1.2 mi. East of Central Sandy Bay
Villas Sur Mer	Villa complex	(876) 382-3717		1.7 mi. South West of Central Negril

Apartments

Apartments in Jamaica provide basic shelter, and while they are fine accommodations, they often have fewer frills than their other rental counterparts. They can be rented with maid service, but do not always automatically include it. Some apartments may not have swimming pools or even a front desk. However, they can be excellent options for longer stays.

Cottages

Cottages are generally small and simple. These rental options will likely contain a bedroom, kitchen and bathroom but little else. Still, they can be extremely popular during the high season in Jamaica and in many cases need to be booked at least five or six months in advance.

Condos and Villas

The most popular rental properties in Jamaica are condos and villas. Condos often have a reception desk, and may seem more like a suite in a big hotel. Most condo complexes have at least one swimming pool.

Villas are generally rented by the week and are often self-catering. They can be as different as a quaint, beach-side building to a mountain mansion. A full staff may be included, but you'll almost always find some maid services, as well as many home essentials.

Villa Rentals

Renting a Villa in Jamaica

Jamaica's all-inclusive resorts seem to overwhelm the hospitality industry, but in truth the variation of lodgings throughout the island is astounding. Villa rentals, which range from quaint cabins to luxury apartments, make up a sizable portion of the accommodation offerings, especially in the less populous destinations where hotels are not as prominent.

Individual Villas

Rental homes are also found to be common on Jamaica. You'll find plenty of choices for different villa styles and feels. View the table below for information concerning rental properties.

INDIVIDUAL VILLAS ON JAMAICA

Jamaica Travel Guide, Caribbean

Name	Phone Number	Bedrooms	Bathrooms	Location
Afterglow	--	3	3	0.3 mi. Northeast of Central Ocho Rios
Beach Haven Villa	(876) 954-2001	3	2	1.5 mi. Northeast of Central Duncans
Cary Island	--	7	7	1.3 mi. East-Northeast of Central Ocho Rios
Casuarina	(876) 954-2001	2	2	1.5 mi. North-Northeast of Central Duncans
Four Winds	--	5	5	2.8 mi. East of Central St. Ann's Bay
Idle Hours Villa	--	1	1	1.5 mi. North-Northeast of Central Duncans
Kai Kala	--	10	10	1.5 mi. East-Northeast of Central Ocho Rios
Rio Chico	--	8	8	3.4 mi. West of Central Ocho Rios
Sundown	(877) 845-5275	5	5	0.6 mi. North-Northwest of Central Discovery Bay
A Summer Place	(305) 767-2596	7	9	0.5 mi. North-Northwest of Central Discovery Bay
Afiba View	(876) 587-4547	2	2	1.5 mi. Northwest of Central Tower Isle
Ah Selah	(305) 767-2596	4	4	1.3 mi. East of Central Runaway Bay
Akwaaba	(876) 954-2001	4	--	1.4 mi. Northeast of Central Duncans
Alice Cottage	--	3	2	1.9 mi. Southeast of Central Treasure Beach
Allamanda	--	5	5	2.1 mi. East-Northeast of Central Montego Bay
Almond Hill	--	4	4	0.9 mi. East-Northeast of Central Hopewell
Almond Tree Villa	--	4	2	1.6 mi. East of Central Ocho Rios
Amanoka	(876) 973-	7	7	0.7 mi. North-Northwest of

Caleb Gray

		2626			Central Discovery Bay
Amedis		(877) 458-2366	3	4	0.3 mi. South West of Central Whitehouse
Anchor Listing Villa		(786) 991-9092	2	2	1.3 mi. South-Southeast of Central Montego Bay
Anchorage Villa		--	3	3	0.9 mi. South of Central Montego Bay
Anticipation		--	6	6	1.4 mi. East of Central Sandy Bay
Azure Sky Villa		(312) 981-6344	4	4	1.0 mi. South of Central Negril Beach Hotel Zone
Bahia		(305) 767-2596	1	1	1.0 mi. East of Central Runaway Bay
Bambu		--	6	6	1.3 mi. East of Central Hopewell
Barukamba		--	2	1	1.6 mi. West-Northwest of Central Treasure Beach
Bay Watch		(305) 767-2596	5	5	1.1 mi. East of Central Runaway Bay
Bay Whisper Villa		(312) 981-6344	5	5	1.0 mi. South of Central Negril Beach Hotel Zone
Belle Abri		--	7	9	0.4 mi. South West of Central Rose Hall
Bienvenue		(786) 991-9092	4	4	1.3 mi. East of Central Great River Bay
Big Grape Villa		--	3	2	1.5 mi. South West of Central Negril
Birds Eye View		(876) 862-9190	--	--	1.2 mi. West of Central Rose Hall
Blessings Villa		(305) 767-2596	4	4	1.3 mi. Southeast of Central Port Antonio
Bliss By The Sea		--	4	3	1.9 mi. Southeast of Central Treasure Beach
Blow Hole		(941) 312-7127	3	5	1.0 mi. Northeast of Central Oracabessa
Blue Heaven		(786) 991-9092	--	3	1.8 mi. North of Central Anchovy

Jamaica Travel Guide, Caribbean

Blue Marlin	(941) 312-7127	4	3	2.0 mi. Southeast of Central Treasure Beach
Blue Moon Villa	(876) 954-7807	5	5	1.4 mi. Northeast of Central Duncans
Bluebird	(941) 312-7127	4	4	2.2 mi. North-Northeast of Central Anchovy
Bogue Villa	--	5	5	0.8 mi. East of Central Montego Bay
Bolt House	--	5	5	1.9 mi. North of Central Port Maria
Bonne Amie	(941) 312-7127	4	5	1.5 mi. West-Northwest of Central Fairy Hill
Bougainvillea	--	5	6	0.6 mi. East-Southeast of Central Sandy Bay
Bumpers Nest	--	4	4	0.8 mi. East of Central Sandy Bay
Butterfly Villa	(305) 767-2596	4	5	1.3 mi. North-Northeast of Central Duncans
Calabash Bay Villa	876-965-300	4	4	0.3 mi. South-Southeast of Central Treasure Beach
Calabash House	(484) 480-3207	5	5	0.5 mi. South-Southeast of Central Treasure Beach
Calypso Shores	--	4	4	2.5 mi. South West of Central Montego Bay
Cannon Cottage	(305) 767-2596	3	3	1.5 mi. North-Northeast of Central Duncans
Carnell By The Sea	--	2	1	1.0 mi. West-Southwest of Central Revival
Casa De Familia	(305) 767-2596	6	4	3.4 mi. Northeast of Central Montego Bay
Casa Espana	(876) 954-2001	3	3	1.4 mi. Northeast of Central Duncans
Castlevue	--	7	7	0.8 mi. South of Central Montego Bay
Cave Canem	--	4	5	0.7 mi. West-Northwest of Central Treasure Beach
Celebrity Villa	(219) 393-	7	7	Clarkson Ville, Central

Caleb Gray

	0507			Jamaica
Chateau Gloria	(876) 953-8383	4	--	0.9 mi. South of Central Montego Bay
Clandestino Villa	--	4	4	1.8 mi. South West of Central Negril
Claremont garden	--	3	1	0.5 mi. West of Central Old Harbour
Cliffside Cottage	(240) 380-3415	5	5	Downtown Montego Bay
Club Paradise	(876) 954-2001	4	--	1.5 mi. Northeast of Central Duncans
Comfort Haven Villa	--	3	2	1.0 mi. Northwest of Central Priory
Coo Yah	--	4	4	0.9 mi. East of Central Sandy Bay
Coquina	(941) 312-7127	3	3	2.0 mi. Southeast of Central Treasure Beach
Coral Cove	(305) 767-2596	8	8	0.6 mi. North-Northwest of Central Discovery Bay
Cottage Cerasse	--	1	1	0.5 mi. South-Southeast of Central Moore Town
Cottonwood Cottage	--	2	2	1.9 mi. North of Central Belmont
Crystal Cove Villa	(305) 767-2596	3	3	1.4 mi. West-Northwest of Central Fairy Hill
Crystal Villa	(876) 954-2001	4	4	1.4 mi. North-Northeast of Central Duncans
Culloden Cove	(941) 312-7127	5	4	1.1 mi. Northwest of Central Whitehouse
Dacha Andrea Villa	--	4	4	0.9 mi. East-Southeast of Central Ocho Rios
Datura Villa	(212) 982-7678	5	5	2.5 mi. North-Northwest of Central Anchovy
Day-O Villa	(305) 767-2596	3	3	1.3 mi. North-Northeast of Central Duncans
Destiny	--	4	4	2.1 mi. East-Northeast of Central Montego Bay

Jamaica Travel Guide, Caribbean

Name	Phone			Location
Doc's on the Bay	(876) 965-0126	5	5	0.5 mi. Southeast of Central Treasure Beach
Doctors Villa	(818) 207-8451	4	4	2.1 mi. West of Central Oracabessa
Dominique's Villa	--	2	2	1.6 mi. West of Central Spanish Town
Doubloon Villa	--	4	4	0.5 mi. Southeast of Central Treasure Beach
Dream Maker	--	1	1	0.9 mi. North of Central Hart Hill
Dreamin Villa	(305) 767-2596	2	2	1.5 mi. North of Central Duncans
Driftwood	--	3	3	1.8 mi. Southeast of Central Treasure Beach
Ebb Tide	(876) 954-2001	4	4	1.5 mi. North-Northeast of Central Duncans
Eden Harbor Villa	(954) 816-0684	2	2	0.8 mi. West of Central Oracabessa
Eight Rivers	--	4	4	1.7 mi. East-Northeast of Central Ocho Rios
Emerald Seas	--	5	5	1.4 mi. East-Northeast of Central Ocho Rios
Emerald Villa	44 79 4671 2415	2	1	0.7 mi. North of Central Tower Isle
Emerald by the Sea	(876) 954-2001	4	4	1.4 mi. Northeast of Central Duncans
Endless Summer	--	6	6	0.5 mi. West-Southwest of Central Rose Hall
Fairhill Villas	(876) 965-3088	--	--	1.5 mi. Southeast of Central Treasure Beach
Fairway Manor	--	7	8	0.2 mi. South West of Central Rose Hall
Fairy Hill Palms	--	3	2	0.4 mi. West of Central Fairy Hill
Fantasy Villa	(305) 767-2596	6	6	0.6 mi. East of Central Rio Bueno
Flower Hill	(800) 387-	5	14	1.1 mi. South-Southeast of

	2726			Central Montego Bay
Folichon	(876) 965-0126	4	2	0.1 mi. South of Central Treasure Beach
Fortlands Point Villa	(305) 767-2596	7	7	0.9 mi. North-Northwest of Central Discovery Bay
Frangipani	--	4	4	1.5 mi. East-Northeast of Central Ocho Rios
Frankfort	--	6	6	1.9 mi. East-Northeast of Central Ocho Rios
Gardenia at Long Mountain	(876) 809-3782	1	1	1.8 mi. South West of Central Papine
Ginger Breeze villa	(312) 981-6344	5	5	0.9 mi. South of Central Negril Beach Hotel Zone
Goat Hill	--	--	--	1.3 mi. East of Central Hopewell
Golden Castle Villa	(941) 312-7127	12	15	1.2 mi. Southeast of Central Montego Bay
Golden Clouds villa	(305) 767-2596	9	9	0.7 mi. North-Northeast of Central Oracabessa
Golden Cove Villas	(877) 458-2366	16	16	1.4 mi. West of Central Oracabessa
Golden Sun Villa	(718) 414-2830	3	3	2.7 mi. West-Northwest of Central Discovery Bay
Good Hope Retreat	(876) 391-3775	1	1	0.8 mi. North of Central Mearnsville
Goodman Villa	--	3	3	0.5 mi. West of Central Rose Hall
Great River House	--	5	5	2.3 mi. East-Northeast of Central Montego Bay
Greatview	--	6	7	0.2 mi. South-Southwest of Central Rose Hall
Grosvenor Retreat	--	3	4	3.5 mi. North of Central Kingston
Halcyon Villa	--	4	4	1.3 mi. East of Central Port Antonio
Hang Time villa	(305) 767-2596	3	3	1.4 mi. Northeast of Central Duncans

Hanover Grange	--	6	6	0.7 mi. East-Southeast of Central Sandy Bay
Hanover House	--	7	5	1.1 mi. South of Central Montego Bay
Harmony Hill	--	7	8	1.0 mi. East-Southeast of Central Sandy Bay
Heron's Reef	(876) 965-0126	1	1	0.1 mi. South of Central Treasure Beach
Highland House	(305) 468-4637	6	7	Downtown Montego Bay
Hill Seaview Villa	001 876 418 22 21	--	--	1.6 mi. East of Central Port Antonio
Hillcrest Villa	(212) 255-8900	5	3	1.5 mi. East of Central Rio Bueno
Hope House	(876) 965-3000	4	4	0.4 mi. South-Southeast of Central Treasure Beach
Hummingbird Hill	(305) 767-2596	5	4	1.0 mi. East-Southeast of Central Runaway Bay
Ian Fleming Villa	--	5	5	0.6 mi. North of Central Oracabessa
Idleawhile	--	6	6	1.4 mi. East of Central Rio Bueno
Idleawile Villa	(305) 767-2596	6	6	2.2 mi. West-Northwest of Central Discovery Bay
Imani Ashia Villa	(305) 767-2596	4	4	0.7 mi. West of Central Rose Hall
Indikanegril	--	4	3	1.2 mi. South of Central Negril Beach Hotel Zone
Infinity	--	5	5	0.8 mi. East of Central Sandy Bay
Island Breeze	(786) 991-9092	3	3	0.6 mi. Northwest of Central Montego Bay
Jamaica Dream Villas	(876) 973-6892	--	--	0.9 mi. West of Central Port Antonio
Jasmin Hill	--	4	4	0.4 mi. Northwest of Central Ocho Rios
Jasmine Hill	(305) 468-	4	4	2.6 mi. Southeast of Central

Caleb Gray

	4637			Ocho Rios
Jawara	--	3	4	0.7 mi. Northwest of Central Montego Bay
Je Suis Content	(305) 767-2596	3	3	1.6 mi. Northeast of Central Duncans
Jubilation Villa	--	6	8	0.9 mi. East-Northeast of Central Hopewell
Katamah	--	4	4	1.2 mi. West-Northwest of Central Treasure Beach
Keela Wee Villa	(305) 767-2596	6	6	0.7 mi. North-Northwest of Central Discovery Bay
Kelso	(305) 767-2596	4	5	1.3 mi. North-Northeast of Central Duncans
Kelso Villa	(305) 767-2596	4	4	0.8 mi. Northeast of Central Discovery Bay
Kima	--	3	3	2.1 mi. East of Central St. Ann's Bay
Kimochii Villa	(876) 890-8315	1	1	1.9 mi. East-Southeast of Central Harbour View
Kingsington Villa	(876) 835-0615	3	4	1.5 mi. North of Central Kingston
Kingston City View	(305) 468-4637	5	5	3.9 mi. North of Central Kingston
L'Dor V'Dor	(518) 907-4865	10	10	0.7 mi. South-Southeast of Central Montego Bay
LDor VDor	--	10	10	1.0 mi. East-Southeast of Central Sandy Bay
La Casita	--	2	2	0.4 mi. South West of Central Rose Hall
La Chez Cherie	(876) 954-2001	4	4	1.5 mi. North-Northeast of Central Duncans
La Hacienda	(876) 954-2001	5	6	1.4 mi. North-Northeast of Central Duncans
La Sirena	--	3	3	3.0 mi. East of Central Treasure Beach
LaSolana Villa	--	4	5	1.5 mi. West of Central Fairy Hill

Jamaica Travel Guide, Caribbean

Lansdowne	--	5	4	2.9 mi. Southeast of Central Ocho Rios
Las Palmas Villa	--	3	3	0.7 mi. East of Central Runaway Bay
Laural's Cottage	--	1	2	4.5 mi. West-Northwest of Central Kingston
Lime Acre	(941) 312-7127	5	5	20.2 mi. Northwest of Central Treasure Beach
Lime Tree	(518) 907-4865	5	5	2.5 mi. Southeast of Central Ocho Rios
Linga-Awile Cottage	(876) 298-9118	3	3	0.6 mi. North-Northwest of Central Discovery Bay
Little Palm	--	2	1	1.1 mi. East-Northeast of Central Sandy Bay
Little Water Villa	(305) 468-4637	3	3	1.6 mi. West-Northwest of Central Revival
Luck Now Villa	(876) 954-2001	3	3	1.4 mi. North-Northeast of Central Duncans
Lyric Villa	--	4	2	0.4 mi. South-Southeast of Central Treasure Beach
Mais Oui	(866) 624-7684	8	7	1.4 mi. East of Central Rio Bueno
Majestic Beach House	--	4	4	1.4 mi. East-Southeast of Central Rio Bueno
Makana Villa	(305) 767-2596	6	6	0.8 mi. North-Northwest of Central Discovery Bay
Malatai	--	6	6	2.9 mi. East of Central St. Ann's Bay
Mamiti Blue	(941) 312-7127	4	5	0.7 mi. West of Central Fairy Hill
Mango Walk Villas	(876) 952-1472	--	--	Downtown Montego Bay
Maranatha Villa	(755) 216-2921	7	5	1.7 mi. East of Central Rio Bueno
Memoriez	(305) 767-2596	1	1	1.5 mi. North-Northeast of Central Duncans
Milestone Cottage	(877) 955-	2	2	2.1 mi. North of Central

	8993			Belmont
Mirador	--	1	2	1.2 mi. East of Central Sandy Bay
Miramar Villas	(786) 991-9092	9	8	0.8 mi. West-Southwest of Central Ocho Rios
Miss P's Place	(305) 767-2596	3	2	1.5 mi. Northeast of Central Duncans
Monicove	(876) 824-8222	3	5	2.1 mi. West of Central Cave
Monticello	(876) 285-3300	6	5	2.8 mi. Southeast of Central Ocho Rios
Moon San Villa	(876) 848-1843	--	--	The vicinity of Jamaica
Moonlight Magic	--	1	1	2.2 mi. West-Northwest of Central Hart Hill
Moves Cottage	(780) 086-6496	2	1	1.4 mi. South West of Central Negril
Mullion Cove	--	5	6	1.9 mi. North of Central Belmont
Negril Beach Villa	(305) 767-2596	3	3	0.5 mi. North of Central Negril Beach Hotel Zone
New Freedom Palace Villa	--	2	2	0.8 mi. Southeast of Central Ocho Rios
New Point	--	3	2	1.2 mi. West-Northwest of Central Treasure Beach
New Point	(240) 380-3415	5	5	Downtown Montego Bay
Noble House	--	--	--	2.2 mi. East of Central Hopewell
Norse Point Villa	(786) 991-9092	--	--	0.9 mi. West of Central Port Antonio
Nutmeg	(800) 387-2726	--	--	0.9 mi. South of Central Montego Bay
Nutshell Villa	(876) 954-2001	3	2	1.5 mi. Northeast of Central Duncans
Ocean Shell Villa & Spa	(305) 767-2596	4	4	2.0 mi. West-Northwest of Central Fairy Hill

Ocean View Guest House Calabash Bay	(876) 369-1859	4	4	0.6 mi. Southeast of Central Treasure Beach
Ocean View Guest House Montego Bay	(876) 952-2662	--	--	1.0 mi. North of Central Montego Bay
Oh Boy Villa	(876) 954-2001	4	3	1.5 mi. Northeast of Central Duncans
One Love Villa	(305) 767-2596	4	4	1.5 mi. Northeast of Central Duncans
One Rhythm Villa	(239) 682-3309	2	2	1.8 mi. Northwest of Central Duncans
Overlook	(518) 907-4865	5	5	0.7 mi. South-Southeast of Central Montego Bay
Paradise Beach Front 1	(305) 468-4637	3	3	0.7 mi. North-Northwest of Central Discovery Bay
Paradise Burlington Villa	(305) 468-4637	3	3	3.4 mi. Northeast of Central Montego Bay
Paradise Clarridge View	(305) 468-4637	1	1	1.5 mi. East of Central Great River Bay
Paradise Drambuie	--	5	5	2.4 mi. North-Northwest of Central Anchovy
Paradise Enchanting	(305) 468-4637	5	4	3.4 mi. Northeast of Central Montego Bay
Paradise Golden Castle Villa	(305) 468-4637	5	5	0.1 mi. South West of Central Rose Hall
Paradise L Horizon	(876) 414-0548	--	--	2.2 mi. East of Central St. Ann's Bay
Paradise Milbrook	(305) 468-4637	4	4	1.8 mi. West of Central Rose Hall
Paradise PGG - 286775	(305) 468-4637	10	10	0.8 mi. West of Central Rose Hall
Paradise PMW - 118228	--	2	2	0.7 mi. North of Central Montego Bay
Paradise Plum	(877) 458-2366	4	4	3.5 mi. East-Northeast of Central Montego Bay
Paradise Skibereen	(305) 468-4637	4	4	1.2 mi. West of Central Rose Hall
Paradise TBB - 84453	(305) 468-	5	5	0.8 mi. East-Northeast of

	4637			Central Hopewell
Paradise TFA - 83497	(305) 468-4637	4	4	0.9 mi. East of Central Hopewell
Paradise TTP - 86366	(305) 468-4637	6	6	1.0 mi. East-Northeast of Central Hopewell
Paradise White House	(305) 468-4637	5	4	0.7 mi. Northeast of Central Tower Isle
Pavilion	(888) 384-5113	5	6	2.3 mi. North-Northwest of Central Anchovy
Pelican Villa	(305) 767-2596	3	3	1.4 mi. West-Northwest of Central Fairy Hill
Pelican's Reach	--	3	3	2.1 mi. Southeast of Central Treasure Beach
Pimento Hill	--	6	6	Central Jamaica
Pineapple Hill Sea View Cottage	--	2	1	0.5 mi. Southeast of Central Port Antonio
Pineapple II	(305) 767-2596	2	2	1.4 mi. North-Northeast of Central Duncans
Pineapple Villa	(305) 767-2596	7	7	1.4 mi. North-Northeast of Central Duncans
Pot O' Gold Villa	--	1	1	1.5 mi. North-Northeast of Central Duncans
Providence House	--	--	--	1.2 mi. West of Central Negril
Quadrille Villa	(305) 767-2596	4	4	1.5 mi. Northeast of Central Duncans
Quarter Deck	(305) 767-2596	3	3	1.4 mi. North-Northeast of Central Duncans
Rainbow Point	(703) 948-0651	3	2	1.7 mi. West-Northwest of Central Treasure Beach
Rainbow Tree	(703) 948-0651	5	5	2.4 mi. Northwest of Central Treasure Beach
Red Fox Villa	(305) 767-2596	4	4	1.5 mi. North-Northeast of Central Duncans
Reef House	(941) 312-7127	4	4	Downtown Montego Bay
Rendezvous Villa	--	5	5	1.0 mi. East-Southeast of

Jamaica Travel Guide, Caribbean

				Central Runaway Bay
Retreat Plantation House	(876) 577-3484	3	2	0.3 mi. West of Central Negril
Rick's Hide Away	--	2	1	0.4 mi. Northwest of Central Negril
Roaring Pavilion	--	5	5	4.7 mi. West of Central Ocho Rios
Rock Hill Villa	(305) 767-2596	5	5	1.3 mi. North-Northeast of Central Duncans
Rose Cottage	--	6	7	0.7 mi. East of Central Sandy Bay
Round Hill Villas	(877) 458-2366	4	4	2.4 mi. Northeast of Central Montego Bay
Russell Hall Villa	--	4	4	2.2 mi. South-Southeast of Central Montego Bay
Rutland	--	1	1	1.8 mi. Northwest of Central August Town
Salt Ash	(305) 767-2596	3	3	1.4 mi. North-Northeast of Central Duncans
San Bar	(876) 929-2378	6	6	1.5 mi. West-Northwest of Central Fairy Hill
San Cove Villa	(876) 930-6738	4	4	1.5 mi. West-Northwest of Central Fairy Hill
San Michele	--	6	6	0.6 mi. Northwest of Central Belmont
Sand Dollar	(305) 767-2596	5	5	1.5 mi. North of Central Duncans
Sanspice Villa	(876) 993-7747	3	3	0.4 mi. South-Southeast of Central Port Antonio
Sanwood Villa	(877) 458-2366	3	3	0.7 mi. West-Southwest of Central Fairy Hill
Scotch on the Rocks	--	5	5	0.3 mi. Northeast of Central Ocho Rios
Sea Breeze Villa	(876) 965-0126	3	3	1.0 mi. Southeast of Central Treasure Beach
Sea Grapes	(876) 979-8080	5	5	0.9 mi. North-Northwest of Central Discovery Bay

Sea Haven	(876) 382-4079	4	4	0.8 mi. North-Northwest of Central Discovery Bay
Sea Spice	(305) 767-2596	2	2	1.0 mi. North of Central Duncans
Sea Spray Villa	(305) 767-2596	3	3	1.5 mi. North-Northeast of Central Duncans
Sea Star	(941) 312-7127	5	6	1.5 mi. West-Northwest of Central Fairy Hill
Sea Wave Villa	--	2	2	1.4 mi. North of Central Duncans
Sea Wyf Cottage	--	2	2	1.5 mi. North-Northeast of Central Duncans
Seagrape	(941) 312-7127	3	3	1.8 mi. North of Central Wiltshire
Seagull Cottage	(305) 767-2596	3	3	1.5 mi. North of Central Duncans
Seascape Villa	(305) 767-2596	3	3	1.3 mi. North-Northeast of Central Duncans
Seaside Cottage	(888) 384-5113	4	4	2.2 mi. North-Northeast of Central Anchovy
Seaview Chateau Villa	(877) 458-2366	9	9	0.5 mi. Southeast of Central Montego Bay
Seaweed Luxury Villa	(877) 458-2366	6	6	0.3 mi. South of Central Treasure Beach
Secrets and Dreams	--	1	1	3.2 mi. South of Central Buff Bay
Serendipity	--	6	6	0.4 mi. West-Southwest of Central Rose Hall
Serenity	(240) 380-3415	4	4	2.1 mi. East of Central Hopewell
Seven Seas	--	4	4	2.1 mi. East of Central St. Ann's Bay
Sevilla Villa	(305) 767-2596	5	--	1.1 mi. East of Central Runaway Bay
Shakti Home	--	2	2	1.0 mi. Southeast of Central Treasure Beach
Shotover Gardens	(876) 298-	4	3	2.3 mi. West of Central Port

Jamaica Travel Guide, Caribbean

		6677			Antonio
Siesta		(305) 767-2596	5	5	1.0 mi. East of Central Runaway Bay
Silent Waters		(800) 387-2726	10	6	2.2 mi. East of Central Hopewell
Silver Pointe Cottage		(305) 767-2596	1	1	1.5 mi. North-Northeast of Central Duncans
Skylark Villa		--	4	4	1.4 mi. West of Central Rose Hall
Sleepy Shallows		(305) 767-2596	4	4	1.5 mi. East-Southeast of Central Rio Bueno
Sol Mar Villa		(305) 767-2596	3	3	1.5 mi. North-Northeast of Central Duncans
Somewhere		--	4	4	1.7 mi. East-Northeast of Central Ocho Rios
Soon Soon		--	3	3	1.3 mi. South of Central Negril Beach Hotel Zone
Spanish Cove		(305) 767-2596	4	4	0.1 mi. Northeast of Central Runaway Bay
Spicy Hill Villa		(876) 968-2934	5	5	2.0 mi. West-Northwest of Central Fairy Hill
Spyglass Hill		(786) 991-9092	8	8	2.5 mi. North of Central Anchovy
Stanford House		--	4	4	2.2 mi. Northeast of Central Munro
Star Apple House		+44 7899 843989	3	3	0.9 mi. South of Central Montego Bay
Stone Harbour		--	4	4	2.8 mi. East of Central St. Ann's Bay
Stoney Gate Cottage		(876) 957-0423	1	1	1.4 mi. South West of Central Negril
Sugar Bay Villas		(305) 767-2596	5	5	0.6 mi. North-Northwest of Central Discovery Bay
Sugar Hill Villas		--	7	7	1.3 mi. East of Central Sandy Bay
Summerhill		--	9	9	0.5 mi. West-Southwest of Central Rose Hall

Summertime Villa Montego Bay	(786) 991-9092	6	6	0.8 mi. East of Central Great River Bay
Summertime Villa Silver Sands	(305) 767-2596	4	4	1.5 mi. Northeast of Central Duncans
Summerwind	(920) 948-8665	--	--	1.7 mi. West of Central Oracabessa
Sundown Villas	(305) 767-2596	7	7	0.6 mi. North-Northwest of Central Discovery Bay
Sunrise Villa	(876) 954-2001	3	2	1.4 mi. North-Northeast of Central Duncans
Sunset 1 Villa	(876) 954-2001	3	--	1.4 mi. North-Northeast of Central Duncans
Sunset 2 Villa	(876) 954-2001	3	3	1.4 mi. North-Northeast of Central Duncans
Sunspot Villa	(305) 767-2596	4	3	0.7 mi. East of Central Runaway Bay
Sweet Spot	(305) 767-2596	6	6	0.7 mi. East of Central Runaway Bay
Tangerine	(305) 767-2596	7	6	1.0 mi. Southeast of Central Runaway Bay
Tek Time Villa	--	5	6	0.6 mi. West of Central Rose Hall
Teresina	--	--	--	1.8 mi. South-Southwest of Central St. Ann's Bay
Terrazas Villa	(876) 965-0126	3	2	1.7 mi. West-Northwest of Central Treasure Beach
The Buccaneer	(941) 312-7127	4	4	1.1 mi. West-Northwest of Central Treasure Beach
The Hermitage	--	4	4	1.9 mi. North of Central Belmont
The Royal Palms	(876) 954-2001	5	5	1.5 mi. Northeast of Central Duncans
Tingalayas Retreat	(305) 468-4637	1	1	1.5 mi. West-Northwest of Central Revival
Tranquility Villa	(876) 993-2213	--	--	3.5 mi. South of Central Port Antonio
Trinity Villa	--	5	5	2.4 mi. West of Central

				Hopewell
Tropical Breeze Guest House	(416) 267-9232	--	--	The vicinity of Jamaica
Tropical Dreams	(876) 954-2001	3	3	1.3 mi. North-Northeast of Central Duncans
Tropical Spice	(305) 767-2596	3	--	0.7 mi. East of Central Runaway Bay
Turtle Beach Towers	(876) 974-2802	--	--	Downtown Ocho Rios
Twin Palms	--	7	--	1.4 mi. East of Central Sandy Bay
Under The Stairs	(876) 545-0735	5	4	1.9 mi. South West of Central Tower Isle
Van Villa Guest House	(876) 957-4963	--	--	The vicinity of Jamaica
Villa Arcadia	--	2	2	2.1 mi. Northwest of Central Treasure Beach
Villa Hikaru	(860) 713-9960	4	2	2.1 mi. West-Northwest of Central Treasure Beach
Villa Lido	--	5	5	5.0 mi. West of Central Ocho Rios
Villa Mara	--	7	7	2.1 mi. East of Central St. Ann's Bay
Villa Marina	(305) 767-2596	3	3	1.4 mi. North-Northeast of Central Duncans
Villa Optima	--	3	3	1.0 mi. Southeast of Central Treasure Beach
Villa Paradiso	--	7	6	2.1 mi. East of Central St. Ann's Bay
Villa Plantana	(518) 907-4865	3	3	2.5 mi. Southeast of Central Ocho Rios
Villa Viento	--	8	7	1.5 mi. Northwest of Central Tower Isle
Villa de l'Ocean	(876) 965-0126	2	2	0.9 mi. West-Northwest of Central Treasure Beach
Villa de la Sable	(876) 965-0126	2	2	0.9 mi. West-Northwest of Central Treasure Beach

Name	Phone			Location
Villa du Soleil	(876) 965-0126	2	1	0.8 mi. West-Northwest of Central Treasure Beach
Villa-forty-two	(519) 266-6711	6	6	0.4 mi. West of Central Montego Bay
Vision Guest House	(876) 972-7175	--	--	The vicinity of Jamaica
Viviana	--	6	6	0.8 mi. East of Central Sandy Bay
Wagwater	--	3	3	1.4 mi. East-Northeast of Central Ocho Rios
Westgate Hills	(305) 468-4637	--	--	1.9 mi. Southeast of Central Montego Bay
Whispering Waters	(305) 767-2596	7	7	0.7 mi. North-Northwest of Central Discovery Bay
Whispering Winds	--	11	9	1.9 mi. West of Central Revival
Whistling Villa	(604) 961-0421	--	--	0.9 mi. Southeast of Central Runaway Bay
Wild Grape Villa	(876) 486-1783	3	3	1.4 mi. South West of Central Negril
Wild Orchid	(877) 458-2366	5	5	1.7 mi. North-Northwest of Central Wiltshire
Windjammer Ocho Rios	--	4	4	0.2 mi. Northwest of Central RioNuoya
Windjammer Villa Silver Sands	(876) 930-6738	--	4	1.5 mi. North-Northeast of Central Duncans
Windrush	(518) 907-4865	5	5	0.7 mi. South-Southeast of Central Montego Bay
Winedown Villa	(876) 954-2001	4	4	1.4 mi. North-Northeast of Central Duncans
Yellow Canary Villa	(876) 954-7922	2	2	1.5 mi. North of Central Duncans

Cruising to Jamaica
Cruises stop at several popular ports in Jamaica

Approximately half of the Caribbean's two million annual cruise travelers visit the island of Jamaica to enjoy the beautiful beaches and warm weather. Many of Jamaica's visitors fall in love and return to the island for a longer stay.

The popularity of cruises stems from their on-board amenities and activities, and their ability to offer travelers the opportunity to visit several destinations on one trip. Jamaica is one of the Caribbean's most visited destinations, so if your cruise is stopping at one of the country's ports, you'll need to plan ahead. This is especially true is you plan to travel during the high season, when cruises are often booked months in advance.

Most cruises to the Caribbean leave from the Florida cities of Miami, Ft. Lauderdale, and Tampa, and dock at Jamaica's largest ports: Montego Bay, Ocho Rios, and Port Falmouth. In March of 2011, after three years of construction a cruise ship specific pier, Falmouth Cruise Pier in Trelawny, officially opened for business. The pier was built in partnership with Royal Caribbean, who's cruise ship Oasis of the Sea (the largest cruise ship on waters as of 2011) made its inaugural trip into the port on March 24, 2011.

When booking your own cruise, you may want to call the cruise line directly, or use their Web site for research. You'll want to think carefully about which line you choose, matching the style of your desired vacation to the style of the ship. While some may choose a family-friendly cruise line, others may prefer a more glamorous ride.

The following cruise lines regularly service Jamaica:

Cruise Lines	Telephone Number	Usual Jamaican Port
Carnival	888-CARNIVAL	Ocho Rios
Celebrity	800-221-4789	Ocho Rios, Montego Bay
Costa	800-33-COSTA	Ocho Rios
Holland America	800-626-9900	Montego Bay, Falmouth
Princess Cruises	800-PRINCESS	Ocho Rios, Montego Bay
Royal Caribbean	800-659-7225	Ocho Rios, Montego Bay, Falmouth

Cruise Classes

Cruises are generally divided into four main classes: contemporary/value cruises, premium cruises, luxury cruises, and specialty cruises. After learning the details on each of these classes, you may find it easier to choose the style of cruise that is best for you.

The most popular type of cruise is the contemporary/value cruise, where reasonable prices and package deals rule. Carnival and Royal Caribbean are two such lines. Together they make up almost 90 percent of the cruise industry.

The next step up in cruises is premium cruises. More expensive, they also offer higher quality service and smaller ships. Celebrity and Holland America offer premium cruises that host larger wait staffs and fewer passengers.

If you're looking for top-notch services and amenities, luxury liners will have what you're looking for. Though the cost may be much higher , the experience is generally considered to be worth the extra expense.

Specialty class ships don't travel as often to popular ports like Jamaica, but those that do typically are themed cruises. Exclusive cruises are available for certain groups, like singles, homosexuals, and senior citizens.

Ships

Ship size is another factor to consider. While travelers wishing to see the sights in Jamaica shouldn't have any trouble, visiting smaller ports would be impossible in some ships because of their size. Travelers on a Panama-class ship will barely squeeze through the ports of the Panama Canal.

Such incredible ships hold a maximum of 3,000 passengers, which may be a consideration for travelers looking for high levels of personalized service. However, their enormous size does make the ships more stable on the ocean during even the most turbulent weather. The following criteria are used to classify ships:

Criteria	Criteria Explained	Meaning
Gross registered tonnage	measurement of the ship's volume/vessel's size	1 gross registered ton = 100 cubic feet
Passenger-to-crew ratio	number of passengers served by each crew member	Smaller ratio = better service
Passenger capacity	based on double occupancy (2 passengers per cabin)	More rooms = more passengers
Space ratio	comparison of ship space/tonnage to passenger capacity	Higher ratio = extra spacious

Cabins

When booking a cabin you'll have two choices. The "run of the ship" cabin allows you to choose between an outside or an inside cabin, but are the less expensive option because they are not assigned until the week you're scheduled to depart. The "perfect" cabin means you'll get the exact cabin you've asked and paid for. It is important to make all requests while you are booking your cabin, to ensure you receive all the desired amenities.

There are a few other considerations you may want to make before picking a room:

- ✓ Cabins near anchors, bars, casinos, elevators, engine rooms, gyms, nightclubs, public rooms, stairways, pools and hot tubs, theaters or thrusters should be avoided, especially by light sleepers as these areas are particularly noisy.
- ✓ Travelers with young children may want to avoid outside cabins with balcony access.
- ✓ Those prone to motion sickness may consider a lower cabin. Travel in the middle of the ship is the smoothest.
- ✓ Take general safety precautions: lock your door when you leave, keep valuables hidden, and avoid flashing lots of money.

When to Go

Wintertime snow and holidays find many northern travelers seeking the warmth of the Caribbean, and cruises between December and early April are extremely popular - a fact reflected by a higher price tag. New Year's Eve, Christmas, Thanksgiving, and Easter are the most popular times for cruises.

Cruising in the springtime is one way to cut costs and still enjoy a cruise in the Caribbean. Cruises booked during hurricane season tend to be less expensive as well, because many travelers try to avoid the waters during this time.

Itineraries

Depending on your vacation time, you can book a cruise that lasts anywhere between a few days and several weeks. First-time cruisers might want to start with a shorter trip, perhaps docking in only one or two spots. Seven and ten day cruises are popular options for many cruisers, offering approximately twice the number of islands. For some a two-week cruise is the most enticing, and two week-long cruises can be booked back to back, or as one long journey.

Wherever you dock, on-shore activities will be arranged by the cruise line. Snorkeling, scuba diving, horseback riding, golfing, and tours are just a few of the options most often offered by cruise lines. Such on-shore activities will cost an extra $25(USD) to $100(USD) per person, and some even more than that. Reserve such activities when you book, or add them on after you board, but remember that space may be limited.

Remember that, when traveling by cruise, your time on the island will be limited. Consult the cruise director to find out how long you'll have on the island, it will help you plan your excursions. If you're less interested in the pre-planned activities, or more interested in exploring Jamaica on your own, you'll find there are plenty of things to do, from site-seeing to shopping. Port Antonio is known for the beautiful nature surrounding it, while Ocho Rios is known for its native dishes and bargains. Montego Bay is a resort town with a little bit of everything.

Cost

Cruise costs will, of course, be different based on any number of factors. The most important of the factors will be luxury level, cruise length, and number of people traveling. Surprisingly for some travelers, a single occupancy rate is higher than a double occupancy rate.

While most of your travel is included in the price of your room, many extras such as shore excursions and beverages, especially alcoholic beverages, are typically not. Make sure you go over which items are inclusive, and be aware of the cruise lines policy on tipping.

What to Bring

When packing there are a few things you'll need to remember. While you'll be spending your days enjoying a sun-filled vacation, your nights will almost inevitably include meals that are classified as evening casual, informal, or formal. This means you'll need to pack diversely, but the caution is also not to over-pack.

Remember that your cabin will likely be small, and you'll need to make the best use of the space you have. It's recommended that travelers include bathing suits, lightweight and light colored shirts, shorts, and other cover-ups, flip-flips or sandals, sunglasses, and a hat with a brim for additional protection from the sun. But for the nights you'll want to keep a pair of nice slacks and a collared shirt for men, and a sun dress or nice pants and a blouse for women. When traveling on a cruise "informal" can mean a suit and tie and cocktail dress, while formal dinners require black tie attire.

Jamaica has its own standards for dress. It is considered inappropriate to wear beachwear into towns. Shorts, pants, and skirts are acceptable, but women should avoid wearing clothing that is too revealing, which is also inappropriate.

Weddings in Jamaica

A wedding in Jamaica transforms your special day into a magical one

If you are seeking an unforgettable wedding experience, you should consider hosting your big event in beautiful Jamaica. From exquisite landscapes and excellent climate conditions to delicious cuisine and a romantic built-in honey moon, a wedding event in Jamaica guarantees to deliver lasting memories.

Have you always imagined saying your nuptials while waves gently lapped onto the shore behind you? Did you dismiss the idea because you thought it would be too complicated and certainly too pricey? Think again. A bit of exploration and heavy helping of meticulous planning can help make your dream come true.

Pros and Cons

Some people find that wedding event planning can be quite stressful, particularly when you have no choice but to place all your confidence in an event manager in a foreign nation. For so many people, the benefits outnumber the negative aspects by far. Still, a destination wedding is not for everyone. The following list of pros and cons will allow you to decide if getting married in Jamaica is the most ideal choice for you.

Pros

- ✓ Cost. While you might not expect it, a Caribbean wedding can actually save you money - including the price of your flight. This is because destination weddings are inclined to be smaller events that fewer guests attend, therefore costing you less money in table settings and food. Many resorts also offer wedding and honeymoon package discounts, thus improving your savings even more.
- ✓ Weather. Climate is a key factor for any event, particularly if you are planning your wedding at an outdoor venue. The average temperature in Jamaica ranges from between 80 and 90 degrees Fahrenheit throughout the year. Rain showers do occur, but they are usually over before they begin.
- ✓ Planning. Couples scheduling a destination wedding commonly hire an event planner (or one is assigned to you by your hotel when you purchase a wedding package through them). This makes certain that a specialist thoughtfully takes every single aspect of your wedding into consideration.
- ✓ Friends and Family. Choosing a destination wedding means that you can scale down your guest list - you don't need to feel obligated to extend an invitation to an uncle you aren't that close to, or your old college classmate.

Cons

- ✓ **Cost.** Many people feel burdened with the responsibility to pay for **air travel** and the hotel stay for their entire wedding party and guests. If you decide to include all these expenses within your budget, a Caribbean wedding will undoubtedly cost more in the end.
- ✓ **Weather.** Jamaica is situated within the hurricane belt; therefore it is absolutely essential to remember that scheduling a wedding celebration during hurricane season (which lasts from the beginning of June through the end of November) presents a slight risk.

- ✓ **Planning.** Because you will not be able to personally see and choose wedding items for the majority of the time leading up to your nuptials, you may find yourself becoming uneasy, feeling as though everything is out of your control.
- ✓ **Legal issues.** While preparing for your Jamaica wedding, an essential concept to keep in mind is that the guidelines pertaining to marriage licenses could differ from those you would come across back home. Obtaining a marriage license in Jamaica calls for time, so a suddenly scheduled wedding may not be feasible.
- ✓ **Family and friends.** Everyone you hope to have at your wedding may not be able to attend a destination wedding.

Why Choose Jamaica

Aside from the obvious beauty and tropical ambiance that hosting a wedding in Jamaica supplies, why would you choose to get married in Jamaica over all of the other options in the world? Because planning a wedding in Jamaica is easy. Jamaica is known as the birth place of the all-inclusive resort, and for as long as these resorts have been around, people have been having weddings at them. This means that the staff at resorts and other local event planners are well versed in planning weddings with couples living in other countries. Their experience and expertise will make it very easy for you to plan a wedding that is right for you and right for your budget.

Local Wedding Customs

A reception in Jamaica is all about the food, and large quantities of it. A great way for you to integrate Jamaican customs into your own wedding is by serving up some of the culinary delights that locals might also provide on their special day. Curried goat dishes, rum punch, and spiced fruit cake are common choices. If you have a sweet tooth, consider this: in Jamaica, numerous cakes are commonly served at the reception, and kept covered until they are served, as a surprise for the bride.

The celebration of a new marriage on the island is traditionally not a one day event. The Sunday after the official wedding ceremony would customarily see the wedding party attend church to pray for the longevity of the new marriage. After church, everyone would retire to the home of the bride's parents for a second reception - typically a larger and more boisterous affair than the first. This was called Tun T'anks Sunday, and if you enjoy a good party, you may consider adding this day to your roster of wedding events.

Types of Ceremonies

Your Jamaican wedding can truly be whatever you want it to be: indoors or out, large or small, extravagant or low key. Many couples choose to marry in Jamaica because they want to say their vows on a beach, or in a garden amid the tropical flowers. Regardless of where you choose to host your ceremony, there is one way to commemorate the start of your union that is perfect for an island locale: with a sand ceremony. The way a sand ceremony works is that the bride and the groom each hold a vial of different colored sand that they will simultaneously pour into a new, clear, container. This represents two separate lives joined together to create one.

Budgeting

Despite the fact that a destination wedding often carries a smaller price tag than an extravagant wedding in your home town, it is still imperative that you take some time to carefully create a budget. To achieve this, take time to plan with your future spouse and crank out a list of everything you imagine you might spend money on, based upon importance to you. These items might include the catering, location, photography, and attire, among numerous others. After doing a bit of quick research, designate a price limitation to each item on your list, then total everything up. This will give you a ball park figure of how much money you can anticipate spending. Bear in mind that this total will change as you prepare for your special day, and the ordered list of key items will help you to know instantly what things you can cut back on and which items you would rather spend money on.

Requirements

The great thing about getting married in Jamaica is that you can file all of your paperwork and receive your marriage license before you even get to the island. If you hire a wedding planner or go through a resort, they will give you a date by which you send them all of your paperwork (usually a month or more before the wedding date), and they will file for you. The documentation you will be required to present will include birth certificates, photo copies of passports, and any death, divorce, or adoption certificates that are relevant.

The day of your wedding is one of the most memorable milestones of your life, and organizing a destination wedding in Jamaica may be an opportunity for you to make that day all the more special. Just imagine getting married on a warm day amid the palm trees, with the sounds of the nearby ocean. If this sounds like heaven to you, a wedding in Jamaica might be just your style.

Budgeting for a Wedding in Jamaica

Make your Jamaica wedding planning stress free by starting early and taking lots of notes

A destination wedding speaks to the idea of getting away from it all; running away to an exotic location to celebrate with the one you love; romance. Choosing Jamaica as your wedding location allows you to experience all of that and more. After making the decision to say "I do" in Jamaica, it is time to begin planning your big day.

What is the biggest secret to achieving a great Jamaican wedding? The key is to begin your planning process as quickly as possible. A good system of time management should be developed because it allows you to save time when researching choices, making reservations, and coping with any complications that may arise. Beginning early also gives you time to take advantage of any possible deals that could become available.

Hired Help

Many couples who are planning a Jamaican wedding find that the most significant obstacle is making the arrangements from afar. This is why so many couples hire a wedding or event planner to do what they do best - make the planning of your wedding as stress free and simple as possible. You can hire someone local, someone in Jamaica, or choose to buy a resort wedding package.

If you choose to hire a wedding planner local to you, make sure he or she has previous experience planning a Caribbean wedding and references available. Connections in the area and knowledge of the local language and customs will help guarantee that your experience is exactly what you want and expect. Remember, if you want your wedding planner to be on site the day of your wedding, be prepared to to pay for her airfare and hotel stay.

You may discover that choosing an event planner in Jamaica is a great option if you're looking for someone on the island to be your eyes and ears. This person will be able to handle every detail of your wedding, and most importantly analyze venues and vendors in person.

WEDDING PLANNERS IN JAMAICA	
Name	Phone Number
A Tropical Weddings	876-407-6767
A Wedding Day Away	862-250-0949
BJs Bridal Fantasies	876-974-6798
Caribbean Dream Wedding Plus LTD	876-403-0137
Destination Weddings in Jamaica	914-709-0457 866-MAISOUI
Helen G Event Planning and Design	876-541-7772 718-880-4067
Negril Weddings	876-957-0392
Tropical Weddings Jamaica	876-407-6767

Wedding packages offered by local resorts are most common and often the most reliable. Accommodations, venue, officiant, catering, adornments, and more are usually included in one flat rate. Read our guide to Jamaica Wedding Locations and Venues for more information on resort weddings.

How to Plan a Jamaican Wedding Yourself

Preparing a wedding in Jamaica may seem stressful but many find it a fun challenge and have successfully achieved their dream event. Stay prepared, write lists, and keep notes of every phone call and transaction you make.

Step One: Structure Your Budget

Developing a sensible budget is essential to any successful wedding. On average, couples in the United States spend between $20,000 and $30,000 on their big day, while a destination wedding in Jamaica can cost you as little as $2,000. Numerous major resorts and hotels have wedding planning services that can prepare your big event down to the very last detail, and charge a single set fee for the entire package. If you decide to arrange the entire wedding yourself, consider the expenses you may encounter.

ESTIMATED JAMAICAN WEDDING COSTS	
Item	Expected Cost
Marriage License	$80(USD)
Officiant	$50 to $250(USD)
Photography	$500 to $3000(USD)
Flowers	$300 to $1500(USD)
Decorations	$300 to $1500(USD)
Venue	$0 to $1000(USD)
Food	$25 to $50(USD) per person
Lodging	$100+(USD) per night

The chart above merely addresses wedding basics, and estimates are based upon average costs of the individual items. Consider other fundamentals such as the bride's gown, the groom's tuxedo, and the wedding rings. Overall, wedding costs will change drastically depending on which items you decide are the most important. You need to stay within a reasonable budget that is based upon your financial situation. List items commonly associated with a wedding from maximum value to lowest value and allocate a price estimate to each item.

Items ranked in order of importance will allow you to see exactly where you may be willing to trim back and where you aren't willing to compromise.

Step Two: Select a Theme

By this point you will have determined what style of wedding you would like to host, and the type of venue you would like to have it in. Options typically include a traditional wedding wedding in a church or historic landmark, an outdoor ceremony in a garden, on a beach, or another beautiful setting, or at sea on a chartered yacht. Making this selection will quickly trim down your list of potential vendors. Consult our guide to Jamaica Wedding Locations and Venues for for more information about the types of weddings available in Jamaica.

Step Three: Do Your Research

Every location, vendor, resort, decoration, and method of transportation should be evaluated. Contact companies for price estimates and inform them that you are arranging your nuptials from abroad, and that they should expect mainly long distance phone calls and e-mail communications. When you contract with vendors sight unseen, ask for references from those who have previously used their services.

Also give consideration to the time of year in which you wish to get married, and the type of events that may occur during that time. If you want you and your guest to have a party environment, getting married in Jamaica during Carnival, for example, may be just the ticket. However, if you would rather have an intimate, discreet event, you should make other arrangements. Additionally, the weather can have a significant impact on your wedding experience, especially if you are looking to host an outdoor celebration.

Don't forget to look into what is required of you to get married in Jamaica. Jamaica is unique among the Caribbean islands, because couples have the option of mailing their documents to the island ahead of time in order to secure their marriage license. After a marriage license has been granted, the couple must be on the island for 24 hours, and then they can legally wed.

While you are doing your research, take the time to learn about local wedding customs and traditions. You may find that incorporating local dishes like ackee and codfish into your reception is a fun way to honor the island on your wedding day. Another simple way to do this is by using the national flower of Jamaica in your bouquet or boutonnière. Jamaica's national flower is the lignum vitae, a dainty, blue (almost purple) bloom. For more information on Jamaican wedding customs, read our guide to Jamaica Wedding Requirements and Traditions.

Step Four: Book Your Vendors

The vendors you select will essentially make or break your wedding event. When you make your final decisions and book your vendors, explain precisely what you are looking for, and the dates you have chosen. Get all of your price quotes in writing (Have them send you a quote through the post office, by e-mail, or by fax). Keep duplicates of everything including invoices of all items that are included the price. Some businesses require a deposit. Do not send anyone payments until you have received a paper statement; protect yourself from any possible misunderstandings.

Step Five: Take Care of at Home Projects

Many couples wish to bring a bit of personal flair to their Jamaica wedding event. If you are creating or purchasing any of your wedding decorations at home, there is no better time than now to start working on this project. This may also be the time to purchase the wedding dress and/or make arrangements to rent a tuxedo. List everything you plan on taking care of at home, and the estimated time it will take you to accomplish it.

Step Six: Follow Up

Although you may think your arrangements are finalized, it is still important to talk to your vendors periodically to review their progress, or to discuss any changes that need to be made. Don't worry about calling too often; they are working for you, and you are paying them to provide these services.

Listed below are a few additional tips that will assist you in planning your Jamaica wedding.

- ✓ Consider the weather. If you are planning a wedding at an outdoor venue, make alternative arrangements in case of stormy conditions. Typical weather conditions for that time of year should be considered when choosing your wedding attire. If you plan to marry on the beach in the middle of a hot afternoon, plan accordingly.
- ✓ Send wedding supplies ahead of time. If you are bringing any wedding items with you from home, consider shipping them ahead to your resort or venue so that you can avoid airport hassles and restrictions. Be sure to arrange for insurance on these items in case they are lost or damaged during shipment.

As your wedding day approaches, all your hard work and effort will finally begin to pay off. As everything falls into place, you can relax and prepare to enjoy the most memorable day of your life - your wedding in Jamaica.

Wedding Locations and Venues in Jamaica

Searching locations and venues for your Jamaica wedding is sure to produce the perfect place to say "I do"

Montego Bay, Kingston, Negril, Ocho Rios, and Port Antonio are Jamaica's bustling cities, and home to the largest concentration of wedding venues. Still, couples who prefer to get off the radar can find reception halls and outdoor locales in smaller and quieter Jamaican towns.

Among the most challenging aspects of organizing a Jamaican wedding is choosing a wedding venue without the chance to visit the site before you reserve it. Recruiting a wedding or event planner is an excellent choice for couples who are searching for someone to take care of everything in Jamaica associated with your wedding prior to the big celebration. These experts work to make sure that your nuptials operate as smoothly and ideally as possible. If you decide to do all the planning yourself, selecting the kind of wedding you would like to have will trim down your possible choices a great deal, rendering the entire process a little less complex.

Types of Ceremonies

When it comes to your ceremony, your Jamaica wedding is only limited by your imagination. While the most common type of wedding planned by foreigners is a beach ceremony, this is not the only option available.

Casual vs. Formal

Whether you're seeking a formal or informal wedding, Jamaica provides choices to suit any couple's wedding needs. Though Caribbean weddings are normally thought of as informal celebrations, you can dress your wedding up with formal wear and elegant adornments. Similarly, you may dress down a commonly formal event such as a church wedding by seeking very simple adornments and permitting your guests to dress in a casual fashion.

Traditional Wedding

The more traditional wedding ceremony customarily takes place in a religious venue, with relatives and companions filling the pews as the bride slowly walks down the aisle toward her handsome groom. As soon as the vows are said, the wedding party and their guests typically continue on to a dining hall to celebrate the memorable event. This is as much a possibility in Jamaica as anywhere else. Your wedding planner can help you locate a chapel or temple that is appropriate for your religious faith; for example, the Lady of Fatima Church in Ocho Rios is the most popular choice for Catholic weddings.

HOUSES OF WORSHIP AND WEDDING CHAPELS IN JAMAICA

Venue	Location	Phone Number
Cathedral of the Blessed Sacrament	Montego Bay	867-952-2481
Holy Trinity Cathedral	Kingston	876-922-3335
Lady of Perpetual Help	St. Ann's Bay	876-972-2279
Mary Gate of Heaven	Negril	876-957-4900
Mount Zion United	Rose Hall area, Montego Bay	876-419-7286
Ocho Rios Baptist Church	Ocho Rios	876-972-2405
Ocho Rios Methodist Chapel	Ocho Rios	876-974-1420
Our Lady of Fatima	Ocho Rios	876-974-2523
Prospect Plantation Chapel	Ocho Rios	1-800-733-5077
Shaare Shalom Synagogue	Kingston	876-922-5931
St. Joseph Roman Catholic Church	Savanna la mar, Westmoreland Parish	876-955-2648
St. Mary's Anglican Church	Montego Bay	876-926-8925
The Chapel at Trident Castle	Port Antonio	1-877-446-7188
Wedding Chapel at Breezes Runaway Bay	Runaway Bay	1-877-273-3937 ext. 4621
Wedding Chapel at Sandals Montego Bay	Montego Bay	876-952-5510

You may also choose to host a more traditionally styled ceremony at a museum, plantation house, or important historical landmark.

TRADITIONAL WEDDING VENUES IN JAMAICA		
Venue	Location	Phone Number
Bellefield Great House and Gardens	Montego Bay	876-952-2382
Devon House	Kingston	876-929-6602
Greenwood Great House	Greenwood, near Montego Bay	876-953-1077
Rose Hall Great House	Rose Hall area, Montego Bay	876-953-2323

Outdoor Wedding

Between the gently lapping waves and soft, sandy shores, it isn't surprising to find that the most popular outdoor weddings are those hosted on the seashore. It goes without saying that a wedding on a Jamaican beach is a beautiful affair. The sea and fine sand deliver such an ideal backdrop that few decorations are needed. Weddings on the beach are also rather simple to organize, and smaller weddings may not even require permits in Jamaica. Gardens and waterfalls also serve as exquisite outdoor locations.

OUTDOOR WEDDING SITES IN JAMAICA	
Site	Location
Blue Lagoon	Port Antonio
Coyaba River Garden and Museum	Ocho Rios
Cranbrook Flower Forest	St. Ann Parish
Dunn's River Falls	Ocho Rios
James Bond Beach	Ocho Rios
Lover's Leap	St. Elizabeth Parish
Negril Cliffs	Negril
Negril Lighthouse	Negril
Seven Mile Beach	Negril

Shaw Park Gardens	Ocho Rios
Somerset Falls	Port Antonio
YS Falls	St. Elizabeth Paris

Marriage at Sea

If you dream of getting married at sea, doing so in Jamaica is one of the most beautiful places on the planet to so. The Caribbean Sea offers some of the most crystal clear, calm waters, and stunning views. You might choose to plan to get married aboard a major cruise line that makes a stop in Jamaica, or charter a yacht for a few hours. You may even rent the boat for an entire day and host the reception on board as well.

Resorts with Wedding Packages

A trendy possibility for couples planning a Jamaican wedding is obtaining a wedding and honeymoon package at a large resort. Jamaica in particular is well known for having a wide range of all-inclusive resorts, and these locations almost all offer wedding packages.

Reserving a wedding package at a Jamaica resort is a surprisingly simple way to plan your big event, because essentially everything is completed for you. Most packages are comprised of the following:

- ✓ Personalized wedding consultant and planner
- ✓ Wedding venue
- ✓ Reception venue
- ✓ Officiant
- ✓ Floral bouquet and boutonnière
- ✓ Cake
- ✓ Reception food and beverages
- ✓ Photography

- ✓ Marriage certificate
- ✓ Government fees

Optional add-ins may include:

- ✓ Accommodations for wedding guests
- ✓ Videography
- ✓ Music and entertainment
- ✓ Wedding favors
- ✓ Honeymoon package
- ✓ Planned excursions and activities for wedding party and guests

Most wedding packages at resorts in Jamaica begin at around $1500(USD) and increase from there, with prices depending upon add ons and number of guests.

JAMAICA RESORTS WITH WEDDING PACKAGES		
Resort	Location	Phone Number
Breezes Grand Negril	Negril	1-877-273-3937 ext. 4621
Breezes Rio Bueno	Runaway Bay	1-877-273-3937 ext. 4621
Breezes Runaway Bay	Runaway Bay	1-877-273-3937 ext. 4621
Breezes Trelawny	Falmouth	1-877-273-3937 ext. 4621
Charela Inn	Negril	876-957-4277
Coral Cove	Little Bay, Westmoreland Parish	876-457-7594
Couples Negril	Negril	876-957-5960
Couples Sans Souci	Ocho Rios	876-994-1206
Couples Swept Away	Negril	876-957-4061
Couples Tower Isle	Tower Isle, St. Mary Parish	876-975-4271
Geejam	Port Antonio	876-993-7000
Half Moon Resort	Rose Hall	800-339-9728
Hummingbird Hall	Rose Hall	876-789-0523
Jamaica Inn	Ocho Rios	876-974-2514

Riu Montego Bay	Montego Bay	888-748-4990
Riu Negril	Negril	888-748-4990
Riu Ocho Rios	Ocho Rios	888-748-4990
Riu Palace Tropical Bay	Negril	888-748-4990
Rondell Village	Negril	876-957-4413
Royal Decameron Club Caribbean	Runaway Bay	876-973-4803
Royal Decameron Montego Bay	Montego Bay	876-952-4340
Sandals Carlyle	Montego Bay	876-952-4140
Sandals Grande Riviera	Ocho Rios	876-974-5691
Sandals Montego Bay	Montego Bay	876-952-5510
Sandals Negril	Negril	876-957-5216
Sandals Royal Caribbean	Montego Bay	876-953-2231
Sandals Royal Plantation	Ocho Rios	876-974-5601
Sandals Whitehouse	Whitehouse, Westmoreland Parish	876-640-3000
Strawberry Hill	Irish Town, St. Andrew Parish	876-944-8400
The Blue House	Ocho Rios	876-994-1367
The Caves	Negril	876-957-0320

Whether you decide to plan your Jamaica wedding single-handedly, or choose to reserve a wedding package at an all-inclusive resort, the venues located on this popular Caribbean destination guarantee to provide everything you need for a picturesque wedding that you'll remember for the rest of your life.

Weddings Traditions and Requirements in Jamaica

Learn about Jamaica weddings, from traditional customs to modern necessities

When asked to describe a wedding, the most common response people give is the image of a bride dressed in white, walking down the aisle to meet her groom and exchange vows.

This notion is a very western one, and certainly not a tradition that every country follows. A look back at the wedding customs of Jamaica will prove that the islanders have, in the past, had a different idea of what makes a wedding great. You may find that these time-honored traditions speak to you, and want to incorporate them into your own wedding, or you may just find it an interesting read. There are a few rules you must abide by, however, if you plan to get married in Jamaica.

Local Wedding Customs

Though weddings in Jamaica are typically a modern affair, similar to what you would be used to seeing back home, there are some customs that remain historically significant. You may find it fun, or important, to incorporate some of these customs into your own ceremony.

Traditionally, Jamaican weddings involve the entire village in which the couple lives. Everyone is invited to celebrate the momentous occasion, and it is not uncommon for uninvited guests from nearby villagers to show up as well. The wedding fruit cakes (there were multiple cakes in order to feed all of the guests) were covered in lace (so that they would be a surprise to the bride), carried to the wedding location by a quiet procession of married women, and the bride would later be paraded through the streets to the ceremony location in what many consider to be the oddest of the Jamaican wedding traditions. As the bride walks through the streets, villagers line up and call out to the bride criticizing her appearance. If she gets a lot of negative feedback, the bride will return home and try to make herself more beautiful before returning to the wedding site.

At the ceremony, the bride was walked down the aisle by both her mother and her father, or just her father. Rarely was a bride escorted by her mother if the father was out of the picture.

After the wedding, the reception would be held at the groom's family home, at which lots of food (curried goat was commonly served), drinks (rum), and cake were consumed, and guests danced and toasted the couple. Guests would give the newly married couple provisions to begin their life together, such as livestock, money, and home decor.

After the reception, the newlywed couple would go to their home and rest for one week.

Though many of these practices are considered archaic, some of these wedding traditions are upheld today, many of which involve food. If you would like to honor Jamaican wedding traditions, consider serving curried goat, rum punch, and fruit cake at your reception. .

Modern Requirements

Weddings in Jamaica can take place every day of the week, including Sundays and holidays, but the bride and groom must have been in Jamaica for at least 24 hours before their ceremony is scheduled to take place. The only exception to this is if the wedding party arrives via cruise ship, in which case they may be married that same day.

There are a number of documents that you are required to produce before you may get married in Jamaica. Many venues and planners will require that you mail or fax them these documents at least 30 days (and often up to 60 days) prior to the event. Check with your venue to be sure.

Required Paperwork:

- ✓ Certified copies of the bride and grooms birth certificates.
- ✓ Certified copies of Divorce Certificate if one or more parties has been divorced.
- ✓ Certified copies of Death Certificate if one of the parties is a widow or widower.
- ✓ Certified copies of adoption certificates that reflect any name changes.

- ✓ Photocopy of photo identification for each party.
- ✓ Notarized copies of English translations for any documents that are not originally worded in English.

The wedding venue or minister should take care of filing all of the paperwork to make your marriage official, and mail it to your home within four to six weeks of the wedding date.

Whether you plan a very customary religious ceremony, a service that includes elements of traditional Jamaican nuptials, or create a whole new wedding concept that works for you, a destination wedding in Jamaica is sure to be a dream. Take the time to make sure you've got all your required documents in order before you head to the island, and your Jamaican wedding can be whatever you want it to be.

Caleb Gray

Why Not Go to Jamaica?

The island of Jamaica boasts a stunning and seductive diversity of culture

Geographically, Jamaica is an island of intense color and contrast with tropical beaches and arid plains set among the misty Blue Mountains. Socially, the same contrasts endure as British ex-patriots mingle with spiritually expressive Rastafarians. Jamaica is one of the most dynamic nations in the Caribbean, which can make it both daunting and endearing to travelers.

Whatever vacationers think of Jamaica, it must be good, because they keep returning time and again. Jamaica is continually named as one of the top destinations in the Caribbean, in fact, between the years 2005 and 2011, World Travel Awards honored Jamaica with the "Caribbeans Leading Destination" award. The island's hotels have also won several awards over the years, and the country itself walked away with awards for the "Caribbean's Leading Tourist Board," and the "Caribbean's Leading Cruise Destination" in 2011. To continue the spree, in 2014, it was ranked as one of the top Spring Break destinations.

Accommodations

The most notable travel fact about Jamaica is that it is the birthplace of the modern all inclusive resort. The north coast of the island, particularly in the area of Negril and Seven Mile Beach, is lined with all-inclusive mega resorts that charge one price at the door to take care of all of your vacation needs, from your accommodations to meals to every imaginable recreational activity, all within a gated, guarded complex, safely sheltered from the outside world. From the colorful family-friendly getaways of the Franklin D. Resort to the racy pleasures of the adults-only Hedonism resorts, there's an all-inclusive to suit your needs. There is also a congregation of mega resorts around Montego Bay. They may not offer as much for one flat price, but you can still enjoy an entire vacation without ever leaving the guarded grounds of the resort.

For some people, this is the ideal Jamaican vacation, and all-inclusive has its merits. Everything you need is provided for you, and at your disposal whenever you want it. The environment is secure and safe, making for a worry-free getaway. However, for those who vacation to see new places and new culture, there is an experience unlike any other in the world waiting outside the resort gates. In December of 2010, Jamaica was honored with the Caribbean's Top Tourist Destination award, solidifying the idea that every type of vacationer can find pleasure in Jamaica.

Geography and More

The island of Jamaica is the third largest island in the Caribbean. A land mass of 4,400 square miles, it's just a little smaller than the state of Connecticut and offers plenty to do for the nature lover. Thebeachesof the north coast are ranked some of the best in the islands, and offshore the island is surrounded by remarkable diving and snorkeling opportunities. In the southwestern part of the island, you'll find semi-arid coastal plains where sugarcane is grown. In the middle of the island, rising to an altitude of 7,402 feet, are the Blue Mountains, where the world famous Blue Mountain coffee is grown. Here, there are rivers for rafting, trails for hiking and of course, gorgeous scenery.

Many traveling to the Caribbean looking for sunbathing opportunities are invariably drawn to the island beaches, but some of Jamaica's prime bathing spots are in the tropical rock pools, many at the bases of waterfalls, to be found along the inland rivers and streams. Here, you can relax in the cool, clear water dappled in sunlight while enjoying the scenery and listening to the sounds of the surrounding jungle. However, Jamaica is also more densely populated than many other islands, so if you're looking for that quiet sensation of complete seclusion, it will be a little harder to find here.

Around the Island

The natural beauty of Jamaica is unquestionable, but the feature of the land that most sets this island apart from the rest of the Caribbean is its people. More than 2.5 million people call Jamaica their home. The people of Jamaica are a strong-minded and vibrant, passionate about social and political issues and outspoken about their opinions, yet warm and fun-loving at heart. They share a spirituality that stands in contrast to the hedonistic lifestyles of some of the upscale resorts, and they have a unique culture with intoxicating music, colorful dress and tantalizing cuisine that is all their own. The streets of the cities are alive with a range of sights, smells and sounds that you won't find anywhere else.

While Jamaica remains a bastion of strength and character, it is not always the paradise promised by resort brochures. Once outside the gates of the all-inclusive, tourists exploring the island on their own should heed proper precautions to ensure a safe and enjoyable trip. Approximately 35 percent of the population lives below poverty level. Many of these people, living outside the large cities, do not have access to proper garbage disposal, so they usually pile it and burn it themselves in their yards or in a hole in the ground. While this does not pose a danger to tourists, it can be disturbing to some to encounter such images of poverty, making for an unpleasant trip to the countryside.

If you love to shop and bargain for prices, the island street markets will be an unforgettable experience. They are loud, crowded, colorful and lively, with countless merchants selling every imaginable product. There will likely be street performers on the corner, calypso bands playing to the crowd and a gamut of tantalizing sounds and smells to draw your attention. However, Jamaican vendors can be notoriously aggressive and will rarely take no for an answer, so be prepared to be firm. For those not prepared to engage in these kinds of social interactions, a trip through the market might not be pleasant.

Crime rates in Jamaica are known to be high, particularly in and around the city of Kingston. There are some areas of the island that tourists should avoid at night and other areas that should be avoided all the time, but as long as you educate yourself and pay attention, they aren't hard to stay out of. While violent crime is on the rise in inner city areas, most of the crime against tourists that occurs on the island is petty theft and pick pocketing. The most important thing to remember is to keep a close watch on your possessions at all times. Always keep cars locked; make use of your in-room safe; and don't leave any valuables in plain sight, even in a locked car. In the end, visiting the island of Jamaica is no different than visiting New York, Chicago, Miami, or any large city because common sense should always guide you away from uncomfortable situations. For more information on crime in Jamaica and how to avoid it, click here.

The climate of Jamaica is an important consideration when deciding to visit as well, and that doesn't just pertain to weather. Although the higher altitudes can get quite cool in the mornings and evenings in the winter, the weather patterns of Jamaica are remarkably mild and temperate. More important to consider is the social climate at the time you visit. Jamaicans are extremely passionate about their politics, and the social environment in the more densely populated areas can become quite heated in the headlights of an upcoming election or other significant socioeconomic event. On the other hand, island-wide events like the annual Junkanoo Festival can bring Jamaica to a fever-pitch of music and dancing that is a sight to see.

There are many faces of Jamaica, many more than can be seen in one visit to the island. 1.2 million visitors travel to Jamaica every year, many of them on return vacations, to bask in the sun, dive in crystal clear waters, hike through misty mountains or talk down prices at the market. Once you're here and you've dined on jerk meats and conch fritters, washed them down with Red Stripe beer and danced to reggae or calypso until the sun comes up, you'll find there's no place on earth quite like the island of Jamaica. If you want to surround yourself with breathtaking natural beauty and vibrant people, Jamaica provides both with bravado. So read up on the risks, educate yourself on the proper precautions and take the trip of a lifetime.

Travel Basics

Learn about the differences and delights you'll experience in Jamaica

Visiting Jamaica is a great experience no matter how much you know before you leave home. Still, a little local savvy will go a long way and help you feel as comfortable as possible on this unique and diverse island.

Etiquette

Jamaicans are easygoing people, but a few codes of conduct will keep everyone smiling. Common courtesy always goes a long way; handshakes and politeness are always respected, especially in business situations. Travelers are reminded that punctuality is greatly appreciated, and when it comes to fashion, locals in Jamaica consider short skirts and shorts for women to be inappropriate.

Regions

Like any other country, each region of Jamaica has its own style. The following chart provides a brief description of Jamaica's larger cities.

City Description

Montego Bay
Affectionately called "MoBay," the community of Montego Bay is one of the most popular resort destinations in Jamaica, especially for American travelers. Here you'll find upscale resorts and all-inclusives

with all the bells and whistles. It has plenty of commercialization and isn't the best spot for authentic Jamaican culture, but it is easily accessible from its own airport, the Donald Sangster International Airport.

Negril

If you want to leave your inhibitions behind, Negril is the place to go. Here, beautiful beaches, some of them clothing-optional, host crowds interested in partying and ganja (marijuana). The East End features upscale hotels, while the West End is a throwback to the popularity Jamaica enjoyed in the 1960s - a more free-spirited and bohemian style of vacation, featuring local restaurants and modest cottages. A word of warning: Walking alone at night, especially outside a resort's secured area, has been greatly discouraged by many.

Ocho Rios

Ocho Rios is most Americans second choice for destinations in Jamaica. It is a popular cruise port and truly thrives on tourism. It is just two hours from Montego Bay and offers a more laid back hotel stay than either Montego Bay or Negril. Beaches here are beautiful, and some people travel here for the history - Ian Fleming wrote his James Bond novels here, and it was a popular spot for Errol Flynn and other legends as well.

Runaway Bay

Runaway Bay is much smaller than Ocho Rios and less popular. It has fewer people day-to-day because it lacks the cruise ship popularity that Ocho Rios holds. However, it does have a few historical distinctions and is the spot where the Spanish fled the island after their defeat by the British. Travelers looking to avoid "tourist traps" may find this their ideal vacation spot in Jamaica.

Port Antonio

A unique destination lacking in posh resorts and crowded streets, celebrities and travelers alike enjoy the peace of Port Antonio. This seaport northeast of Kingston is also north of the Blue Mountains. Known as one of the more lushly beautiful sections of the island, it is also popular among explorers. Visitors here are more often European than American, and the atmosphere is extremely relaxed, especially when it comes to nightlife, upscale dining and shopping. Don't visit this part of Jamaica, however, if you're looking for all-inclusives and mega resorts.

Kingston

Kingston is the city most vacationers avoid, whether because they've been warned away by its bad reputation or because it simply doesn't offer the resort amenities vacationers are looking for. Business travelers are generally the only travelers visiting Kingston. However, it is a major urban center and the cultural center of the island with a large number of artists and artisans among its inhabitants. Nightlife can be great, but travelers are warned to take extra caution - as in any major metropolitan area - and avoid certain neighborhoods, especially at night. Just outside the city are the Blue Mountains, where Jamaica's trademark coffee is grown. It's also easily accessible through its own airport, though it is often recommended that tourists stick to Montego Bay's airport unless visiting Kingston or surrounding areas.

Along with these tips on etiquette and overview of Jamaica's main cities, we offer numerous articles of information regarding many of the most important basic travel tips. Learn about any documentation you may need to enter the country, which clothing is appropriate, how you can call home, and more by selecting an article from our list of "Travel Basics" to the left.

Clothing

The right clothes can help make your vacation to Jamaica a breeze

In some of the most secluded resorts on Jamaica, clothing may not be required at all, but if you're staying where clothing is not optional, keep some of the following fashion tips in mind.

The clothing you'll see around Jamaica is vibrant and striking, but the overarching theme in this tropical climate is comfort. No matter your plans, comfortable clothing is essential. Lightweight cottons and linens are advisable, while light woolens are suggested for evenings. Try to avoid synthetics, which may not be as breathable as woolens and linens.

Hats, particularly with large brims, and sunglasses are also highly recommended for travelers to keep the unrelenting sun at bay. Sun block is also a must-wear for most vacationers. Some have also said that, while skimpy clothing may sound appealing to those looking to tan, the mosquitoes can be as much of a deterrent as social custom. Sundresses and lightweight pants are particularly recommended, though sweaters may be a necessity in the evening.

Additionally, waterproof clothing and rain wear are a necessity all year long. Rain showers in Jamaica usually come up suddenly, come down hard, and then are over fairly quickly, so you need to be prepared with a waterproof jacket or umbrella everywhere you go. Opt for attire that is easy to carry around that you can quickly slip on and then put away again when the sun reappears.

What to Wear

Although one of the most culturally independent islands in the region, Jamaica still retains some of the influences from its days as a British colony. The following tips will help you fit in, and avoid accidentally offending more conservative islanders:

- ✓ If you are traveling for business, a suit jacket and tie are expected, and the usual formalities and courtesies are observed;
- ✓ Shorts and bathing suits are acceptable on beaches, but should be avoided in town without cover-ups such as a long t-shirt of sarong;
- ✓ Generally speaking, travelers should consider long shorts or skirts and pants, and men may want to bring button-up shirts;

- ✓ Club attire is generally more revealing than clothes worn any other time during the day or night, particularly for women (but it is best to err on the side of caution!).

As always, it's best to be aware of the attire expected at a specific location. Many all-inclusive resorts have little to no dress code in place, but some resorts and hotels require women to wear dresses or slacks and men to wear suits and ties at their restaurants. Kingston is known for being a bit more upscale, and women particularly may want to avoid wearing jeans in this city, meanwhile Negril has a more laid-back side. To be safe, stick to packing clothing that is considered to be resort casual -- that is, collared shirts, sundresses, an linen or khaki bottoms that are clean and pressed. Bright prints and bold colors are welcome.

Traditional Clothing

While visitors may want to come prepared for all possible weather, there are many styles of island dress that are appropriate. Traditional garb may be worn by some, but Rastafarian wear is also well-known. No matter what the clothing, you can be sure it will always be infused with color.

Although these days it has become commonplace to see men and women in global fashions, traditional clothing remains popular among a decent amount of locals. The traditional clothing style of Jamaica draws from both British and slave culture.

Commonly, traditional garb for women was made from calico cloth and was always very colorful, from the tiered dresses to the ever-important head scarfs, which helped to keep hair in place and protect from the heat of the sun. These scarfs were very specifically wrapped and placed by folding a piece of material in half, tying it around the crown of the head, and then tucking it in in a particular way to keep it from slipping off. Clothing of the past was always loose and comfortable.

Men's clothing tended to be loose fitting pants and shirts made of natural, organic fabrics. They did not dress as colorfully as women, and bold designs and clashing colors were rarely found they preferred a more subdued style in their every day dress, but also chose comfort over all else.

In more modern times, Rastafarian-influenced clothing has become a part of the culture. These items are colored to represent the Ethiopian flag in red, green, and gold, and are made of natural fibers to reflect the views of the religion. To top it all off, the tam hat would be worn on the head to cover the dreadlocks.

Remember that Jamaican locals have adopted many of the same Western trends and fashions that you are used to back home, so fitting in should not be a problem. As long as you pack clothing that is cool and comfortable, you won't look back and regret the clothes you wore on your Jamaican vacation.

Currency

Learn more about the currency in circulation in Jamaica

The official unit of currency in Jamaica is the Jamaican dollar. As of December 2011, $1 USD equaled approximately 89.10 JMD, but the rate of exchange changes almost daily, and visitors are advised to wait until they arrive in Jamaica to exchange their money. This will ensure they receive the most up-to-date rate.

Jamaican currency is issued in increments of one cent, ten cent, twenty five cent, one dollar, five dollar, and ten dollar coins; as well as 50, 100, 500, and 1,000 dollar bills. All coins feature portraits of historic Rt. Excellents; except for the one cent coin, which showcases an image of Ackee, the Jamaican national dish. Bills are colorful, with portraits of historic figures on the front of the bill, and images of popular locations on the back.

Jamaican law requires that Jamaican currency be used when paying for all goods and services, though that law is followed very loosely and the U.S. dollar is accepted almost universally. Keep in mind that this does not mean you will receive your change in US currency. Credit cards may also be used, with Visa and Mastercard being the most widely accepted.

There are exchange bureaus in airports, hotels, and commercial banks, and ATMs can often be found at gas stations. When you make an exchange, keep all receipts because you must present them upon departure when you reconvert unspent currency.

Customs

Getting Through Customs in Jamaica

Customs procedures are designed to help you bring home all of those souvenirs you picked up in Jamaica

Avoid long delays passing through Customs by brushing up on some basic information for international travelers headed in and out of Jamaica.

The island's expressive culture makes Jamaica a paradise of arts, crafts and souvenirs for any and every taste. Knowing the customs regulations for Jamaica and your home country will guarantee a hassle-free travel experience. As a visitor, be aware of the following customs, tips and rules before entering the region:

- ✓ You may bring up to two liters of alcohol and two cartons of cigarettes to Jamaica;
- ✓ You may bring a "reasonable" amount of duty-free goods for personal use; anything deemed in excess of "reasonable" may incur an import tax;
- ✓ All prescription drugs must be accompanied by an official prescription;
- ✓ Firearms and recreational drugs are not permitted;
- ✓ United States citizens can avoid paying duty on foreign-made high-ticket items, such as laptops, cameras and watches, by

registering them with customs before leaving the country. Consider filing a certificate of registration for items identified with serial numbers or other permanent markings; you can keep the certificate for other trips. Otherwise, bring with you a sales receipt or insurance form to show you owned the item before you left the United States.

As an island shopper, and before returning home, remember these tips:

- ✓ You should keep receipts for all items you buy in Jamaica;
- ✓ When departing, make sure your purchases are easily accessible in case your home country's customs officials request an inspection;
- ✓ If you have any questions or complaints about your customs experience, write to the port director at your point of reentry.

The following additional re-entry rules apply for United States citizens traveling to Jamaica:

- ✓ You may bring back to the U.S. up to one liter of alcohol (if you are 21 or older) or perfume containing alcohol, up to 200 cigarettes, and up to 100 non-Cuban cigars. If you stay fewer than 48 hours, you may bring home up to 150 ml of alcohol, 50 cigarettes, and 10 non-Cuban cigars;
- ✓ You may bring home original works of art, such as paintings, drawings and sculptures, and antiques (officially defined as objects more than 100 years old) duty-free;
- ✓ You may send packages home duty-free, with a limit of one parcel per addressee per day, with the exception of alcohol or tobacco products or perfume worth more than $5(USD);
- ✓ You can mail up to $200(USD) worth of goods home to the U.S. for personal use; be sure to write "PERSONAL USE" on the parcel and attach a list of its contents and their retail value;

- ✓ If you send home a parcel containing personal belongings that have been used, write "AMERICAN GOODS RETURNED" on the package to avoid a duty fee;
- ✓ You may send up to $100(USD) worth of goods as a gift to someone in the U.S. provided you write "UNSOLICITED GIFT" on the package.

Although ganja (Marijuana) is highly common in Jamaica, it is still illegal, and trying to leave the country with it will be met with harsh penalties. There are drug-sniffing dogs at every airport and harbor, and you can expect for your luggage to be searched.

Since customs regulations are subject to change from time to time, it is best to check with your country's specific entry requirements before you leave, and keep your knowledge current using the following contact information:

Country	Contact
United States	U.S. Customs Service 1300 Pennsylvania Ave., NW Washington, DC 20229 Tel: 877/227-5511 http://www.cbp.gov
United Kingdom	HM Customs & Excise Tel: 0845/010-9000 http://www.hmrc.gov.uk/index.htm
Canada	Canada Customs and Revenue Agency Tel: 800/461-9999 www.ccra-adrc.gc.ca
Australia	Australian Customs Service Tel: 1300/363-263 www.customs.gov.au
New Zealand	New Zealand Customs Service Tel: 04/473-6099 www.customs.govt.nz

Don't spend hours waiting in customs because you didn't know the rules. Arrive prepared, and exiting and entering the country will be a breeze.

Driving

Roadway Guidance in Jamaica

When driving in Jamaica, patience is a virtue

International visitors should be prepared to encounter a few differences when driving in Jamaica.

Road conditions in the larger cities and the more tourist-frequented areas of Jamaica are fair to good, but bumps and other roadway nuisances can be extreme in the more rural areas.

If you decide to rent a vehicle for exploring the countryside and seeing the smaller towns, an SUV is probably your best bet. A U.S. driver's license is valid in Jamaica for one year, but you must be 21 to drive. Driving is on the left-hand side of the road with steering wheels on the right.

Traffic is fairly light, but roads in the countryside are frequented by domestic animals and can become narrow and winding. Be prepared to give up the right of way to both livestock and oncoming traffic. Most locals don't think twice about stopping in the middle of the road to carry on a conversation with a bystander, and don't be put off by honking horns; it's a Caribbean way of saying hello.

Not everyone feels confident driving in a foreign country, especially in one like Jamaica where the driving is done on the opposite side of the road than their home country. Instead of chancing it, you can opt to leave the driving up to locals who know what's what. Getting around the island can be as simple as hopping aboard a bus, or hailing a cab. Fear of navigating the island on your own should not hinder you from having a great time.

Sometimes driving is unavoidable, and many tourists are up for the challenge. If you're going to get behind the wheel, just be sure you are aware of local driving laws, and follow all safety precautions. This will make driving in Jamaica a smooth ride every time.

Electricity

Outlets and Voltage in Jamaica
Electrical service varies across the island of Jamaica
A difference in the types of electrical outlets all over the island means that Jamaica's vacationers will need to carry adapters wherever they go.

Electrical outlets on Jamaica do not follow a standard. They could be 110 volts or 220 volts AC (50 Cycle), depending on your location. Whether you are a vacationer from Europe, the United States or anywhere else it's a good idea to be prepared for the chance that you'll need adapters and transformers in order to convert the electricity for your own appliances.

Call ahead to your hotel to find what, if anything, is needed. Many of the larger-scale hotels and resorts may provide these for you, but there's always the chance that they could run out, so you should probably be prepared anyway.

Embassies

Embassies and Consulates in Jamaica
Consulates and embassies offer important information for those in Jamaica
An embassy or consulate can provide a friendly face abroad and assist travelers with lost or stolen passports, emergencies, or just general information.

Local consular offices can also provide a list of local doctors, dentists, and medical specialists. Calling an embassy or consulate in Jamaica can be a challenge because the telephones aren't always immediately answered, but once contacted, they can be valuable travel resources.

If you are involved in an emergency, go to the nearest embassy or consular office for your native country and register as a citizen in the region. If you are injured or become seriously ill, a consul will help you find medical assistance and, at your request, inform your family or friends. It is unlikely you'll receive government financial assistance from an embassy if you need an emergency trip back home, but pre-purchased travel insurance will cover such expenses. Travel insurance is a wise provision for an unforeseen cancellation or incidental medical expenses. Purchase travel insurance directly or through your travel agent rather than a tour operator.

On the Island:

Embassy	Address	Contact
Embassy of the United States of America	2 Oxford Road Kingston 5, Jamaica http://kingston.usembassy.gov/	935-6053 935-6054 929-4850-9 (visa section) 935-6019 (visa section fax) E-mail: opakgn@pdstate.gov
British High Commission	28 Trafalgar Road Kingston 10, Jamaica PO Box 575 https://www.gov.uk/government/world/organisations/british-high-commission-jamaica	510-0700 510-0737 511-5335 (consular section fax) E-mail: bhckingston@mail.infochan.com
Canadian High Commission	3 West Kings House, Waterloo Road Entrance Kingston 10, Jamaica PO Box 1500 http://www.dfait-maeci.gc.ca/jamaica	926-1500 511-3494 511-3480 (consular section fax) E-mail: kngtn@dfait-maeci.gc.ca

Abroad:

Embassy	Address	Contact
Jamaica High Commission	1-2 Prince Consort Road London SW7 2BZ, UK http://www.jhcuk.com	020-7823-9911 020-7589-5154 (fax) E-mail: jamhigh@jhcuk.com
Jamaican Embassy	1520 New Hampshire Avenue, NW Washington, DC 20036, USA http://www.emjamusa.org	202-452-0660-9 202-452-0081 (fax) E-mail: info@emjamusa.org
Jamaican Consulate	767 Third Avenue, Second and Third Floor	212-935-9000 212-935-7507 (fax)

General	New York, NY 10017, USA http://www.congenjamaica-ny.org	E-mail: registry@congenjamaica-ny.org (general inquiries) passport@congenjamaica-ny.org (passport/visa information)
Jamaica High Commission - consulates in: Toronto, Winnipeg, and Edmonton	275 Slater Street, Suite 800 Ottawa, Ontario K1P 5H9, Canada http://www.jhcottawa.ca	613-233-9311 747-5354 (24 hour information service) 613-233-0611 (fax) E-mail: hc@jhcottawa.ca

Although you will likely never have to contact your local embassy during your trip to Jamaica, knowing where to find them is a good precaution to take. Include these numbers on a list of emergency contacts that you bring with you to the island, so if an emergency does occur, you can get in touch without panic arising.

Health

Staying Healthy in Jamaica

When traveling to Jamaica, consider these tips for a safe, healthy, and enjoyable trip

Health and medical considerations are a concern whenever traveling abroad, but for the most part, you'll find good quality health care in Jamaica.

Travelers heading to Jamaica are required to meet only one health requirement: anyone above the age of 1 must obtain a yellow fever vaccination certificate only if traveling to Jamaica from a contaminated locale. Jamaica has no other health requirements before arriving on the island, but Hepatitis A is a frequently occurring disease, and acquiring proper vaccinations is advised before traveling.

If you are traveling with prescription medication, carry it in its original, clearly marked container (avoid designer pill boxes) alongside a prescription slip and note from your physician stating your medical need for the medication. It will also be wise to pack a Travel Medical Kit with the following items:

- ✓ Painkillers including acetaminophen, aspirin, ibuprofen;
- ✓ Antihistamines;
- ✓ Topical disinfectant;
- ✓ Antacids;
- ✓ Rubbing alcohol;
- ✓ Bandages;
- ✓ Thermometer.

For health and medical treatment while staying in Jamaica, first consult the hotel for recommendations regarding a medical clinic, dentist or doctor. The majority of hotels keeps doctors and dentists on call, so check with the concierge in non-emergency situations before making the trip to the hospital. If you need urgent medical attention, visit one of Jamaica's 16 public or six private hospitals located around the island. The following list provides the names, locations and phone numbers of the primary medical facilities tourists should visit if necessary:

Hospital	Location	Telephone
University Hospital of the West Indies	Mona, Kingston	876-927-1620
St. Ann's Bay Hospital	St. Ann's Bay	876-794-8565
Port Antonio Hospital	Naylor's Hill, Port Antonio	876-715-5778
Mo Bay Hope Medical Center	Half Moon Resort, Montego Bay	876-953-3981
Cornwall Regional Hospital	Mt. Salem, Montego Bay	876-952-5100

For an ambulance, dial 110 immediately. Also, be sure to check if your insurance policy covers medical expenses incurred while traveling. Medical expenses in Jamaica can be costly, so if your insurance company does not provide sufficient coverage, you should obtain traveler's insurance before visiting the island.

Many larger hotels and chains in Jamaica will have a doctor on-call at all times. It is best that you have any paperwork from your own doctor if you may need it on your travels, including prescription information.

Drinking Water

Piped-in water is usually safe to drink because it is filtered and chlorinated. However, the chlorination could cause mild abdominal upsets, so if you're prone to stomach problems, it may be wise to drink bottled water, which is readily available.

It is not in anyone's big vacation plans to fall ill while they are visiting Jamaica, but it is always a possibility. When you arrive on the island prepared to take steps should illness occur, handling the situation will be that much easier.

Hours of Operation

Have the Time of Your Life in Jamaica

Visitors in Jamaica will avoid hassle if they know the hours of operation
The laidback attitude may be easy for travelers to adjust to, but business hours are another matter entirely.

Although some establishments in Jamaica run on inconsistent business hours, consult this list for the standard hours of operation for businesses and services on the island. Be sure to check with the hotel once you arrive in Jamaica, however, as these hours may change from business to business, or season to season.

Establishment	Days	Hours
Banks	Monday - Thursday Friday	9:00 a.m. - 2:00 p.m. 9:00 a.m. - 4:00 p.m.
Government	Monday - Thursday Friday	8:30 a.m. - 5:00 p.m. 8:30 a.m. - 4:00 p.m.
Post Offices	Monday - Friday	9:00 a.m. - 5:00 p.m.

Stores	Monday - Friday	8:30 a.m. - 4:30 p.m.
	Saturday	8:00 a.m. - 1:00 p.m.

Don't let a "Closed" sign deter your vacation plans. Knowing the basic operating hours on the island will help you to successfully plan your trip.

Languages

Can We Talk in Jamaica?

When visiting Jamaica, the language you'll encounter is English - with a local flair

The Jamaican accent is one of the most recognizable in the world, and luckily for most English speaking vacationers, it is also very easy to understand.

The official language of Jamaica is English, and native islanders generally look towards British English for spelling and dialect, though the island's locale near the United States and increasing business with the country has created a slight shift towards American English.

Additionally, most Jamaicans speak Patois on a more regular basis, amongst their family and friends. In Jamaica, Patois refers to Jamaican Creole, which is a combination of Spanish, English, and an assortment of African tongues. When you listen to Jamaican music, this is what you are hearing.

Almost everyone on the island speaks a familiar form of English, so tourists have nothing to worry about. If you find yourself having a conversation with a local, and they are speaking in an unknown slang, just ask them to either repeat themselves or speak slower. Jamaicans will often have a good sense of humor about the situation.

When traveling abroad, language is a common concern. Happily, English speakers from around the world will find that there is no need to prepare for a trip to Jamaica with special classes or dictionaries filled with translations. Simply show up, enjoy the soothing lilt of the Jamaican accent, and enjoy your time spent on the island without the worry that you will be hindered by a language barrier.

Passports

What Do I Need to enter Jamaica?

The requirements for entering Jamaica include a passport
When you arrive in Jamaica, you'll be required to present a few a documents before you may start exploring the island, including an onward or return ticket and a valid passport.

Citizens of the United States and Canada are required to submit proof of citizenship, such as a government-issued photo ID. A passport is also now required for citizens of both countries to enter Jamaica.

After all travelers' items are checked, officials in Jamaica will issue you a tourist card valid up to six months for $27(USD). When leaving the island, vacationers must return the tourist cards and pay a departure tax of $27(USD) in cash. Since some airlines include the departure tax in the price of the ticket, look over what your airfare includes to determine if you can spend that last $27(USD) on a souvenir or if the money will be used toward getting you home.

Visas are not required from citizens of Australian, British, Canadian, Japanese, U.S., and many European nations. The following chart will help you to determine if you will be required to obtain a visa to enter Jamaica. In some cases, visitors will be able to obtain their visa at the port of entry.

COUNTRIES REQUIRING A VISA TO ENTER JAMAICA		
Country	Cost (USD)	Notes
Andorra	$20	Visa obtainable at Port of Entry.
Afghanistan	$30	Referral required.
Albania	$20	Visa obtainable at Port of Entry.

Algeria	$10	
Angola	$30	
Argentina	$30	Visa required for stays longer than 30 days.
Armenia	$20	Visa obtainable at Port of Entry.
Austria	$38	Visa required for stays longer than 90 days.
Azerbaijan	$20	Visa obtainable at Port of Entry.
Bahrain	$20	
Belarus	$20	Visa obtainable at Port of Entry.
Belgium	$38	Visa required for stays longer than 90 days.
Benin	$20	
Bhutan	$20	
Bolivia	$50	
Bosnia/Herzegovina	$20	Visa obtainable at port of entry.
Brazil	$60	Visa required for stays longer than 30 days.
Bulgaria	$20	Visa obtainable at port of entry.
Burkina Faso	$20	
Burundi	$15	
Cambodia	$35	
Cameroon	$20	
Cape Verde	$13	
Cayman	$102.40	
Central African Republic	$60	
Chad	$6	
Chile	Free	Visa required for stays longer than 30 days.
China	$25	
Columbia	Free	Visa required for stays longer than 30 days.
Congo	$70	
Costa Rica	$20	Visa required for stays longer than 30 days.

Croatia	$20	Visa obtainable at Port of Entry.
Cuba	$35	
Czech Republic	$20	Visa obtainable at Port of Entry.
Denmark	$38	Visa required for stays longer than 90 days.
Djibouti	$30	
Dominican Republic	$10	
Ecuador	$50	Visa required for stays longer than 30 days.
Egypt	$25	
El Salvador	$20	
Equatorial Guinea	$50	
Eritrea	$25	
Estonia	$20	Visa obtainable at Port of Entry
Ethiopia	$70	
Fiji	Free	Visa required for stays longer than 90 days.
Finland	$38	Visa required for stays longer than 90 days.
France	$38	Visa required for stays longer than 30 days.
Gabon	$50	
Georgia	$20	Visa obtainable at Port of Entry.
Germany	$38	Visa required for stays longer than 90 days.
Greece	$38	Visa required for stays longer than 30 days.
Guinea	$25	
Guinea-Bissau	$45	
Guatemala	$10	
Haiti	$18	
Hong Kong	$25	
Honduras	$20	
Hungary	$20	Visa is obtainable at Port of Entry.
Iceland	$38	Visa is required for stays longer than 90 days.

Indonesia	$25	
Iran	$3.50	
Iraq	$3.50	
Israel	$13	Visa is required for stays longer than 90 days.
Italy	$38	Visa is required for stays longer than 90 days.
Ivory Coast	$25	
Japan	$38	Visa required for stays longer than 30 days.
Jordan	$28	
Kazakhstan	$20	Visa required for stays longer than 30 days.
Korea (North)	$30	
Korea (Republic of)	$30	Visa required for stays longer than 90 days.
Kosovo	$20	Visa obtainable at Port of Entry.
Kuwait	$20	
Kyrgystan	$20	Visa obtainable at Port of Entry.
Laos	$35	
Latvia	$20	Visa obtainable at Port of Entry.
Lebanon	$20	
Liberia	$40	
Libya	$7	
Liechtenstien	$38	Visa required for stays longer than 90 days.
Lithuania	$25	Visa obtainable at Port of Entry.
Luxembourg	$38	Visa required for stays longer than 90 days.
Macedonia	$20	Visa obtainable at Port of Entry.
Madagascar	$74.50	
Mali	$20	
Marshall Islands	$50	
Mauritania	$10	
Mexico	$71	Visa required for stays longer than 90 days.

Jamaica Travel Guide, Caribbean

Micronesia	$10		
Moldova	$20	Visa obtainable at Port of Entry.	
Monaco	Free	Visa required for stays longer than $30 days.	
Mongolia	$45		
Morocco	$15		
Myanmar	$30		
Nepal	$15		
Netherlands	$38	Visa required for stays longer than 90 days.	
Nicaragua	$25		
Niger	$35		
Nigeria	$20	Referral necessary.	
Norway	$38	Via required for stays longer than 90 days.	
Oman	$9		
Pakistan	Free	Referral necessary.	
Palau	$50		
Palestine	$20		
Panama	$32		
Paraguay	$8		
Peru	$27		
Phillipines	$25		
Poland	$20	Visa obtainable at Port of Entry.	
Portugal	$38	Visa required for stays longer than 30 days.	
Qatar	$33		
Reunion	$20		
Romania	$20	Visa obtainable at Port of Entry.	
Russian Federation	$20	Visa obtainable at Port of Entry.	
Rwanda	$30		
Samoa	$47		

Country	Fee	Notes
Samoa (Western)	$20	
San Marino	$20	Visa required for stays longer than 90 days.
Sao Tome & Principe	$20	
Saudi Arabia	$54	
Senegal	$27	
Serbia & Montenegro	$20	Visa obtainable at Port of Entry.
Slovak Republic	$20	
Slovenia	$20	Visa obtainable at Port of Entry.
Somalia	$30	
Sudan	$49	
Spain	$38	Visa required for stays longer than 30 days.
Sri Lanka	Free	Referral required.
Suriname	$30	
Sweden	$38	Visa required for stays longer than 90 days.
Switzerland	$38	Visa required for stays longer than 90 days.
Syria	$16.50	
Taiwan	$40	Affidavit of Identity required.
Tajikstan	$20	Visa obtainable at Port of Entry.
Thailand	$20	
Togo	$10	
Tokelau	$50	
Tonga	$40	
Tunisia	$15	
Turkey	$38	Visa required for stays longer than 30 days.
Turkmenistan	$20	Visa obtainable at Port of Entry.
Ukraine	$20	Visa obtainable to Port of Entry.
United Arab Emirate	$10	
Uruguay	$6.50	Visa required for stays longer than 30 days.

Usa	$140	Visas are required for students and workers.
Uzbekistan	$20	
Venezuala	$25	Visa required for stays longer than 15 days.
Viet Nam	$40	
Yemen	$50	
Zaire	$20	
Zimbabwe	$100	

If you will be traveling to Jamaica on business, the application requires the following materials: one passport-sized photo and valid passport, and proof of return or onward ticket. Business travelers may only stay for 30 straight days, and a total of 180 days per year.

Consult the your nation's embassy or the Jamaican embassy for further information on passport and visa requirements and stipulations.

Telephones

Wanna Talk in Jamaica?

Local, long distance and cellular telephone services are available across Jamaica
Jamaica's telephone systems are not hard to understand, and are in fact so similar to those in the United States that you won't have any issue making phone calls while on vacation.

Most hotels permit travelers to make telephone calls from the hotel with direct-dial services. Pay phones are dispersed throughout the island if vacationers choose to use this method to generate local or long-distance calls. However, be cautious when making "local" calls in Jamaica because calling between towns counts as long-distance.

Like the United States, Jamaica is a part of the North American Number Plan, and the island's country code is "1." Unlike the United

States, which has over 250 different area codes, "876" is the only area code in the country. To call Jamaica from the United States, dial 1, then 876, then the number you are trying to reach. In order to place a call outside of Jamaica, to a foreign country such as those in Europe, Asia, or Africa, you would first dial the "011" exit code, then the number you are trying to reach.

Business travelers who require fax facilities are in luck because most local businesses allow travelers to send and receive faxes for a small fee. Additionally, the Cable & Wireless Caribbean Cellular office in Kingston at 26 Trafalgar Road provides fax equipment and is open from 7:00 a.m. to 10:00 p.m. daily. Call their office at 876-968-4000 or fax them for information at 876-968-3999.

Mobile telephone service on Jamaica is available through the local GSM 900 network, Digicel. To learn more about Digicel's network services, check out their website at www.digiceljamaica.com. Cable & Wireless Caribbean Cellular rents mobile handsets but requires a deposit, registration fee, per-day access charge and per-day hire charge. Travelers may register for a rented handset prior to arriving in Jamaica to save time. Contact Cable & Wireless at 888-225-5295 or visit their website at www.cwc.com for more information on renting mobile telephones.

Tipping

How Then Shall We Tip in Jamaica?
Guidelines for tipping help travelers to reward the good service they receive in Jamaica
Every country has its own traditions and rules about what is customary when it comes to tips and gratuities. In Jamaica the percentage and procedure differs from hotels to restaurants.

While tipping throughout the United States is compulsory, in Jamaica tipping may be less common. Gratuities are often included in the bill, or in the original price quoted to you. The following are a few simple guidelines to demystify tipping in Jamaica.

Restaurants

While some restaurants take the liberty of including a 10 percent to 15 percent gratuities charge into the final bill, others do not. So it is wise to thoroughly review the final bill or ask your server about the charges incurred. If a gratuities charge is not incorporated, a 10 percent to 20 percent tip on the total cost is expected depending upon the level of service. Like always, tipping is based solely upon the diner's discretion.

Hotels

Similar to restaurants in Jamaica, many hotels tack on a service charge for food, beverage, and room expenses. Then again, other hotels do not include this charge. At the time of check-in, consult the front desk employee regarding the hotel's policy on gratuities and/or service charges. Otherwise, tip helpful service employees an adequate amount. Bellhops expect $1(USD) to $2(USD) per bag, and maids anticipate $1(USD) to $2(USD) per day.

A word of caution for those travelers staying in all-inclusive hotels: most of these establishments strictly do not permit tipping.

Taxis

Taxis in Jamaica are either metered or non-metered. Rates go by the car, not by the passenger. Check with the driver before starting your trip so you will know if you need to arrange a flat fee or if you will be paying according to the meter. To arrange taxi services, JUTA (Jamaica Union of Travelers Association) is a highly recommended service because it is the largest on the island and is well-regulated. Contact JUTA in Montego Bay at 876-952-0813, in Negril at 876-957-9197 or in Ocho Rios at 876-974-2292.

Vacationers may also summon a taxi on the street. Either way, a 10 percent to 15 percent tip for taxi drivers is customary. Trips taken between midnight and 5:00 a.m., however, run on a standard tipping rate of 25 percent on top of the metered fee. When taxis are not metered, the price must be negotiated and may not include tip. Also, make sure that the price is negotiated in a specified currency, as several different types will be accepted in Jamaica.

The End

www.ingramcontent.com/pod-product-compliance
Lightning Source LLC
Chambersburg PA
CBHW031058080526
44587CB00011B/737